ENJOYING ARCHIVES

ENJOYING ARCHIVES

What They Are · Where to Find Them
How to Use Them

DAVID IREDALE

David & Charles : Newton Abbot

ISBN 0 7153 5669 0

Set in 11/13 Imprint
and printed in Great Britain
by Latimer Trend & Company Ltd Plymouth
for David & Charles (Holdings) Limited
South Devon House   Newton Abbot   Devon

MATRI MEAE . . . 'bonis studiis serviens, domus curam bene gerens, sua cum discretione dispensans atque conservans, bonae matris familias officio fungebatur; mores erant probi . . .' from EADMERI monachi cantuariensis *Vita Sancti Anselmi Archiepiscopi Cantuariensis* written about AD 1100.

CONTENTS

INTRODUCTION

'AND THE Archives hold my great-great-grandfather's will, all written on vellum and in the Latin tongue.' The retired village postman paused for my comments. I hesitated so he continued. 'You can't see it because it's locked away but my mother once visited Lambeth Palace and was shown a copy. She always insisted he left a lot of money which Lord Russell took after he got a copy of the will. . . .'

How could I explain that the ancestor, a tenant farmer of the Duke of Bedford, left no will? His inventory, hastily scrawled in English round hand, almost illegible but entirely legal, lay open for all to consult at the county record office. Documents, archives, muniments are still a mystery to many people.

This book deals with the great heritage of documents in England and Wales, and with a few of the archives where documents are stored. It aims to describe, in outline, the work of the county record office, the repair of manuscripts, and the method of reading old records.

A document is something written to provide evidence or information upon any subject under the sun. Coins, gravestones, films or Brueghel paintings are documents, though this book will refer mainly to manuscript (handwritten) or printed papers and parchments like maps, correspondence and deeds of title. When a document is drawn up or used in the course of a public or private transaction and preserved in the custody of the people responsible for the transaction, it becomes part of an archive. An archival document is frequently no longer in current business use but set aside for permanent preservation. Thus a letter written to the Earl of Derby concerning estate affairs, and held at Knowsley since 1764, forms part of the archive or family muniments of the Earls of Derby; but a single love letter from Tom to Sally or the haphazard purchases of an antiquarian cannot be an archive.

The archives is the office or repository where are stored documents of all types, whether archival or not. Many archives are now called record offices because here are found parish, legal and official records. Any document created as authentic evidence of a matter of legal importance is known as a record: a marriage register at the church for example. A muniment is a document preserved as evidence of rights and privileges. Families and boroughs therefore own muniments.

Documents have varied uses. Books cannot supply all the answers. Is your family tree in print? Has someone written the history of your house? Can the origin of the local smith be traced? Do you know the names of all inhabitants of your town in 1851? Which London livery company did great-great-grand-father join? You can almost certainly answer these questions by going to the archives, and in no other way whatsoever. Library, local soothsayer, Citizens Advice Bureau and historical society will generally yield disappointingly small amounts of information.

Documents are stored in several thousand different buildings in England and Wales, ranging from the British Museum to the local solicitor's office, from country mansions to factory cellars. Obviously only a few dozen buildings are in any sense adequately planned and staffed as archives offices. Visiting the remainder can be disheartening. Fortunately many documents have been printed, and are thus obtainable in libraries, saving visits to archives themselves. Many records in print are listed in E. L. C. Mullins, *Texts and Calendars* (1958).

The following chapters attempt to describe those archives accessible to professional and part-time historians alike. The term historian to my mind includes all individuals interested in reading documents about the past; and includes, therefore, the genealogist whose work is regarded so often by other students with the condescension that rock climbers reserve for fell walkers; includes the retired ICI worker leafing through a vestry account book; the housewife following the history of her cottage; the sixth-former examining an 1842 tithe map; the social scientist reconstituting families in the Stuart village. There is no reason to leave out occasional historians like the solicitor tracing deeds, the civil engineer following the track of an old road, the architect or landscape gardener studying Georgian building plans and estate surveys.

Most people visiting archives are indeed part-time amateur historians and my advice takes this into account, leaning heavily on title deeds, wills and inventories, parish registers and quarter-sessions records. For this reason, too, record centres like the royal archives at Windsor, not readily accessible, do not appear here. Original Anglo-Saxon charters at the British Museum are a specialised study, a wide knowledge of diplomatic, old English, palaeography and history being called for. Most historians will turn to edited and translated versions, whose commentaries adequately replace my type of guide. Domesday Book, a most difficult source to translate and understand, is discussed because it does figure in histories, though much of its information is ignored or maltreated. My book is obviously biased towards documents most commonly studied by the majority of historical researchers. With exceptions, the chapters aim to report on types of documents you find in archives once you arrive there, not with individual documents, apart from a few exceptions like Domesday Book.

Following this recitation come hints on how to use documents. It is all very well to requisition land taxes of Bucklow Hundred for 1790–1820, but without guidance you may not realise how to turn land taxes into means of plotting the history of every parcel of land in your village. General remarks on research methods are in the opening chapter. These are intended for the local historian, as, obviously, the professional is more than capable of using source material to best advantage, and his research students lean on their professor for advice. The local historian should also read the chapter on county record offices which deals with use of manuscripts. It is of course just as important to know for what purposes various types of document are being employed by historians nowadays. You may broaden your own field of interests as a result. A friend of mine, an avid peruser of old wills and inventories, was led by such suggestions to extract information on seventeenth-century cottage interiors. The historical significance of this type of record has only recently begun to be appreciated. People have in the past been content only to copy down names and legacies and lands from probate documents. Obviously without a sound historical sense—common sense as much as book learning—you can easily overlook the wood for the trees and end up with a garbled knowledge of both archives and history.

So I seem to have returned to my retired village postman. 'Why they can't give me the will, I don't know. No one else would want it,' he told me, his mind only on the supposed fortune mentioned therein, presumptuously ignoring the needs of historians who do use probate records for other purposes. But for some people, the past is not only dead but was never alive, its people figments of a schoolmarm's imagination, its records as expendable as a packet of cigarettes and not half as precious. Archives are not trusted to speak for themselves. It is always 'ask old Bill, he knows everything' or 'Grandma's the only person who can tell you about the building of the new road'. There is a curious fatalism abroad that we are almost too late to rescue the past from oblivion because old folk are dying every day. To suppose that this generation can study archives and learn more about the past than Bill or Grandma ever knew is incomprehensible to many people.

Chapter 1

RESEARCH METHODS

HISTORICAL research nowadays calls for organisation of material as well as dedication to detail; a regard for method as well as for truth. A scientific approach to original documents and an artistic style of writing usually results in worthwhile and readable history. Not that the itch to burst into print is the sole reason for consulting archives; many people do so purely for interest or entertainment. I did not write screeds when I wandered round the Louvre or Hermitage. I was content to admire; I took away memories of outstanding exhibits and a general impression of European culture. In the same way one of my acquaintances, a regular county record-office visitor, loves to read old manuscripts just for the pleasure of learning about the past, of seeing old family surnames and archaic place-names. She has no thought of taking notes, writing or lecturing. My acquaintance and others like her should find in parts of this book—the description of documents deposited in various archives centres—the stimulus to further browsing.

But I presume that others do have a specific object in sight: writing a family history, laying claim to a plot of disputed land, or lecturing on railway history. For such research, careful organisation alone results in successful conclusions. It is essential at the outset to define your object, to be clear in the mind about the scope of your work. Write your aim down and then

consider if this statement really meets your requirements. What
is your field of interest? Is it genealogy, local history, national
politics, the story of religious development in England, biography
of a famous Cornishman or Essex probate records? In what
period of time are you specialising; the Iron Age, 1558–1603,
1945–65, Renaissance? Are you sure of the relevance of the
period with regard to your chosen topic? Yes, the period 1558–
1603 is most pertinent for a religious and political history of
England; but how meaningful is that period in Puddlecombe's
history? From the religious angle Puddlecombe's significant day
came much earlier than 1558. Back in 1536, its small abbey was
dissolved and the reformed religion accepted so wholeheartedly
that not even Bloody Mary's persecutions altered local affairs one
jot. And a closing date, 1594, might open a new chapter. In that
year came to the village an enthusiastic Puritan family whose
activities thrust the parish into the era of religious and political
controversy that culminated in the 1688 Revolution.

Furthermore when you consider periods for study remember
that archives have in general nothing to say, as far as primary
source material goes, about pre-Saxon England. The period
before the seventh century belongs to the province of archae-
ology. Classical and medieval writings refer to those centuries,
but do require expert interpretation. Archives too are rarely
available for the decades immediately preceding the present.
Government reports and newspapers are exceptions to the avail-
ability rule, but must be taken with a pinch of salt. The most
useful private documents are usually held by people who themselves will write memoirs and autobiographies. It would be
foolish indeed to commence a history of the Labour party or
Puddlecombe Grammar School for the period from 1945 unless
you have written permission to gain access to all relevant archives,
something difficult to obtain even by professional historians of
repute.

Should you be studying a particular place you must next ask:
what are the physical bounds of my chosen district? The answer
is simply arrived at if you are writing about a county, township

or parish because the boundaries of these units are generally definable at any specified date. An economic unit like Merseyside or a political-social grouping such as Greater Manchester demands more careful definition. When contributing to a history of Congleton published in 1970, I soon became aware that the borough of Congleton, the political unit as far as many documents are concerned, was not the Congleton of the economic historian. A neighbouring township, incorporated politically in the borough only a generation ago, economically formed an integral part of the town from the eighteenth century. Its industry grew with Congleton's; its houses spread to meet Congleton's; people daily crossed the river (the borough boundary) both ways, living in one place, finding a livelihood in the other. A political study of Congleton in the nineteenth century would, of course, not include the industrial suburb outside the borough boundary. What to include and exclude does therefore entirely depend on the title and scope of your history. It can and will be argued that the historian must consider almost the whole world before he understands Congleton. Indeed Congleton's silk-mills were merely a minute proportion of an important industry. Then too, England's free-trade policy which destroyed the silk industry must be studied; and to study free trade the historian needs to appreciate the economic and political framework of the Victorian world. Every student knows the importance of setting a subject in its context; a context which ought to be as wide as subject, time and place demand for the reader's enlightenment. None the less this never cancels the task of setting physical bounds to your district.

When you have chosen your subject and period carefully, the next job is to grasp the historical background and context. To comprehend any religious changes in your township in 1532–59, you must know about Henry VIII and the Reformation, Luther and Wolsey and Ann Boleyn, the medieval church, and England's opposition to foreign control of ecclesiastical affairs. But do not spend too long widening your knowledge or you will never get back to your locality. It is as well not to choose a topic that does demand too much background delving. For instance, the medieval bishop's court sounds a romantic piece of research but you must know how medieval catholicism was organised, at what point state administration took over from the church, why the bishop possessed certain powers and not others, why church and state were continually at loggerheads; you will have to study ecclesiastical law, discover the meaning of all technical terms employed in court, learn both medieval Latin and court hand, resolve why and how the various types of documents were produced. All problems can be overcome, however, if you work in an orderly way and allow yourself plenty of time; for part-time projects something like five or six years.

Historians themselves are men, not computers. Theirs is an imperfect science, in the sense that both raw material and workers are biased. To know all might occasionally mean to forgive all; but the historian acts as a man of his time; reading accounts of the overseer of the poor, he possibly feels a ready pity for the unmarried mother or orphaned child or father with ten starving children, and consequently soundly berates the parsimony of prosperous farmers and hard-hearted churchgoers. The records are open to this interpretation, even though they are written by those farmers and churchgoers themselves. But it is not impossible for the researcher to be himself a comfortably-off middle-class churchgoer, sceptical of the benefits of the welfare state. He sees in the accounts living proofs of his contention that people are improvident and thoughtless of the burden imposed on the few thrifty ratepayers. Some bias is inescapable and adds spice to lectures and histories.

The historian admits that his original material may be just as prejudiced, or at least not exactly what it claims to be. Medieval inquisitions *post mortem* were supposed to be produced by a sworn local jury; in fact the family steward supplied needful information. Tudor documents dealing with Richard III's reign exhibit an unabashed bias against every action of the former king. The report in 1834 of the commissioners inquiring into the poor laws has a definite axe to grind. Inquests about enclosure of open fields and wastes are sometimes persuasively one-sided.

History must be rewritten periodically and from country to country. This is no dispiriting state of affairs. History is for our present enjoyment, use and understanding, not for the future.

Local history tells us how men have travelled the road from primitive life to today; why our village bears its present pattern of church, enclosed fields, village green, woodland; how Baker and Jones have replaced de Courtenay and Fitznigel in village counsels; when county council replaced highway supervisor. Local history, following the definition of Professor H. P. R. Finberg, describes and explains the foundation, rise, periods of stability and depression, and (where relevant) subsequent decline and fall of a discrete community. It is an old saying that we understand the present by learning about the past. The consequent responsibility of the historian may be somewhat worrying, but encourages a more dedicated approach to scientific methods of research, as set out below.

A number of books on historical research are essential reading. V. H. Galbraith's *The Historian at Work* (1962) concisely defines history and explains historical research methods. Books specifically on the local historian's problems and duties include H. P. R. Finberg, *The Local Historian and His Theme* (1952), W. G. Hoskins, *Local History in England* (1959), R. B. Pugh, *How to Write a Parish History* (1954), F. G. Emmison, *Archives and Local History* (1966). L. Redstone and F. W. Steer in *Local Records* (1953) cover in more detail some of the ground of this present book. Recent research in your chosen field can be followed in the relevant periodicals. As an economic historian you will read the *Economic History Review*; as a local historian your own county's historical society journal. *Ulrich's Periodicals Directory* arranges journals according to subjects and provides an alphabetical index to titles. To know what books have been published on your subject you need a standard bibliography; that is a list of books on history or demography or archives. Theodore Besterman's *World Bibliography of Bibliographies* is the classic list of these book lists. Most libraries provide catalogues of books by subjects.

B

Books are of course merely compilations, albeit from original sources, possibly mistranslating documents, lacking footnotes, turning out old-fashioned theories. But they usually contain some worthwhile pointers. Even if you gain just one idea for further research from an odd footnote, your reading will not have been wasted. If you are in doubt about the value of a certain book, check to see if the indexing is thorough, the bibliography reasonably lengthy and footnotes explicit about the whereabouts of documents. Should these factors appear satisfactory, the book itself may be relied on.

Take especial care with any documents that have been transcribed and printed by editors. Transcribers sometimes add punctuation marks and inverted commas, which is usually fair enough, but omit large chunks of what they consider uninteresting, without noting this is the text. They add dates on excellent, but not conclusive, evidence to undated manuscripts. They leave out obscene, libellous, indecorous and embarrassing phrases. Even when editors admit this, the later student wants to see for himself what the original stated in full in order to comprehend the writer's character. Words are not infrequently wrongly read or transcribed or translated. There is an example where the editor of Lichfield Cathedral register quotes a letter of 1183, from the archbishop of Canterbury, commanding men to meet him in Caen 'at the sign of the Man of Galilee' (*ad viri Galilee*). But the archbishop is referring not to an inn, but to the introit for Ascension Day: *viri Galilee* . . . ye men of Galilee why stand ye gazing up into heaven? 'Meet me,' he writes, 'in Caen on Ascension Day.' This was at that period an accepted means of referring to a feast day, and a medievalist must know little background facts of this kind. Finally, before visiting any archives centre or library to commence work, read its official guide and rules so that you will know what types of material to inquire after and will not get off on the wrong foot.

Once you have chosen your subject and period, and have done some general background reading, you will want to start tackling the sources. Only two destinations can generally be recommended to the student who does not know where relevant material is deposited. First, you may visit the reference librarian of a city or university library. He may immediately inform you that an excellent book is already in print on the very topic. More likely, he will have printed books that will give you all you will need. Your task would therefore consist in culling information from various works, to be put together in your own thesis. The latter, though built up from the researches of others, ought to be in itself a unique piece of research with its own theme and conclusions. Do not denigrate printed works as bases for research. Parliamentary sessional papers, to take one example, are printed but will for a long time yet afford information for research.

Second, you should visit the county archivist in the county record office. Although the record office is placed behind other repositories in this book, it is none the less more important nowadays than most. Ask the archivist for advice on the type of manuscripts needed and available for your work, the location of documents, and any problems of use and access. The archivist will probably tell you if the relevant papers lie in his own or a neighbouring record office, in a great house like Chatsworth, in a factory strongroom, or elsewhere.

It is usually a mistake to take advice from anyone else, when you are beginning research. Do not rely too much on the local schoolmaster, the girl behind the library counter, the parish priest or even the village postman's mother, well-read though she may be. Everyone could help, of course, and advice should be politely heard; but until you have consulted either a professional reference librarian or the county archivist do not let yourself possibly be hindered by well-meaning friends. Should you be willing to alter your topic of study, the archivist usually is prepared to suggest suitable research projects within your capabilities. He may feel that you will not cope with Latin or old handwriting or intricate administrative backgrounds. He may realise that documents will not be available for your purpose. He will certainly know if someone else is already engaged on similar lines of study. But millions of documents await detailed examination,

and the archivist would be only too pleased to indicate collections
that will form the basis of a worthwhile history. Even if you just
transcribe a parish register, the resulting typescript will be used
by hundreds of later researchers. If you co-operate with the
archivist, he and his staff can make your task not only all the
easier but thoroughly enjoyable too. Finally do not wander into
any of the repositories (other than county record office) mentioned in this book, whether parish church vestry or House of
Lords Record Office, until you have taken advice from reference
librarian or archivist.

Now that you have established where the raw material of your
work is to be found, you will be faced with your first actual
document. A pencil is better for taking notes than a pen, because
ink damages documents too easily and pencil is swiftly erased if
need be; I also take plenty of quarto-sized paper, an eraser for
rubbing out mistakes, and a large number of 5 × 3 inch white
indexing cards and a small filing cabinet to match. The first
document I study is numbered 1, the second 2, and so on. Even
if the document proves useless, it is worth recording that fact. Of
course a collection of documents, like wills at the diocesan
registry, or settlement certificates in the parish chest, may be
given one number, each item in the collection being sub-
numbered. Provide yourself with a list of sources in numerical
order, so that immediately on seeing a reference to note 212, you
know that this is from the 'COUNTY RECORD OFFICE: QUARTER
SESSIONS: PETITIONS'. Each set of notes must be clearly labelled
with name of archive, its location and present owner, covering
dates of documents and subjects covered. Head your notes as
follows:

Source 74
  1. Location of document(s): 1 Millbank, London
  2. Owner: the Church Commissioners
  3. Type of document(s): minute books, letters, surveyors' reports
  4. Dates: 1818–56
  5. Subjects: new churches, parsonages, burial grounds

Then make detailed notes of each document you study, choos-
ing points relevant to your research project, quoting words

accurately. No rule can be proposed about taking notes: your purpose is the ruling factor. But for an example there follows an archivist's calendar of one document in Chelmsford settlement papers (source 92). This attempts to exhibit the gist of document 92/41 dispassionately, without regard to this or that student's interests.

Source 92/41

Examination prior to removal of Robert Bond late of Coggeshall but now a prisoner in the House of Correction at Chelmsford.

About 27 years old, born Broom, co Suffolk; about 7 years ago at old Michaelmas let himself to Mr William Grimwood of Wetheringset near Debenham, co Suffolk, farmer, for one year at £10 wages, board and lodging; worked one year till next old Michaelmas day, received full wages, and no further settlement gained; about 5 years ago went to board and lodge with Mr William Bacon at the *Black Boy Inn*, Chelmsford, engaged by George Wilson, head waiter, as boot catcher, for what he could get of customers for cleaning their boots and shoes; served 15 or 16 months, absent only 4 days; married about one year ago in parish church of Great Coggeshall to Sarah Scott, his present wife.

Mark of Robert Bond X

23 Nov 1821

Now the genealogist would probably need all the above details since he is seeking information on Bond and Bacon. But the student of wages and prices would be quite content to note:

Source 92/41

Examination prior to removal of Robert Bond late of Coggeshall. Wages £10 + board and lodging at age 20 (1814) in service of William Grimwood of Wetheringset near Debenham, co Suffolk, farmer.

No wages. Free board and lodging. Paid direct by customers. Engaged by George Wilson, head waiter, as boot catcher, at William Bacon's *Black Boy Inn*, Chelmsford (1816–17).

23 Nov 1821

The student of social mobility records the document at length.

Source 92/41

Examination prior to removal of Robert Bond late of Coggeshall. Born Broom, co Suffolk, about 1794. Service of farmer at Wetheringset near Debenham, co Suffolk, about 1814 for one year.

Service of innkeeper (as boot catcher) at Chelmsford, co Essex, about 1816–17, for 15–16 months.

Married at Great Coggeshall, co Essex, about 1820.
Chelmsford House of Correction 23 Nov 1821.

23 Nov 1821

A man studying literacy, after duly noting the document's subject
heading, writes down:

Source 92/41
Robert Bond (born 1794), farm labourer 1814, boot catcher
1816–17   Mark X

The student of occupations will be similarly brief.

Source 92/41
Examination of Robert Bond, 23 Nov 1821 mentions—
Decade 1810–19: farm labourer 1814–15, boot catcher 1816–17,
(the latter lived free in inn 'being engaged there as Boot Catcher by
George Wilson the Head Waiter . . . for what he could get of the
Customers for cleaning their Boots and Shoes').

The social historian comparing Preston's and Chelmsford's
settlement cases will probably work through the settlement
papers at Chelmsford, noting names to ensure that two or more
individual papers do not refer to one case. His only note need be:

92/41   Robert Bond.   23 Nov 1821.   Out of Chelmsford.

So far then, we have followed the progress of several different
students as they tackled one document. The information in the
notes varies tremendously. It is worthwhile remembering this,
because to take notes haphazardly without purpose leads to un-
satisfactory final results; just as the attempt to squeeze every
ounce of information from a document is too burdensome if you
do not need ninety per cent of the facts. So there next follows an
example of a genealogical and topographical abstract of a will;
not a full calendar of a will but a sifting of the record in order to
extract firstly people's names and personal details, secondly notes
of property and places. The testator's religion, the conditions
attached to legacies, his wretched spelling—all significant in some
studies—are irrelevant here.

Genealogical and topographical abstract of the will of Thomas
Henshall of Little Hey Side, yeoman, dated 21 June 1740, died
2 May 1761, not proved.

Mentions sons William of Stockport, butcher, and his
wife Mary;
Thomas of Barbados, merchant
daughter Elizabeth wife of William Johnson
servant Letice Purnell
Property: farm at Little Hey Side with newly-built farmhouse; freehold dwellinghouse in the market place of
Manchester; meadow adjoining the old mill at Hey held
for remainder of 21 years of Mr William Armstrong.
Witnesses: Matthew Hand and John Jolley (both sign
with marks).
Testator signs personally.

Probably more people examine registers (or transcripts) of
baptisms, marriages and burials than any other type of document.
Rules for studying, taking notes, transcribing and indexing
registers hold good for other archives too. Adopt the following
hints to suit particular conditions. If you are taking notes of
certain surnames for genealogical purposes, you will not of course
copy down the whole register. But it is essential to record every
mention of the surnames during the relevant period, even if some
of the families seem unrelated to your own, except in name. First
copy down general remarks:

Parish register of—Brockhampton 1733–1855
Years searched—1733–1812 (baptisms only)
Years missing—1752
Years illegible or damaged—none
Surnames sought—Cook, Fisher, Lambert

Use abbreviations with caution when taking notes, because these
can be a source of future error. Make sure, for example, that the
typist or reader of your notes knows that *c* means baptism or
christening, *b* means burial, *m* marriage, *d* died, *bn* banns, *brn*
born, *dau* daughter and *s* son. I take the first three letters of the
names of months, clearly writing Jan or Jun, Mar or May. There
are variations just as acceptable, but as long as you know what
you are doing and make your method and rules crystal clear, your
ways are as good as any. Never abbreviate names of people or

places or alter spellings (except for the possible exception of Christian names). Relevant entries should be set out horizontally across the page, so that further ones can follow in columns. Examples below record the minimum detail to be extracted.

BAPTISMS AT BROCKHAMPTON

Date	Surname	Christian Name	Parents	Abode	Father's Job
brn 1 Sep 1735	FARR	James	Henry & Mary	Langstone	not recorded
c 4 Sep 1735 (private)					
c 18 Sep 1735					

MARRIAGES AT COLYTON

Date	Surname	Christian Names	Abode	State or Job	Licence or Banns
21 Feb 1574	TOCKER	Robert	otp	bachelor	bn
	NEWTON	Susan	otp	spinster	
			(of this parish)		

BURIALS AT HAVANT

Date	Surname	Christian Name	Abode	Age	Job or State
d 16 Oct 1788	SMITH	Maurice	Langston (from Ireland)	ab 56	seafarer married man

If from these entries you go on to construct a family tree, use a wider variety of sources to prove the steps taken. You are, for the sake of an instance, tracing the pedigree of John Richardson of Houghend, shoemaker, who died in 1785, aged sixty-four. There are obviously going to be many John Richardsons born around 1720–22; but even in the one parish where John lived, there are two:

John son of James and Mary Richardson c 15 Apr 1721

John son of Matthew and Mary Richardson c 16 Jun 1721

Quite obviously the pedigree can from here take two very different lines, unless you bring other evidence to bear. John himself served as overseer of the poor in 1760, according to the town book, 'for Richardson's tenement'. The leases of the tenement in the squire's family muniment room at the old manor house go back to 1680. In 1695 Henry Richardson the younger takes a lease on a tenement 'lately in the possession of Elizabeth Woodeson' which later was known as Richardson's. There are no further leases till 1775, far too late to be of use. But Henry died in 1750 and in his will mentions his son James 'lately deceased'. It is reasonable therefore to link Henry, James, and our John through their connection with the tenement; reasonable but not yet certain. Now in 1734, John Bryant, a local shoemaker, took as apprentice John Richardson, aged thirteen, whom he describes as 'my nephew'. John Bryant was son of John and Ellen Bryant and grandson, through his mother, of Thomas and Elizabeth Woodesen. John Bryant had a sister Mary who, in 1718, married James Richardson. Bryant's will, dated 1776, mentions John Richardson of Houghend 'my kinsman' but no other John Richardson. The link is acceptable at last; though not of course perfect.

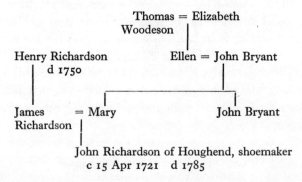

An edited transcription of the register demands a somewhat different approach since, theoretically, your work should be good enough to present to a publisher. In such cases, quarto paper must be used, special lined paper for the working manuscript and typing paper for a typescript. Always make a top copy and at least two carbons, and present the register's owner with one copy. Give others if available to the county record office and Society of Genealogists. Use one side of the paper only, and never write in the 1½ inch margin. Place on the title page the name of parish or chapelry; describe the size and condition of the

register, whether its pages are parchment or paper, type of cover
and binding, legibility, covering dates of volume with notes of
missing or indecipherable pages, name of transcriber and date of
the work.

Each subsequent page ought to be headed with name of parish
and must indicate whether page contains baptisms, marriages,
burials or all three. When entries are in Latin, translate the date:
octavo die aprilis becomes 11 Apr. If there is no doubt about the
Christian name, this may be translated: *Gulielmus* is always
William. But *Anna* may in English be Ann, Anne, Hannah and
could be left in the Latin form. There is a list of Latin equivalents
in the first volume of the *National Index of Parish Registers*, pages
110–12. Surnames are rarely Latinised, but great care is needed
with any that are. *Filius Gulielmi* could be Williamson or Fitz-
william or even 'son of William' (Smith or Brown or whatever).
Occupations should be translated, unless you are transcribing
exactly what stands in the register and it seems to you important
to leave whatever is in Latin as a contrast to what is in English.
If, by reason of illegibility or damage to document, you supply
missing information by guesswork, even on the surest of grounds,
you must state what you have done clearly, so that future researchers never mistake your interpolation for the words of the
document.

LIGHTFOOT, Martha (Matty) of Barnton	
daughter of Samuel & Sarah Burgess of	
Anderton, born 1801	55
married Ashton Lightfoot of Barnton 1822	55
received legacies from William Leigh and	
residue of Ashton's goods 1845–6	11/44
resident of Barnton 1846	20
purchased Leigh's property 1832	64/21
lived at Leigh's Brow 1841	107
died 1854 aged 54 years	164
	/over

Obviously a very large pile of information will soon accumulate.

The notes are in no sequence except the haphazard order in which records were examined. Thus Chelmsford settlement papers were ninety-second, not in importance but in order seen. Such an arrangement is difficult to organise without an adequate card index. Here then the small cards come into their own the object being to form one very condensed alphabetical sequence of people, places and subjects mentioned in your notes. Numbers refer to the following documents:

11/44   Will of Ashton Lightfoot of Barnton, watchman at the salt works, proved 1846

20   Tithe apportionment 1846

55   Great Budworth parish registers

64/21   Papers of William Leigh at Messrs Chambers, solicitors

107   Census of Barnton, 1841

164   Death certificates at superintendent registrar's

MILLING—FLOUR	
John Ross, miller, 1832	172
Petition complains of high prices, 1637	212/86
Situated in Blacklock's meadow, 1596	42
In land tax list, 1732–1831	68

STONEY HEYS FARM FARMHOUSE	
Property of Marbury family 12th–17th C	64/15
Paid land tax 1732–1831	68
Occupied by Richard Steele, 1758–87	68, 64/17
House on tithe map 1843	20
Land in Bertintune in fine 1374	133/11
House newly built 1710	89
Estate outside Townfield 1620	79
James Johnson repaired chimney 1667	147
	/over

Notes taken from documents over several years should provide a reasonably complete basis for local history. Every inhabitant that lived in the township ought to be mentioned somewhere, if

merely as recipient of a pauper's funeral. This is certainly true
for the period after 1740, when no one inhabiting the place for
six months or more ought to be missed; and is almost true for the
period after 1600 too. For this modern age, then, draw up one
card for each man and woman fourteen years old or more. In
addition create one family unit card for each couple and their
children, showing dates of baptism and burial (or birth and
death).

```
BOWYER
   Thomas of Netherton, gardener 1695-1757
   Mary (Williamson) 1691-1751
                  m 16 Sep 1717
   Thomas        c 12 May 1718        died about 1790
   William       c 17 Nov 1719        b 22 Nov 1730
   James         c 14 Apr 1721        b 19 Apr 1721
   Mary          c 22 Apr 1722        m 1748
   James         c 26 May 1723        b 21 Dec 1757
   Betty         c  1 Nov 1724        m 1748
   Philip        c 27 Feb 1726        b 10 Oct 1731
                                      /over
```

Such cards are essential tools for the genealogist. He takes all
cards of one surname from the index, sorts in chronological
order, and sees the outline of a family tree in ten minutes. Links
between generations are immediately apparent. But drawing up
these cards is not just the genealogist's work. Most local historians will have to create some such record in order to learn
about population changes, characteristics of the family, migration
and other subjects.

When therefore you have collected a complete set of family
unit cards by indexing all your notes (all notes, be it repeated, not
merely parish registers), you can find yourself in a position to
answer some fifty or sixty questions on the following lines: what
was the average age of marriage, what the average number of
children per family, what the village population in March 1731?
Take just the last question as an example. Use the Bowyer family
card as an instance. You notice that father and mother Bowyer

are in residence or at least alive in 1731, so they are two people in the village.

1   Thomas Bowyer   1695–1757
2   Mary (Williamson) Bowyer   1691–1751

Of course, they may have been temporarily visiting friends in another town in March 1731; but of this we have no evidence either way. Our listing cannot therefore take the place of a census conducted on the spot on one day. But for our purpose, the parents can be called residents. Visitors in their house in March 1731 will be similarly unnoticed. Be this as it may, now move on to the children.

3   Thomas   1718–90

But William died in 1730 and James in 1721.

4   Mary   1722   m 1748
5   James   1723–57
6   Betty   1724   m 1748

Philip did not die until October of 1731.

7   Philip   1727–31

Hence seven members of the Bowyer family are to be added to the list of inhabitants. The figure is very accurate, provided you have patiently examined most township records, taken detailed notes and indexed thoroughly. You actually count a few people in the list who may have been temporarily absent in March 1731, perhaps visiting a daughter in the city or doing a month's hard labour in the house of correction; but you miss others who are in town for only a matter of weeks, Irish labourers, vagrants, travellers, mothers-in-law. The two balance in some cases. Certainly, when I checked my card index against the figure in the 1801 census, I had two more people in a population of over four hundred. Historians do not consider the 1801 census to be absolutely accurate, so the card index figure might well have been right.

The needs of the researcher decide the form and detail of the cards themselves. The student of place-names can ignore people and topics. Another historian may study wages and prices. The manner of indexing depends on the specific angle the man is

taking. If he is going to adopt a chronological approach showing
the movement of wages and prices over several decades, he may
well choose to head his cards with dates, all information for 1814
appearing on one card or on several immediately adjacent ones.
This method would help in drawing up chronological tables and
graphs.

1814 MALE WAGES

Farm labourer—£10 + board & lodging—Suffolk 92/41
Canal boatman—1s 6d a day—Worcester   312
Salt waller—1s 4d a day—Cheshire   71
Schoolmaster—£30 a year—Cheshire   112
Road labourer—1s 2d a day—Lancashire   197

Some final but very important points must now be stressed.
Notes and card indexes should never be destroyed. If you have
lost enthusiasm, preserve whatever you own in case other people
are interested. If the notes are reasonably scholarly, deposit them
in the county record office, just as the solicitors of Richard
Cookson of Goosnargh placed his unfinished history of Goosnargh in the Lancashire Record Office. Instead of transcribing
documents, consider photocopies. These are perfectly accurate,
whereas transcripts may contain mistakes. Record-office hours
are not extensive, and copies can be completed in the record office
as you sort out interesting documents, and then studied at leisure
on your return home. Good photocopies may be stored after use
and read by later researchers with complete confidence.

Remember to inquire about copyright. Public records are
usually freely available, but estate records and correspondence
may be subject to copyright. You can publish only with the
owner's consent which is obtained for you by the county archivist
or other custodian of the records. It is an archivist's job to
produce records from the strongroom for you, but his goodwill is
still needed for transcribing, translating, obtaining permission to
publish, and so on. It is no part of the job of a solicitor, company
secretary or landowner to make documents available for you. If

you upset anybody you cut yourself off from access to vital records and spoil the chances of access for future researchers.

The study of archives and books does not guarantee the production of worthwhile history, even with a scientific approach and artistic style of writing added. It is vital to be clear in your mind what are the significant and essential aspects of your subject, to see the wood for the trees, and to investigate as far as possible your history on the ground. Do not include too much ephemeral material or facts common to every community. It is unworthy of much stress that village tithes were commuted for a rent charge in 1838; as a result of an act in 1836 several thousand parishes commuted tithes. But if tithes were commuted in 1538, this fact demands investigation and explanation because it is out of the ordinary. That one-third of the population asked for poor relief in the period 1800–12 is not surprising; what would be worth detailed study is a community with virtually no paupers during that period. Differences rather than similarities make men and places worth investigating.

No firm rule can be laid down about what should be included and what excluded. Do not therefore throw into your account all facts discovered just to save wasting them, because there is little more boring (or unpublishable, if that is relevant) than a history choked with meaningless details. On the other hand do not leave out any evidence needed to prove your thesis.

Finally, investigate all physical survivals connected with your topic—village houses, present field pattern, the church, railway, castle, portraits, coins, the millrace, drainage ditches, abandoned factory and almshouse. Study the local museum's exhibits and ask the curator to comment on your present or other earlier relevant investigations. I was once told that the main street of a certain village suffered a semi-circular diversion when an eighteenth-century squire took it into his head to build his hall in the middle of the old road. Although there was no longer a house there, the spot in question clearly appeared on all the maps half surrounded by the curving road. But investigation on the ground revealed a treacherous marsh that must in the past have been even worse, certainly boggy enough to encourage surveyors to divert their road. Whether in fact the bog is natural or the result of quarrying or digging a moat might be solved by excavation. Seeing for yourself does therefore explain many a village layout, route of railway or road, location of factory or forge, and rise or decay of market town.

Chapter 2

NATIONAL ARCHIVES

British Museum

THE British Museum was founded in 1753 following Hans Sloane's bequest and sale of his library and museum to the nation. Into this institution was incorporated the older collection of books, manuscripts, and 'other rarities and curiosities' left to the country by the Cotton family. The government purchased the Harley manuscripts, containing many local history documents, at the same date. In 1757, George II donated the Royal Library with its privilege of compulsory deposit of all copyright books published in Great Britain. The museum, financed by lottery, opened at Montagu House, London, in 1759. Two of the departments are vitally important to historians: Printed Books (state paper room and map room included) and Manuscripts.

Documents alone are numbered in millions. Of great use to local historians are the Egerton, Cottonian, Harleian and Additional manuscripts, artificial collections which place side by side documents from Cheshire and Essex, title deeds, muster lists, sketches of villages, petitions to the Commons and monastic charters. Most collections are to some extent listed or calendared, though not adequately indexed. It is as well to work through the printed lists yourself. The museum has never taken public or local government records. It owns few archives, that is entire

manuscript collections of families or businesses, preferring these
to be deposited locally.

Among the Harleian manuscripts are returns from eight dioceses to the 1563 general census. In that year the Privy Council
asked all bishops to make a survey of their dioceses, and the final
statistics survive. For an example of this census see J. Cornwall,
'An Elizabethan census' in *Records of Buckinghamshire*, volume
XVI, part 4 (1959). Returns from the dioceses of Gloucester,
Norwich and Winchester to the official registers of Anglican
communicants, papist recusants and nonconformists compiled in
1603 are also among the Harleian collection.

It is always tempting to commence research on the museum's
series of charters, chronicles, monastic records and autograph
letters of the renowned. But it is wise to recall that many of these
documents are now in print; others have been studied and ex-
ploited by great scholars; while the majority provide palaeographical and linguistic problems of some magnitude. Take for
instance the romantic-sounding and certainly interesting Anglo-
Saxon charters which record the conveyance of property or rights
over land. They date from about 680 to 1100, are written in
Saxon and later in Latin and Saxon, and become very elaborate
in form. They should be studied not at the museum but in the
three books on charters available at reference libraries: J. M.
Kemble, *Codex Diplomaticus Aevi Saxonici* (1839–48), W. de G.
Birch, *Cartularium Saxonicum* (1885–99), and the Royal Historical Society's *Anglo-Saxon Charters* (1968). Their diplomatic
and linguistic aspects should be studied only by expert Saxon-
ists.

The ordinary historian should confine himself to a more super-
ficial study, seeking for instance names of petty kings, nobles,
church dignitaries and landowners as well as families and tribes
from the seventh to eleventh centuries, adding to general knowledge of social and political history in those shadowy times. Try
to identify townships and estates, mapping the progress of settlement. Detailed descriptions of town bounds are worth noting:
'from the stone on along the highway to the ditch thence down

to Wealdenesford thence on to the hollow way'. Evidence for place-name research is important in illustrating Celtic survivals and earliest forms of English names. It is possible also to trace Viking and Danish penetration from personal and place-names. Features like the hollow way or the ford above mentioned continue to figure in documents down to the nineteenth century, so it is interesting to have a pre-Conquest origin for such man-made points.

Anybody may wander into the museum in order to examine the massive display of antiquities, valuable manuscripts and books. But to work in the library and archives you must possess a reader's ticket, countersigned by a person of repute in your community. On account of the value of manuscripts and books, you will be strictly supervised; never resent this care. The museum issues a short guide to the use of the reading room and catalogues of the printed books and manuscript collections. Document collections themselves are being slowly calendared and many volumes are in print.

Somerset House

Since 1 July 1837 the General Register Office at Somerset House has recorded all births, marriages and deaths in England and Wales. The whole country has been divided into local registration districts each with a superintendent registrar. This official must by law be informed of all births, marriages and deaths, and he can indeed perform marriages himself. In the early years of registration, many people neglected to obey the law, and records therefore are not absolutely complete from 1837. None the less by far the greater number of vital statistics are entered in local registers and indexed. Periodically, register entries have been sent to Somerset House for inclusion by the registrar-general in the national register and index. Indexes are there arranged in huge quarterly volumes with surnames in alphabetical order, which are available for public perusal. These provide the necessary reference which enables officials either locally or at Somerset House to locate the volume in which is recorded the original certificate. The latter can be copied, for a fee. Birth certificates state registration district; name, sex and birthplace of child; date of birth; parents' names; mother's maiden surname; residence and job of father; name and address of person who informed the registrar. Marriage certificates show date, town and place of marriage; names and ages of parties with residence and occupations; marital status of both parties; names and jobs of both fathers. Death certificates provide name, address, date, age and cause of death; if known the registrar adds the occupation of the deceased; the name and description of the person who informed the registrar is given. The registrar-general holds a marine register book of births and deaths at sea since 1837; consular returns of births, marriages and deaths of British subjects abroad date from 1849. Somerset House has been, since 1858, the Principal Probate Registry where wills and administrations are proved, registered and indexed. Local probate registries possess copies of all the registers and indexes.

House of Lords Record Office

The House of Lords Record Office was established in 1946 as the repository for records of parliament. Before that date, documents had been preserved by good fortune as much as by foresight in various offices within the Palace of Westminster. Not all records survived: in 1834 a fire destroyed most of the Commons papers, as well as the palace itself. Then after World War II parliament converted the high Victoria Tower into a twelve-storey archives centre with well-designed strongrooms and a search room. The name of the record office reflects the preponderance of House of Lords documents in the strongrooms. Commons papers date mainly from 1834, Lords papers from 1497. Medieval records are in the Public Record Office. Maurice Bond has written an excellent *Guide to the Records of Parliament* (1971), which supplies detailed information.

The daily business of parliament—motions, resolutions, debates, consideration of papers and bills—is recorded shortly in the *Journals of the House of Lords* from 1510 and *Journals of the*

House of Commons from 1547. Both are printed in huge volumes
and indexed thoroughly. Some large libraries and record offices
possess sets of these journals. If, therefore, in the index for 1722
you find mention of an enclosure of land in your village, you are
led from the journals to the original private enclosure acts and
other documents at the Lords Record Office. Journals up to 1803
must serve as the best source for parliamentary activity, because
before this it was a breach of privilege to report on debates.
Unofficial reports were of course written, and William Cobbett
edited these in thirty-six volumes as the *Parliamentary History*,
ostensibly from 1066 to 1803. In 1803 the press gallery was
opened and Cobbett's *Parliamentary Debates* begin, T. C. Hansard taking over in 1812. Speeches of national interest alone were
included in the early days; but more detail gradually crept in,
until in 1909 each House decided to publish reports of its own
debates word for word. These are indexed by subject, person and
place.

Some 60,000 acts of parliament are in the record office. Although public acts (known as statutes) like Habeas Corpus spring
most readily to mind, the bulk are local and personal acts concerning town corporations, naturalisation, divorce, drainage of
fens, harbours, enclosure, estate settlements, repair of roads.
Original public acts on parchment rolls date from 1497 to 1849;
in vellum books from 1849. Texts are in English. Acts are printed
after 1849. Original acts differ from printed versions because
punctuation and general editing of the latter are the work of later
editors; more important, the final printed version either omits
clauses originally engrossed on parchment after the report stage
and subsequently abandoned or alternatively contains additional
new matter. Original private acts on parchment rolls survive for
the period 1497–1850, in vellum books from 1850.

The full, edited and printed text of public acts is in the Record
Commissioners' *Statutes of the Realm* (1810–28). For acts of
1714–97 the full text is printed in *Sessional Volumes of Public
Acts*, very rare but available at the Lords Record Office and
British Museum. A somewhat shortened text of most acts from

1235 is printed in the more common volumes known as *Statutes at Large*, available at local libraries. Since 1798, the final text of all acts has been printed in the *Sessional* (now *Annual*) *Volumes*. Private acts prior to the year 1714 remained unprinted. A number of acts from 1714 to 1797 were published for local or private use and copies survive in local record offices, family muniments and town records. The majority of modern private acts are available in the two series known as local acts (beginning 1798) and private acts (1815). In order to find an act, whether printed or in the original, the student uses various lists. A chronological table to the public general statutes is kept up to date by Her Majesty's Stationery Office and refers by a short title to each act, giving regnal year and chapter (or act) number in the form 'c 12'. No alphabetical index to the acts themselves is available, though *Halsbury's Statutes of England* sets out acts according to an alphabetical order of subjects. The government also issues a printed and indexed list of local acts from 1801 which divides acts into fifteen subject headings; number one reading 'Bridges, Ferries, Roads, Subways and Tunnels'. All acts, both public and private, are listed chronologically in the introductory portions of the eighteenth-century editions of *Statutes at Large*.

The progress of a public bill is followed in the journals of both Houses as the measure receives two readings, consideration in committee, a report stage, third reading, final amendments and royal assent. For greater detail the Lords manuscript minutes of proceedings and draft journals from 1621, the *Parliamentary History* and *Hansard* should be read. Bills which failed to pass the Commons are not preserved before 1834; but Lords failed bills are available and many are printed in the *Calendar of the Manuscripts of the House of Lords*.

Private bills, benefiting or at least affecting local communities, trades, families and individuals, deal with enclosure of open fields, divorce, naturalisation, compulsory purchase of land for railed-ways or borough water supply. Because proposed changes upset or disturbed customary or statutory privileges, a parliamentary measure alone could set matters straight. The process

began with petitions for and against the bill, and these are preserved from 1572. Bills themselves are copied in the form in
which they were introduced or are engrossed after changes in
committee. Committee proceedings are recorded in Lords committee books from 1660. Proceedings on divorce matters are
particularly full from 1669 to 1857 (when general divorce legislation was passed). Discussions on estates took up much time:
settlements, mortgages, mineral rights, entails, succession, all
exercise the minds of Georgian parliaments. After 1706 all petitions to the Lords for estate bills were investigated by two judges
who summoned witnesses and reported opinions to the House.
Naturalisation records show the full name, parentage and place
of birth of the applicant. They date from 1600 to 1844.

In 1792–4 both Houses, worried by the number of navigation
and canal bills, ordered that plans, sections and other documents
be drawn up and presented for parliament's perusal prior to
discussion of the measure. Other public works were later included
in the standing orders. After 1794, the deposited plans and
related material refer to bridges, ferries, roads, tunnels; all transport undertakings (railways, tramways); canals, rivers, navigations; lighting (electric, gas); water supply; drainage. Plans are
usually on a very large scale (some buildings are shown at 44
inches to the mile), in ink, coloured, and usually manuscript
though often printed. Ordnance maps are employed ordinarily as
base plans, after about 1850. Each parcel of property affected by
the proposed development is numbered on the plan, and refers to
a reference book in which are listed names of owners and occupiers with descriptions (acreage and land use) of the property.
Sections across and along the proposed works accompany these
plans. Then follow lists of people consenting to the works, subscription contracts showing how much each person promised to
pay; detailed estimates of cost of buying land and constructing
the works; estimates of time to be taken till completion. In the
course of these investigations the two Houses heard witnesses for
and against the changes. Hundreds of huge volumes in manuscript, and still largely unused by students, exist to record com

mittee evidence in the Lords from about 1800 and in the Commons from 1835.

Parliamentary papers concern nearly every aspect of life since 1531. Parliament is not restricted in the subjects members may raise for investigation or have brought to their attention, and as a result its papers are massive in bulk and alive with interest. Original papers of the Lords, from 1531 to date, are in the record office. These are calendared in *Manuscripts of the House of Lords* for 1531–1714 and printed in full in *House of Lords Sessional Papers* from 1801. A few important eighteenth-century papers for 1788–1801 are available, in printed form, in the House of Lords library. Most original papers of the Commons are either destroyed or unavailable to researchers, though a number dating from 1593–1649 do survive in the record office. Papers of the period up to 1714 have been calendared in *Manuscripts of the House of Lords*. Those for 1715–1801 may be read in the sixteen volumes of Commons reprinted papers. For 1731–1800 you may also use the 110 volumes of collected papers in the Abbot collection (available at the British Museum). From 1801 papers are printed in full in *House of Commons Sessional Papers*. As a key to the papers, employ the journals of both Houses; the two series of indexes to the Commons and Lords sessional papers; W. R. Powell, *Local History from Blue Books: a select list of the sessional papers of the House of Commons* (1962); *Hansard's Catalogue and Breviate of British Parliamentary Papers 1696–1834* (1953); P. G. Ford, *Select List of British Parliamentary Papers 1833–99* (1953).

Petitions form a most important section of the papers. Originating from communities or individuals who found something to say to parliament these documents date mainly from 1621 onwards. Nearly every town, trade and class at one time or another addressed itself to parliament about (to take just four examples) episcopal government in the church, trade practices, wages and political reform. In 1833, petitions began to be recorded in various reports of the select committee of the Commons on public petitions. Only from 1950 are original petitions preserved. Reports are available in the record office on loan from the library of the Commons. Indexes, by subject of petitions and organisations responsible, appear in the sessional papers.

Command papers are presented to parliament by government departments and bodies like royal commissions. The earliest, dated 1641, concerns Anabaptists in Southwark. House papers of both Houses are laid before members at their own request by any type of organisation including committees of either House as an aid to parliamentary deliberation. The earliest concerns the relief of London poor afflicted by plague in 1626. Papers deposited under terms of acts of parliament include annual reports of statutory bodies like the Poor Law Board. These three types of papers were at first in manuscript on paper or parchment, though by 1750 most were printed as White Papers (if not separately and specially covered) or Blue Books (if of sufficient importance and bulk to warrant separate publication within a blue cover). From 1801 all command, House and deposited papers have been annually collected together as sessional papers.

Sessional papers concern national and global affairs like imperial expansion, the navy, colonial government, trade, poor law, industry, coal supplies and education. Eighteenth-century papers especially are almost entirely of this type. Tudor and Stuart papers do, however, embrace more local affairs like borough government, prices, markets and craft guilds. The 1642 returns of protestations against Charles I's leaning to arbitrary government serve as parochial census lists of men over eighteen who protested (or refused to protest). Occasional details of jobs and religious affiliation appear. Some thirty counties are represented in whole or part and certain parish lists are fully printed. Parishes represented in the returns are noted in the Historical Manuscripts Commission's *Fifth Report* (appendix) and in volume 5 of the *Calendar of the Manuscripts of the House of Lords*. Returns of papists for 1705–6, 1767 and 1781 cover the whole country and remain largely uncalendared. Though not naming people, each anonymous person's age, occupation, residence and other details appear thus enabling identification by the local historian.

From 1801 sessional papers are voluminous, touching nearly

every topic of historical and legal interest, though not all papers are printed and published. Both the Lords (1817, 1831, 1847) and the Commons (1813–14, 1817, 1818, 1828, 1847) set up committees to investigate the working of the poor laws. The report of the poor-law commissioners of 1834 criticises administration as conducted at that time and proposes reform, appending as proof, answers to questions posed to hundreds of parish officials. Annual reports of inclosure commissioners run from 1846–82. These books list enclosures that do not require parliamentary approval. Reports of charity commissioners are arranged by counties and parishes, describing local charities in existence between 1819 and 1840. The Commons inquired about educational charities also in 1835; and from 1839 there are minutes of the Privy Council committee on education, detailing grants to individual schools, names of student teachers and inspectors' reports. Reports on factory and mining conditions, children's employment, trade and industry, agriculture, sanitary condition of Victorian towns, and hundreds of other papers could be reviewed, but this gives a fair sample of the thoroughness and liveliness of papers. Most are printed and thus available in some large libraries, if not as books then on microcards. A number of purely local papers remain unprinted and must be consulted in the record office: in 1818 for example these deal with Shoreham harbour, Scottish whale fishing and London docks, among other matters.

The House of Lords has since late medieval times acted as a court to hear cases of law, hearing appeals from lower courts and sorting out points of error in law. The volume of work grew enormously after 1720, when Scottish, industrial and commercial problems began to arise. In 1873 the hearing of appeals was abolished by act, but a later act of 1876 gave the Lords the duty of receiving appeals from the newly created courts of appeal in civil cases. In 1907 criminal causes were added. Documents in appeal cases include petitions, proofs, counsels' speeches, records of opinions and judgements from 1624 to date. For a key to all cases see the indexes to the Lords journals. Since 1865 Lords cases appear in annual *Law Reports*.

The investigation of peerage claims from 1628 to date has unearthed a mass of genealogical information. Families are traced back many generations and, horizontally so to speak, from branch to branch till ordinary yeoman or trading stock is reached. Many family legends concerning rights to baronial halls, coats of arms and aristocratic titles might well be authenticated or disposed of by referring to these cases. Original petitions, minutes of hearings, pedigrees, evidences and such like are preserved. There is a card index to claims though once again the journals are the surest guide.

Parliament's records are in fact private, not being within the scope of the public records legislation, and are primarily for the use of members of the legislature—though all researchers are welcomed by the trained staff. The office is open on weekdays throughout the year, and although no appointment is necessary, it is as well to arrange a visit in advance so that requisite documents can be made ready. The office supplies many lists and calendars of documents. Photocopies are produced at modest cost.

Original acts and related documents are essential sources for the historian of family estates. Problems of succession, the disposal of entailed property, settlements on minor branches and estate administration are dealt with. Evidence of ancient local customs is most important and most useful for the period 1700–1840. Deposited plans showing all public works and neighbouring property on a very large scale often ante-date ordnance and estate surveys. The local historian finds evidence of long-forgotten lanes, houses, factories and place-names on these plans. Financial statements reveal the identities of shareholders and the extent of their contributions (though some large subscribers may never actually have handed the money over). What class of people supported public works in your locality? From what source had they raised their money? In the evidence given to committees you discover by reading between the lines the real motive of promoters, the advantages, the case for opponents and extent of disruption of old ways and customs. By the way, emerge lists of local wages, prices, traders, crops, manufactures, gentry, paupers;

descriptions of local practices unrecorded elsewhere; the state of
harvests and factories.

Public Record Office

The Public Record Office in Chancery Lane, London, was established by an act of parliament of 1838, to preserve all state
records. Documents had of course been collected by various
government departments for centuries before this, but storage
facilities were poor and limited. Each department tried to hold
its own records: Chancery, for instance, in the King's Wardrobes
in the Tower of London and the New Temple and later in the
chapel of the master of the rolls (on the site of the present Public
Record Office); and Exchequer at Westminster. Other archives
lay in the Westminster chapter house and King's Mews, ravaged
by rats, insects, damp and souvenir hunters. Some papers were
customarily removed by outgoing ministers. Lord Burghley,
Elizabeth's lord treasurer, and his son Lord Salisbury, secretary
of state, took home to Hatfield a mass of correspondence of far
greater importance to political historians than what remains in
London.

In order to control all these repositories of public records and
to calendar and publish documents themselves, the government
appointed a royal commission in 1800. The commissioners did
little in the way of controlling or arranging archives but published
quite a number of transcripts of documents. The famous typeface
employed by the record commissioners attempted to copy the
appearance of original documents. Thus abbreviation marks are
all preserved, while contractions or suspensions are not extended.
Unfortunately transcripts abound in inaccuracies and indexes are
inadequate. Then, in 1838, the Public Record Office Act provided
for the centralisation of 'all rolls records writs books proceedings
decrees bills warrants accounts papers and documents whatsoever
of a public nature' in one office where the master of the rolls, his
deputy keeper and assistant archivists should care for the records
and define terms of public access. A new repository was erected
in 1850-3 and records were slowly collected together.

By 1862, for instance, the contents of the State Paper Office (which had since about 1603 preserved records of the internal and external affairs of the kingdom) had been transferred to the Public Record Office. Government departments despatch documents no longer in regular use for administrative purposes. Access to the records is limited to students with reader's tickets. A ticket is obtained after filling in a form stating name, address and nature of research project and having the form countersigned by a person of repute in the community (a justice of the peace, schoolmaster or librarian). Provided research cannot as easily be completed in a local library or record office, the issue of a ticket generally follows.

Of course not all documents are available for research. Sir Roger Casement's diaries, 1901–11, and census returns, to name just two archives, stay closed for one hundred years. Other papers may be inaccessible for thirty years (as laid down in the Public Records Act 1967) or during the lifetime of people mentioned in the documents. Certain of the public records like Domesday Book are permanently displayed in the record office museum which is open to all visitors without ticket.

Reading pre-eighteenth-century public records will demand a knowledge of Latin and palaeography, because comparatively few documents are fully published in translation. Calendars sometimes provide all the details a student needs but the majority of records are not yet even calendared. If you purchase a photocopy of a significant document, your county archivist might agree to transcribe and translate for you. All records are arranged by departments, the earliest being Chancery, Exchequer, King's Bench, Common Pleas and the courts of itinerant justices. Later come Admiralty, War, Agriculture, Home and Foreign Offices, and of course many more. Individual series may therefore be calendared in alphabetical order of subject or title within each department's archive. Domesday Book appears under Exchequer, ships' musters under Admiralty.

For a full list of departments whose records are available for study, and an alphabetical list of documents, types of document,

persons, places and subjects, consult the published guide to the
Public Record Office. See sectional list 24 (issued by the record
office) for details of state records that have been edited, calendared, transcribed and published.

The Exchequer was the department where the king's debtors
were called to account and also a court of law for revenue matters.
All the great officers of state originally attended in the Exchequer.
The office was early in the twelfth century known as the Tallies,
from the notched stick cleft in two that was the original method
of accounting. The tallies remained in use till 1826, and their
subsequent destruction in 1834 incidentally burned down the
Palace of Westminster too. The treasurer gradually took control
of this department. (The Prime Minister is still First Lord of the
Treasury.) Other officials then stayed away. Even the chancellor
sent only his clerk, known as the chancellor of the Exchequer.
The law court extended its business from revenue to most
common-law problems touching land, goods or profits. On the
equity side any person could file a bill against another merely by
claiming to be a king's accountant. The Court of Exchequer, the
finance department of government, took its name from the large
tablecloth marked with squares like a chequerboard on which
officials performed their calculations. The use of Roman numerals
meant that arithmetic had to be simplified with the aid of
counters or suchlike.

The upper department or exchequer of audit was subdivided
into the treasurer's remembrancer's office and the king's remembrancer's office. Among records of these offices are the pipe rolls
1129–1832, audited accounts of county sheriffs; foreign rolls containing all other accounts; originalia rolls, which are extracts from
Chancery rolls sent to the Exchequer for information; memoranda rolls with copies of correspondence; vouchers and audited
receipts of expenditure; judicial records concerning treasury legal
tussles. The lower department or exchequer of receipt accepted
money brought to London by accountants, persons rendering
account; and paid out to claimants on government orders. These
transactions are recorded on issue and receipt rolls.

After the break with Rome, Henry VIII seized church property and established new financial organs like the Court of First Fruits and Tenths to administer church revenues. This court's records include the Valor Ecclesiasticus of 1535 (printed by the Record Commissioners), a survey of the value of all ecclesiastical benefices. Exchequer absorbed the Court of Augmentations, which had been founded to deal with the property of suppressed religious houses. It therefore holds monastic muniments, leases of monastic lands, particulars for grants of crown property, documents concerning schools and colleges and certificates of dissolved chantries.

Domesday Book has its origin in William the Conqueror's decision in 1085 to send his commissioners 'all over England into every shire to find out how many hundreds of hides of land were in each shire, and how much land and livestock the king himself owned in the country, and what yearly dues were lawfully his from each shire'. The Anglo-Saxon chronicler records the thoroughness with which the king set about his task 'so that there was not even one ox, nor one cow, nor one pig which escaped notice in his survey'. The survey of 1086 is primarily a personal inquiry into those holding land in chief of the king. To this end the king's men assembled juries in each place consisting of sheriff, priest, lord of the manor, reeve and six villagers; and on oath the juries answered the set questions.

1 What is the name of this manor?
2 Who was tenant in 1065 when King Edward died?
3 Who is now tenant?
4 How many hides in the manor? (A hide is a unit generally reckoned at around 120 acres.)
5 How many ploughteams are working in the lord's demesne and in the villager's lands?
6 How many family units specified by social class (serf, villein, cottar, priest, and so on)?
7 How much pasture, meadow and woodland?
8 How many mills, fishponds and other assets like salt-pans? What is their value?
9 What was the total value of the manor in 1065?
10 What is the value in 1086?

Answers were despatched to the king and eventually written up in clear abbreviated Latin in double columns on parchment. Most answers were somewhat inaccurately condensed, though fuller versions survive for East Anglia and the West Country. The four northern counties do not appear at all and Yorkshire and Lancashire are hastily sketched. The parchments were arranged by counties, each county's entries beginning with a survey of ancient local customs especially concerning tax assessment and payments, individual schemes for administering justice and inquests and rights of military service. Then comes a list of landowners: king, bishops, abbeys, laymen. Then, under the heading of each individual proprietor, follow surveys of manors which he owns. A township divided among three lords therefore appears in three different places in the survey. Domesday is available in facsimile prepared by the Ordnance Survey in 1861–4 and in translation in the *Victoria County History* for each county. V. H. Galbraith's *The Making of Domesday Book* (1961) explains why and how the survey was produced. H. C. Darby and others have since 1952 been publishing a series of regional Domesday geographies of England.

Subsidy rolls date from the late thirteenth century until 1689. Documents record money raised by the government from clerics and laymen to pay the cost of administration and war. The lay subsidy was supposed to represent a proportion of annual value of moveables belonging to people in boroughs, cities and counties, the proportion being a tenth, fifteenth or similar amount. Tax assessors tried to arrange a meaningful tax, varying from time to time with fluctuations in annual value. But this attempt was abandoned in 1334. Later subsidies fall far below true annual values. Clerical subsidies represent one-tenth of annual value of moveables, based on the valuation of Pope Nicholas IV in 1291, modified for the northern province in 1318. The 1291 taxation of all parishes in the country has been printed by the Record Commissioners. It well illustrates the disparity of wealth between the barren northern province and prosperous Canterbury.

The poll tax of 1377 sought four pence from each layman over the age of fourteen, one shilling from beneficed clergy. In 1379 assessors tried to grade the poll tax according to wealth but failed. Hence in 1380 the government asked for a shilling a head from all people. A peasant man and woman had to find two shillings. It cannot have been a matter of surprise to the administration when the population suddenly dropped by one-third, or so it seemed in taxation returns. Collectors in 1381 could not discover the names and whereabouts of thousands of people. Their attempts indeed partly caused the Peasants' Revolt.

Richard II and Henry VIII levied a subsidy of four shillings in the pound on land and 2s 8d on goods. All these taxes soon became fixed sums in fact and do not record real annual values. It seems to have been possible not merely to be undervalued but to escape paying tax altogether. The most reliable and complete tax lists are for 1295, 1327, 1334; the poll taxes of 1377–81; and the comprehensive and very thoroughly collected lay subsidy of 1524–5. Subsidy rolls are generally arranged by counties and parishes. Under each named parish appear all taxpayers and the amount of their tax: 'de Willelmo molendinario vs (from William the miller 5s) . . . de Agnete de Neuton iijs (from Agnes Neuton 3s) . . . de Ricardo tannario iiijs (from Richard Tanner 4s)'. A few documents for certain counties are in print. Since rolls are merely lists of names and sums (in Latin), it is not difficult to transcribe and translate a particular township entry.

Between 1662 and 1689 parliament tried to levy a tax on hearths. Everyone who owned property worth more than twenty shillings a year was liable to pay two shillings on each of his hearths. Paupers alone could seek exemption. The town constable noted the name of each householder liable to the tax, searched the house if dissatisfied with the stated number of fireplaces, and collected the cash. The constable wrote on paper the name of the township, then listed householders with numbers of their firehearths. List and money were taken to the justices at quarter sessions to be enrolled by the clerk of the peace. The latter sent a duplicate list and the money to the Exchequer in London. Widespread evasion, false returns and downright refusal

D

to co-operate vitiated the government's efforts and in 1689 the tax was abolished. Some original returns still lie in parish chests or among quarter-sessions records. Detailed tax lists for most townships are available at the Public Record Office from 1662 to 1674, the fullest return generally being that of Lady Day 1664 which lists paupers and thus theoretically notices every household in the community.

Certificates of musters name adult males between sixteen and sixty years old, liable to serve in local defence forces. The earliest document dates from 1522 when Cardinal Wolsey ordered an inquiry into the military preparedness of the nation for the French war. Wolsey particularly wanted a true valuation of property, intending to levy a forced loan of great proportions. Returns of only five counties have survived in the public records. In 1544 officials listed the whole male population between sixteen and sixty. Again in 1558 commissioners of the muster survey all men of military age to decide between those 'unmeet to serve' and those 'able and chosen'. Further returns are available for 1559, 1560, 1569, 1570, 1573, 1577, 1580, 1583, 1587 and 1588, though none are complete. Thus, only from 1569 is there a house by house enumeration of men. Even then many males escape notice, the 1569 return noticing no member of the Shakespeare family in Stratford. Sixteenth-century muster documents are among Exchequer (king's remembrancer's) records and in state papers (domestic). Calendars have been published for the latter series. Some lists are in print: the Somerset Record Society published the 1569 list for that county.

The chancellor was originally king's chaplain. Because of his book-learning the chaplain became private secretary and adviser on all aspects of foreign and home affairs. He thus looked after and cared for the royal seal which authenticated charters and letters of the administration. He gradually organised a civil service. The chancellor's department finally became settled in London, in Chancery Lane, during the fourteenth century and no longer followed the royal court around the country. Chancery ran its own financial office, the hanaper, accepting large sums as fees or fines for grants under the Great Seal, though accountable finally to Exchequer. The law department, however, extended its jurisdiction from matters arising out of Chancery administrative activities to all cases for which common law offered no remedy. Equity jurisdiction indeed became almost the main function of the court, and Chancery's rules of procedure and slow pace caused bitter recrimination right into Victorian times when the court was included in the Supreme Court of Judicature in 1873. Chancery's administrative business slackened considerably as the king's clerk or secretary took over much of the chancellor's work, and in Henry VIII's reign the principal secretary superseded the chancellor for all practical governmental purposes.

Since the chancellor acted as king's secretary, Chancery records from 1199 include copies of all letters and charters sent out and originals of those received. Letters patent (1201–1920) were despatched open and deal with grants of land, offices and privileges; crown leases; licences and pardons for alienation; special liveries; charters to towns; presentation to benefices; correspondence relating to foreign treaties, inventions (until 1853), denisation (until 1844) and creations of nobility. Letters close addressed to individuals are usually a prime source of local history and genealogy. They concern provisioning of castles, payment of government officials, aids, subsidies, restitution of confiscated land, pardons of state prisoners.

On the back of the close rolls are orders about coinage, wine, ships, armed forces, bankrupts' estates, parliament, records of livery of seisin, enrolments of title deeds, awards of arbitrators, wills, charity papers, deeds of papists, trust conveyances of charity land including nonconformist chapels and village schools. There are over twenty thousand close rolls, mentioning nearly every place in the kingdom. Charter rolls (1199–1516) detail grants of lands, offices and privileges.

Proceedings of commissioners for charitable uses ran from the end of Elizabeth I's reign until George III's reign. They are inquiries into abuses of charitable donations. Chancery possesses over eleven thousand miscellaneous title deeds which were ac-

quired in the course of legal cases, often about charities. The
deeds date back into early medieval times and relate to most parts
of the country. Special commissions of Chancery date from the
early fourteenth century. Of most significance are the returns to
inquisitions about decay of tillage and depopulation through con-
version of arable into pasture. Initiated by Cardinal Wolsey and
taken pursuant to act of parliament, the inquests investigate the
establishment of hunting parks and laying down of sheep pasture
in the generation prior to 1517. Ejected tenants as well as enclosing landlords petition Chancery. Proceedings against landlords
may best be studied in Exchequer records, at least until 1568, on
account of the wealth of detail there provided. This so-called
Domesday of Inclosures (1517–18) was transcribed by I. S. Leadam
in two volumes (1897).

The bundle of various commissions also embodies returns
relating to colleges and charities (1545), forests, sea-banks and
sewers. Commissioners of sewers dealt with sea-walls and the
cleansing of rivers, public streams, ditches and other drains.
Their records include laws and ordinances, decrees and petitions
created mainly between 1600 and 1871. Inquisitions *ad quod
damnum* were taken in medieval times when any grant of fair,
market or other privilege might threaten previously-granted
rights. There is a published calendar covering the thirteenth to
fifteenth centuries. Miscellaneous inquisitions of Chancery start
in 1219 and examine manors, churches, parks, bridges, commons
and boroughs.

Inquisitions *post mortem* were similar inquiries by Chancery
writ after the death of tenants in chief of the crown to ensure that
all the monarch's rights as overlord—especially wardship and
escheat—were respected. Such a process yielded an acceptable
source of royal income from 1066 till the abolition of feudal
tenures in 1660. A tenant in chief holds directly of the king for
rent or service. He may possess very little land in fact. Even so
his heir will succeed—take seisin, as the lawyers say—only by
paying a relief. If there is no heir, land escheats or reverts to the
king. Should the heir be a minor the king claims wardship,

administering the estate, taking the profits, disposing of the heir in marriage.

On a tenant's death a writ is thus sent to the district's escheator. The sheriff summons a jury. In fact the family steward supplies the needful answers on the jury's behalf. The steward states the name of the tenant; date of death; description of his lands; names of various lords of whom property was held; value of individual properties; services due; and heir's name and age. If appropriate, family history is recited. The inquisition is returned to Chancery, the heir appears in court, performs homage to the king, and pays a fine or relief. Livery of seisin follows. The heir's admission may be seen in Chancery fine rolls. If the heir is still a minor, eventually a writ *de aetate probanda* will be issued.

Inquisitions were held in Chancery but copies often went to the Exchequer because money was involved. From Henry VII's time copies were always written for the Exchequer, from 1540 also for the Court of Wards and Liveries. Various orders to escheators concerning livery of seisin, wardship and arrangement of dower are in fine and close rolls. Inquisitions are enrolled in Chancery though related documents are in Exchequer records. Calendars of inquisitions from Henry III to Edward III and for Henry VII's reign are printed. These calendars show if documents known as manorial extents accompany the inquisitions. There are printed registers of tenants' names for the reigns of Henry VIII to Charles I. Palatinate inquisitions are listed separately. All the foregoing are published by the Public Record Office. In addition many local societies have issued calendars or lists, for instance, Bedfordshire Historical Record Society for 1250–86. All publications are presented in E. L. C. Mullins, *Texts and Calendars* (1958).

Proofs of age or proceedings *de probatione aetatis* are inquiries to ensure that heirs are of full age before succeeding to land held in chief of the king. The sheriff summons a jury who try to prove the heir's age by recalling events in their own lives. Thus William Archer was born at Dover three weeks before Edward I came from Winchelsea and two years after the burning of Dover by the

French. Proofs of age exist for most counties and are filed among inquisitions *post mortem*.

Chancery heard law cases from the fourteenth century and its records cover the years 1386–1875. Bills, answers, depositions, title deeds, courts rolls, charters, wills, affidavits, agreements, awards and decrees are among the mass of papers accumulated in the course of centuries, referring to many persons and places in the country. Chancery procedure, its methods of keeping records, its own departmental script, its legal terminology and its general use of Latin ensure that study of Chancery cases is no simple matter for the non-specialist. Some calendars, lists and indexes help the student, providing in most cases names of parties and places as well as dates, but thousands of bundles remain virtually untouched. For proceedings in the reign of Elizabeth with earlier examples, see the Record Commission's *Calendar* in three volumes (1827–32). You will find that all Chancery records, not merely the proceedings in equity cases, demand scholarly treatment, a wide knowledge of legal and administrative history, local background, Latin (for studies prior to 1733) and palaeographical skill. Records should be consulted only in calendar form except by the specialist, though in certain cases like subsidy rolls the local historian may be able to cope himself.

The royal court served as highest common-law court in the land. Cases came to this court (which eventually established itself in Westminster) from an early date, though *curia regis* rolls begin only at the end of the twelfth century. During the next century this royal court divided into three courts of record: Common Pleas, Exchequer and King's Bench. Plea rolls of the Common Pleas actually start in 1194 and continue till 1875. This court specialised in disputes between subjects and thus in its rolls are recorded thousands of title deeds, descriptions of estates, family pedigrees, common recoveries and fines. Fines (which will be discussed in the chapter on family muniments) deal with land transfers, were enrolled from 1182 to 1834, and are reasonably indexed.

King's Bench concerned itself with matters affecting the king's peace such as trespass *vi et armis*, with force and with arms. It heard actions brought by or against its officers, especially cases against people held by the marshal of the court for some offence. By a legal fiction, jurisdiction was extended to cover every kind of personal action on the presumption that the defendant was in fact in the marshal's custody. Records of King's Bench begin in Richard I's reign and continue till 1875. They include depositions, pleas, affidavits, indictments and inquisitions. The three courts of Exchequer, King's Bench and Common Pleas were merged in the High Court of Justice by acts of 1873–5.

Medieval royal judges also went on circuit to hold eyre and assize courts. The eyre court took place at intervals of several years to hear cases affecting the king's peace or revenues, as well as civil pleas. The earliest roll is dated 1194 (actually among *curia regis* records). The eyre system virtually ended in 1294. Assizes were held from the mid-thirteenth century as justices travelled the country hearing inquests, emptying gaols, fixing sentences and imposing penalties. Rolls are arranged by circuits and within circuits chronologically. Records begin in 1248 but there are many gaps before the rolls end in 1482. From 1305 justices also travelled the country to hear and determine ('oyer and terminer') a long list of trespasses and other cases committed since 1297. Records continue until the fifteenth century. Modern justices of assize travel the country in circuits to hear and determine serious offences that quarter sessions could not deal with. Records consist of rolls or files which include indictments and verdicts, coroners' inquisitions, minute books, gaol calendars and various proceedings. All documents dating from before 1800 have been preserved, but after 1800 only those relating to cases of treason, riot, murder, sedition, conspiracy or other historically interesting subjects.

The king in medieval times exercised rights over the livery of lands to heirs of tenants in chief. He took minor heirs as wards and arranged their marriages. These rights as feudal overlord brought in substantial profits. But the Tudors first organised the rights to yield a regular source of income by creating central

government courts which were supposed to miss no chance of
extorting money. Records of Henry VIII's Court of Wards and
Liveries include title deeds and inquisitions *post mortem* brought
into court as evidence; government collectors' accounts; books of
views of liveries, surveys, accounts, decrees, leases, bargains for
sale of wards and petitions. There are some seventy bundles of
miscellaneous extents, valuations of wards' property, particulars
for dower and surveys of tenants' estates. Most documents date
from 1540 to 1650 and are preserved as the archive of the Court
of Wards and Liveries.

In 1715 Commissioners of Forfeited Estates were appointed by
act to inquire into estates of all popish recusants and traitors,
whether implicated or not in the Old Pretender's rebellion. The
commissioners might after 1719 sell estates for the benefit of
creditors. The archive of the commission was placed in the record
office in 1856. Among the most useful of records are returns by
clerks of the peace of names and estates of all popish recusants in
England and Wales county by county. Rentals, deeds and other
documents, dating back in some cases to Tudor times, concern
estates forfeited as a result of the 1715 uprising, arranged under
names of attainted persons. Registers of claims upon the various
estates and minute books of the commissioners meeting in London and Preston, Lancashire, date mainly from 1716–26. All
estates 'given to Superstitious Uses' are described and registered.

The Home Office was established in 1782 under a secretary of
state for Home Affairs who took over business concerning the
internal state of the country that had previously been completed
by the two principal secretaries of state. The secretary's duties
included transmission of petitions from subjects to sovereign and
the issuing of instructions from government to local officers. He
later dealt with aliens (1793), naturalisation (1844), police (1829),
the penal system (1823), elections, care of children, civil defence
and many other problems. His records, complete from 1782,
relate to every place in the kingdom and virtually every happening
of note from crops grown in 1801 to vivisection in 1910, Bedlam
in 1823 and inebriate reformatories in 1905.

Much of the Home Office's business concerned crime and punishment, and the archive includes many calendars of prisoners at quarter sessions and assizes, setting out names, charges, ages, verdicts and sentences as well as complementary lists of convicts on board ships and in all state prisons with ages, sentences, health and behaviour. Lists of convicts in the Australian colonies from 1788 to 1859 provide details of sentences, employment, people's settlement in the colonies (usually as farmers) and eventual pardons granted. Convict transportation registers name every ship and every convict with dates of convictions from 1787 to 1870. Some 280 volumes record personal information on all persons charged with indictable offences and set out results of trials for the whole country between 1791 to 1892. Correspondence with police, prisoners and other state departments, mostly unindexed, supplements all the criminal registers. Police letters are particularly valuable in stating exactly the state of each locality in the country, especially in times of political and economic disturbance.

The home secretary corresponded with politicians, magistrates, government spies, clergymen, trades unionists, manufacturers and labourers, among others, on every aspect of national life: shopping hours, mines, liquor laws, factories, explosives, coroners, children, strikes and lock-outs, railway accidents, political conspiracies. Among the home secretary's miscellaneous records are acreage returns of 1801, parish by parish, showing the different acreages in each devoted to various crops; the ecclesiastical returns of 1851, naming each place of worship in the country used for worship on 30 March 1851, with endowments, sittings, attendances at services that Sunday, and average numbers during the year 1850–1; and census returns for 1841 and 1851. Most of the Home Office archive is available for study on the ordinary record-office conditions, but some seventeen sections are restricted for a century.

The War Office was established in 1794 at the beginning of the French Revolutionary wars to deal with most administrative problems of waging war. From 1801 to 1854, the secretary of

state for war was also in charge of the colonies. In 1855 he took
over the Board of Ordnance which had existed in one form or
another since the fifteenth century. He merged his office with
that of the secretary-at-war (an administrative post created in
1661) during the same army reforms of 1855. In 1870, the War
Office Act gave the secretary of state direct control of every
aspect of army administration. War Office papers are as accessible
as any public records. Various sections are open from five to
thirty years after creation, though certain records are available
only after a century has elapsed in order to obviate distress or
embarrassment to people mentioned therein or to preserve
national security. Army correspondence concerning home,
foreign and imperial affairs dates from 1732 and is to some degree
indexed. Huge bundles or volumes of army lists provide names,
birth and death dates, civilian trades, physical descriptions of
individuals, service histories and pension records of officers and
men in every regiment, usually from the middle of the eighteenth
century onwards. Thus records of service for Royal Artillery date
from 1791–1855 and contain each soldier's name, date and place
of birth, description, trade, dates of service and promotions.
Records of militia regiments throughout Great Britain and Ireland take up 564 volumes and include enrolment and description
books, pay lists, nominal rolls, and registers of marriages, births
and baptisms. Monthly returns of every regiment at home and
abroad from 1759 to 1865 (in 2,812 volumes) set out the effective
strength in all ranks and names of officers. Since 1866, this
information has been printed in abstract in the army's annual
return. Chelsea Hospital admission books commence in 1715. But
War Office records are too voluminous to discuss further; for a
general list see volume 2 of the *Guide to the Contents of the Public
Record Office*.

The king's principal secretary, or secretary of state as he was
probably first called in Elizabeth I's reign, took over much of the
chancellor's work during the sixteenth century. Indeed the press
of business demanded a second principal secretary before Henry
VIII's death. Both officers dealt jointly with the entire field of

domestic and foreign policy until, in 1640, Charles I separated foreign affairs into what became known as the southern and northern departments. In 1782 the southern department was given only home affairs, the northern only foreign. The officers themselves provided for the safekeeping of records in Tudor times which meant that documents went home to places like Salisbury House. In 1603 Sir Thomas Lake received an annuity for 'keeping airing and digesting' various state papers and seven years later two keepers were for the first time appointed. Between 1610 and 1782 the State Paper Office preserved its records in reasonable condition and order based on a division between domestic and foreign papers with special sections for colonial, Irish and Scottish papers.

Documents themselves date from Henry VIII's reign into the nineteenth century. English is used in most domestic papers. John Milton's letters of state are in Latin. State papers include abstracts of all crown grants, army and navy accounts, records of the dissolution of the monasteries, grants of arms, proclamations, lists of judges, musters, returns of aliens and Jesuits, correspondence about church affairs, and reports of government agents on local conditions. Local historians frequently study the order, correspondence and miscellaneous papers of the two Commonwealth committees for the sequestration of delinquents' estates, 1643–53, and for compounding with delinquents, 1643–60. The first seized and confiscated royalist, papist or recusant estates on the information of an informer. The second relied on confessions of delinquents, a full account on oath of their possessions, and the confiscation of a proportion of the property. These documents not only name entire families of royalists but minutely record and value the estates down to the description of each house. A calendar of the proceedings of the committee for compounding is in print, and further calendars are available for various other Commonwealth papers. After the Restoration state papers become more voluminous. Some 450 volumes relate to Charles II's reign (1660–85) and these include Navy Board records for 1664–73. Copies of letters despatched by the two secretaries of state

concerning military, naval, criminal, treasury and church affairs
(among many other matters) take up 418 volumes between 1661
and 1828.

State papers relating to other countries are arranged under the
names of those countries. England's relations with Poland from
1577 to 1781 are set out in 118 volumes with miscellaneous letters
and papers. Other records are bundled by subjects like treaties,
news letters of English agents overseas, entry books of letters
despatched, and archives of British legations abroad. Colonial
papers relating mainly to North America and the West Indies
from 1574 concern trade, politics, land settlement, revenue and
suchlike. These early records with documents of later colonies
have been placed with Colonial Office papers. This last department was set up in 1768, abolished in 1782, and re-established in
1854. The Public Record Office has been publishing calendars of
domestic, colonial, foreign, Scottish and Irish state papers for
many years. These are available in all large reference libraries.
But calendars are not full transcripts though containing virtually
all that the ordinary historian demands. Most documents are still
uncalendared, however, and must be consulted in the original.

The king in council managed naval affairs until 1546, when
Henry VIII established a group of officers of marine causes under
the governance of the lord admiral. Between 1546 and 1832 naval
policy, strategy and personnel remained the province of the lord
admiral (later the Board of Admiralty). Material, civil servants
and general administration was the concern of the Navy Board.
This latter was abolished in 1832 and its duties given to the
Admiralty. All navy records are accessible on the same terms as
other public records. Documents prior to 1546 are among Privy
Council, Exchequer and Chancery records. From 1546 to 1660
most are in state papers domestic, others in the Exchequer, a
number in Admiralty papers proper.

From about 1660 Admiralty records are reasonably complete.
Naval correspondence, orders and instructions, minutes and
court papers concern naval policy, convoys, discipline, pay, ship-
yards, relations with foreign powers, privateering, to mention

just a few of the subjects covered in some fourteen thousand volumes between 1656 and 1934. Various registers contain nominal rolls of personnel: passing certificates of lieutenants, pursers, boatswains and gunners date (with gaps) from 1691 to 1902; pension records of naval widows from 1732–1830; registers and indexes of convicts on the convict ships *Cumberland* and *Dolphin*, 1819–34. Officers' reports of their marriages detailing maiden names of wives, dates and places of marriage and other facts are complete for the period 1806–1902.

For the historian following certain ships and their captains between 1669 and 1920, the record office holds over sixty thousand logs and journals. Ships' musters include description books, which record physical appearance of men, previous service, birthplace and age. Some forty thousand musters are preserved from 1667 to 1878. Pay books record names of all officers and men on board each ship from 1669 to 1856, as well as dockyard personnel 1660–1857. Greenwich Hospital, the home for invalided and retired naval men, possesses fairly complete records. The entry book of pensioners dates from 1704–1869, and is a very detailed and indexed record of careers. Correspondence begins in 1685, accounts in 1695, estate deeds in 1340. Records of the surveyor and (from 1860) the controller of the navy contribute to a history of shipbuilding. Hull, machinery and armament are followed from drawing board to breaker's yard in mainly nineteenth-century papers. Medical records from about 1700 provide sad reading about the sufferings of sick men and prisoners of war and include journals of convict ships, 1817–53, and emigrant ships, 1815–53. Navy Board papers concern the organisation in England from 1658 to 1837 that placed the navy on every ocean of the world. Records of the commissioners of victualling, beginning in 1683, concern the supply of food and equipment to ships, yards and stations.

Among the records of the General Register Office (registrar general's department at Somerset House) are census returns from 1861 and many non-parochial records. England's first census was taken in 1801, but this and subsequent returns of 1811, 1821 and

1831 provide only numbers of persons and houses, not names, ages and other personal details. Returns of 1801–31, consisting of totals for each township, are in print. Returns from 1841 are handwritten by enumerators on printed forms arranged by counties and parishes and taken from householders' schedules; 1841 is in pencil, 1851–61 in ink and the general condition of records is good. One hundred years after the census was taken, records are moved from Somerset House to the Public Record Office for open access. Returns of 1841 and 1851 are actually among Home Office records, but 1861 and following are with the General Register Office archive.

The 1801–31 census returns show size of male and female population by townships, parishes, boroughs, hundreds and counties. The 1801 census attempts to enumerate people engaged firstly in agriculture, secondly in trade, handicraft or manufacture, and thirdly not comprised in either of the two classes. But enumerators sometimes tried to include women in the categories, sometimes left all women out, often put children in category three, neglected to count servants, and so on. Thus the total of the three classes should really equal the number of people employed excluding children or housewives. This most schedules fail to do. The 1811 and 1821 census forms thus asked for numbers of families employed in each class, and figures exist by township, parish, hundred and county.

In 1831 the form split the males aged twenty and over into seven classes: agriculture; manufacture; retail trade and handicraft; capitalists, bankers and professional men; industrial labourers of all types; servants; and all others. For each county and large borough there is a detailed list of all trades and handicrafts with the numbers of men assigned to these trades. Only the 1821 census asks for ages. Age and sex structure tables were compiled for counties, hundreds, large towns and boroughs, but not for parishes. The 1801 census asked for the number of inhabited and uninhabited houses in each settlement. This number can be tied in with information from land taxes and title deeds as a starting point from which the two last-named types of document can be used to trace backwards the history of each local dwelling. In 1811–31 the forms also asked for houses 'building and not yet inhabited', indicating the extent of building activity in some thriving communities.

The 1841 census returns note the address of each household with the name, age, occupation and sex of all people in residence on census night. Ages for persons over fifteen are given to the lowest term of five. The householder states whether each person was born in the same county, elsewhere in England and Wales, in Scotland, Ireland or foreign parts. From 1851 in addition to these questions appears a recording of exact birthplaces, the marital condition of each person and his relationship to the householder, and exact ages of all persons.

Non-parochial registers of christenings, marriages and burials were deposited at Somerset House under an act of 1840. They are now at the Public Record Office. Some seven thousand registers of Methodist, Roman Catholic, Society of Friends (Quaker), Baptist and Independent congregations are now available and cover the period 1567–1858. In addition students may consult records of Bunhill Fields burial ground; Greenwich Hospital registers; original certificates and authenticated registers from both the Wesleyan Methodist Metropolitan Registry and the nonconformist registry at Dr Williams's Library.

Records of clandestine (or semi-secret) marriages, 1667 to about 1777, are among the most useful though not the most used of collections. They concern hundreds of thousands of marriages. At St James's, Duke's Place, London, some forty thousand weddings mainly of this type took place between 1664 and 1691. So many people recount family legends about runaway marriages, so many genealogists compile lists of unlocated marriage entries, that these documents are invaluable, solving at least a proportion of the queries. Most couples seeking to avoid undue expense, publicity or family interference, or to commit bigamy, underwent a clandestine celebration, quietly conducted by an ordained priest without banns or licence in so-called 'lawless churches'.

An act of 1696 laid a penalty of £100 on a priest performing each such marriage. Priests in gaol for debt were hardly likely to be worried by this penalty; so Fleet debtors' prison became an important marriage centre. In consequence of a further limiting act of 1711, most ceremonies took place in the neighbourhood called the Rules or Liberties of the Fleet, within marriage-houses (usually inns), because debtors could pay a security and live in that district immediately outside the prison. Most parsons in the Liberties were not, however, debtors themselves, merely poor clergy seeking profit out of marriage-houses. Their customers too were generally impecunious seamen, soldiers and labouring poor hoping for a quick and cheap ceremony. It is estimated that possibly 180,000 couples married in the Fleet up to 1754. From 25 March 1754, an act recognised as legal only those marriages contracted after banns or licence in the parish church of one of the parties. Marriages accepted as legal abroad (that is, in Scotland) were still accepted in England.

Marriages certificates were handwritten on paper or printed on parchment; but few survive. Huge register books were kept by parsons and marriage-house keepers showing full names of both parties, chronologically arranged, marital status, parishes of residence and the man's occupation. There are a few indexes, both separate and bound with registers alphabetically arranged by male surname. Rough notebooks of pocket size also cover the period 1710–50. Drawn up by the priests, these drafts sometimes provide fuller information about ceremonies than the registers. Fleet records lay in private hands until 1821 when they were bought by the government. They were transferred to the registrar-general in 1840 and are now in the record office, where a catalogue is available. Included with these records are marriage registers from other centres like May Fair chapel, the Mint and Savoy chapel. There is a list of London's lawless churches in *National Index of Parish Registers*, volume I. Clandestine marriages took place throughout the country, and certain clergy as at Peak Forest, Derbyshire, became renowned for their willingness to perform ceremonies without banns or licence. After March

1754, couples had to leave England for such places as Gretna Green or Jersey to be married without solemnisation. Only in 1856 was this possibility closed for English, though not for Scottish, people. Some Gretna registers are at Gretna Hall, some in Carlisle.

National Debt Office records include life annuities and tontines mainly of use now to genealogists. A life annuity is a specified income paid at stated intervals for a fixed or contingent period, usually for the nominee's lifetime, in return for a stipulated premium payable in one lump sum or in prior instalments. A tontine is an annuity scheme in which subscribers or their nominees share a common fund, the survivors' shares increasing as members die until the whole fund goes to the last survivor. Annuities and tontines were popular in Georgian and Victorian times, being organised by governments, local clubs and privately. Some thirty thousand people appear in government documents alone between 1693 and 1789. Life annuities were granted between 1745 and 1779. The master ledgers at the Public Record Office show names of subscribers and nominees with addresses and occupations.

Ledgers of the first tontine of 1693 are lost, but there is at the British Museum an alphabetical list of nominees (usually children) with age, address, occupation of nominee's father, sum paid by the subscriber and date. Ledgers of the English tontine of 1789 (and Irish tontines of 1773–7) show name, address and status of subscriber; name, address, status, age, parentage of nominee (possibly a grandchild of the subscriber); then many years later are recorded date of nominee's death, names of his executors and attornies, with date the account was finally closed. For the 1789 and Irish tontines there is an alphabetical list of nominees at the Public Record Office.

Records of crown lands as well as duchy and palatinate jurisdictions form substantial archives alongside the public records. Crown estate records concern all hereditary lands as well as property falling to the king through forfeiture or escheat and monastic possessions confiscated in 1536–9. Documents are scat-

E

tered among various sections of the public records and it is
essential to use the index to the record office calendar in order to
extract exactly what you need.

Thus the Exchequer Pipe Office preserves some leases of crown
lands from the sixteenth to nineteenth centuries. Original deeds
of monastic property with particulars for leases and for grants,
accounts, surveys and valuations are in the Augmentation Office
of Exchequer. This latter department also holds the detailed
Commonwealth surveys taken prior to leasing or granting former
crown lands to tenants or purchasers. Enrolment books of grants,
leases, inquisitions, surveys, probate records and decrees from
the thirteenth century to 1831 with particulars for grants and for
leases from the fifteenth century to 1841 are among records of the
auditors of land revenue (created in the sixteenth century).

A large archive including modern rentals and surveys is held by
the Crown Estate Commissioners, 55 Whitehall, London SW1;
though many of the commissioners' documents up to about 1900
are now in the Public Record Office. The Duchy of Cornwall
records are mainly at 10 Buckingham Gate, SW1; but various
series lie among the public records too. Duchy of Lancaster
muniments in the Public Record Office relate to ancient possessions of the duchy throughout England, the county of Lancashire being merely a subordinate part of the whole. The county
palatine of Chester was another independent district from the
Conquest to Henry VIII's reign. Records were transferred to the
record office in 1854. Durham, the most ancient and the wealthiest
of exempt jurisdictions, developed courts of law modelled on
Westminster patterns but independent of them until 1536. The
palatine jurisdiction of the bishops was finally taken away in 1836.
Judicial records including feet of fines, inquisitions *post mortem*,
and the register of Bishop Richard Kellaw, 1311–16, alone remain
in the record office. Estate muniments of the bishops have been
deposited by the Church Commissioners in The Prior's Kitchen,
The College, Durham.

Among the record-office special collections are the hundred
rolls, the records of Edward I's fiscal inquiry of 1274–5 in thirty-

two counties where men had usurped liberties, appropriated valuable services and neglected duties. Accompanying this inquiry are returns to the inquisitions of 1255 and 1279–80 on the same lines. Most of the documents were published by the Record Commission in 1812–18. Action on the returns of 1255 and 1279–80 is to be sought in Chancery and Exchequer records, on the returns of 1274–5 in crown pleas on the next eyre roll for the appropriate district. Also in special collections are 505 bundles of court rolls of manors, hundreds and honors from the thirteenth to nineteenth centuries; ministers' and receivers' accounts of manors and land of the ancient demesne of the crown outside the sheriffs' control, thirteenth to seventeenth centuries; accounts of alien priories, 1294–1483; over one thousand rolls of rentals, terriers, surveys, extents and valuations of monastic and other property at one time or another in the king's hands and dating from the thirteenth to nineteenth centuries.

State Papers Domestic normally deal with the peace and prosperity of most localities from Henry VIII's time till 1782. Census returns of 1841–71 provide the material for a social survey of the Victorian community. Law cases in Chancery about the enclosure of open fields, moor and pasture for private farming and especially reports of inquests into the problem from 1517 to 1607 provide the agricultural and social research worker with a wealth of somewhat biased and suspect, but very essential, information.

Subsidy rolls are studied for their evidence of the local economy. It is possible to assess wealth of individuals and communities in comparison with other people and places or with an average figure worked out for a whole county. Tax dodgers must, however, always be allowed for, especially in poll taxes of 1381. Compare the wealth of places owned by ecclesiastical and by lay lords. How did the wealth of market towns compare with surrounding villages? What local trades and occupations are noted from indexes of surnames? It is always impossible to be sure whether the word following a Christian name is a surname or descriptive of a job. In the example quoted previously it is known from other sources that William worked as corn miller; he is both William the miller and William Miller. But Ricardus tannarius was a shoemaker; his father may have been a tanner but he is definitely Richard Tanner, shoemaker, in manorial records. Despite this drawback it is worthwhile noting all the names descriptive of work.

Genealogists of course will be interested in all surnames, if they have been fortunate enough to trace a pedigree into medieval days. The 1524–5 lists are close enough to parish registers to be a basic source of a family tree. Surnames with a place-name element (as Agnes Neuton in the example) illustrate the mobility of population, even in the middle ages. Agnes or her forebears came originally from Newton. It is worthwhile plotting on a map the places from which people in your community travelled. Subsidies can also provide a basis for estimating population of towns and villages, though many pitfalls await the careless worker. How many people escaped taxation? How many people were dependent on each taxpayer? Did the poor pay tax?

Hearth taxes show the number of houses in a township, presuming that each householder lives in a separate dwelling which is nearly always true. Some of the lists, and especially 1664, include pauper households too. Thus no house in the settlement should be missed. This is not impossible to prove from your study of old maps, probate records, estate rentals and the history of individual houses. By multiplying by 6 in towns, by 4·5 in villages where servants and lodgers are fewer, you have an approximate population figure.

Domesday describes the country at the end of five hundred years of English settlement when, by sweat of the brow, men had cleared the woodland and founded nearly all our present-day townships. The economic pattern is by no means easy to interpret without expert guidance; not only because archaic measurements are employed but equally on account of the vagueness of the jury and the condensation of their original answers. This is where the various Domesday geographies should be resorted to. The survey names landowners great and small. It is one means of assessing the extent of Norman penetration and English survival by 1086; of working out the size of Norman holdings; and of estimating the size of various economic groups in local society. Genealogists find interesting the few surnames here recorded for the first time, and several families trace their descent from Domesday men. More important the book puts in writing, often for the first time, the early forms of English place-names. But never theorise on these names yourself unless you have studied E. Ekwall's *Concise Oxford Dictionary of English Place-names*, fourth edition (1960), and the county volumes issued by the English Place-Name Society.

Inquisitions *post mortem*, in mentioning services by which property is held, introduce historians to local customs like the duty of certain estates to victual armies (a great saving of taxpayers' money) and entertain the royal court (saving the king's and thus the taxpayers' money). They note the extent of royal forests, growth of local industries, existence of the wind or water-mill, employment and jobs of town dwellers. They document the descent of certain properties from 1066 onwards and provide a family tree for not a few families, tracing the rise and fall of famous and obscure people alike. Inquisitions are invaluable in place-name study of townships, fields, lanes and estates. J. C. Russell in *British Medieval Population* (1948) even used them in a demographic study.

Census records, especially of 1841-61, provide much information on industrial England and Wales. Details of occupations, houses building, persons per house, number of household servants and migrations come straight from the registrar's surnames. As a model study see R. Lawton's article on 'The Population of Liverpool' in *Transactions of the Historic Society of Lancashire and Cheshire*, 107 (1955). To go a stage further and provide an unrivalled statistical framework for historical interpretation is a fascinating task. Choose an area that interests you: parish, town or county and if large in population (say over 6,000) take a sample only. A ten per cent sample of a city of 40,000 is sufficient. Record every tenth household in a notebook ruled in up to eighty columns showing, for instance, birthplace of head of household; ages and birthplaces of all children, servants, lodgers; number of domestic servants; and so on. The information partly numerical, partly in words must be re-written later in a similar notebook using a number code in place of words. Thus shopkeepers can be 2, factory labourers 3, miners 4; or born in same town 2, in rural parishes beyond 3, in adjoining county 4, and so on. All this information will be transferred to standard eighty-columned punched cards suitable for computerisation. It is of course not impossible though time-consuming to work manually and a sample of three thousand persons would be more than enough to tackle. But universities, colleges of technology and some firms may make a computer available for an evening; it takes only a few minutes to deal with several thousand household cards.

Documents in the Public Record Office are so numerous and far-reaching in subject-matter that few students can leave the archives unenlightened. Before beginning personal research it is essential to study the revised *Guide to the Contents of the Public Record Office* (1963) and *Maps and Plans in the Public Record Office Relating to the British Isles c1410–1860* (1967). Many calendars of public records are available in print.

National Library of Wales

The National Library of Wales at Aberystwyth was founded in 1907. Because Wales has been since 1536 politically united with England, government records are created and preserved in London. But the National Library has been designated by the Lord Chancellor as a repository for public records such as those of the courts of Great Sessions for Wales (1536–1830), of quarter sessions for Cardigan, Montgomery and Radnor (these counties having no record offices of their own), and pre-1858 probate records for Wales. Nearly all Welsh legal records dating from 1536 to 1830 have now been transferred from the Public Record Office, London.

Welsh bishops encourage incumbents to deposit ecclesiastical parochial records like registers, vestry minutes and church-wardens' accounts in the Library. Many collections of estate and family papers are deposited on permanent loan from the whole country, the owners deciding to use the National Library rather than local repositories. But county record offices alone take civil parish records like accounts of overseers of the poor.

Catalogues of material are generally in typescript, but a number have also been printed. The *Handlist of Manuscripts* has been published in parts from 1940 on. There are calendars of muniments of families like Wynn of Gwydir and estates like Hawarden. Documents at the National Library are essential sources of any Welsh history.

Bodleian Library

Sir Thomas Bodley (1545–1613) re-established the university library of Oxford, originally founded by Humphrey, Duke of Gloucester. Bodley's library opened in 1603 with manuscript and printed books. Since 1610 a copy of every book published in Great Britain has been deposited at the Bodleian.

The Bodleian library has been given important family archives and thousands of other documents relating to the whole country. Many Oxfordshire estate muniments came in after World War II, though these will in due course be transferred to Oxfordshire Record Office. The Bodleian usually accepts only collections closely connected with its existing archives or with University members and institutions. The library is the repository for records of the diocese of Oxford, archdeaconries of Oxford and Berkshire, Oxfordshire parishes, and peculiars of Oxford, Buckingham and Berkshire. The Bodleian is used by Oxfordshire local historians for village and family histories. There is material for studies of University graduates and teachers as well as of the University itself. There is no charge for access to the archives, though readers must have signed an application form.

Cambridge University Library

Cambridge University Library dates from the first part of the fifteenth century. Like the Bodleian this library exercises the copyright privilege. Many thousands of manuscripts are preserved at Cambridge, some relating to English local history but many being of more national or specialist interest.

Chapter 3

FAMILY MUNIMENT ROOM

ESTATE and family archives, accumulated by a family in connection with a private estate, may date back a thousand years. The family in this sense can include the local squire, monastery, industrial company or Oxford college. The property involved could be Windsor Great Park, Yorkshire moorland, a cotton factory or just a single cottage. John Worsley of Salford's papers going back three generations to 1870 are the same in essence as those of Worsley of Hovingham, stretching to medieval days.

Family muniments are essential sources of local history not only of the family estate itself, but of the village or town nearby also. If the family interested itself in politics or county government the correspondence will be useful to political historians. Documents provide information about genealogy, rents, prices, wages and industries; about church tithes, quarter-sessions meetings, neighbourhood scandals, canals and road travel and patronage of art.

Some family archives are still in the possession of the family that accumulated the documents; others are held by descendants or successors. Several landed families therefore now own monastic archives, while industrial firms possess archives of superseded estates. It is very difficult and often impossible to consult such privately owned archives. Obviously with the best will in the world, no landowner can spare time to receive hundreds of

72

students a year. Access is even more difficult when muniments are preserved at the offices of estate agents and solicitors. Only deposit in a county record office solves the problem.

Almost every manor house has its muniment room, though documents are not always preserved there any longer. Archives are frequently taken elsewhere by a new owner or deposited at a county record office. For help on location of family records, consult the Historical Manuscripts Commission at Quality Court, Chancery Lane, London, WC2. The commission has since 1869 reported on local archives. It now has two off-shoots:

1   Manorial and Tithe Documents Registers
2   National Register of Archives

The registrar of this latter body will advise if the location and scope of a particular family or estate archive is known.

Title deeds

Deeds of title include every document that has been used to prove ownership to property. Many owners keep bundles of deeds to their parcels of land providing a handy history of the property. A title deed is the document by which one man records his transfer to another of his title to property. In medieval times it was considered sufficient for people to transfer title by removing from the land a stick or piece of turf and handing this to the purchaser who thereby gained seisin or possession, on condition he performed specified services to the lord of the fee or fief. Since witnesses to this act might later lose their life or memories, men began to record on parchment the fact of transfer and such deeds sometimes survive from pre-Conquest centuries. Most title deeds, however, are no earlier than 1150, and were not legally necessary until 1677. The ordinary medieval feoffment, gift or grant recording that A has sold or given property to B creates a fee simple absolute in possession; that is an estate of inheritance unencumbered by entails or trusts and therefore disposable at will. This gift names donor, donee, witnesses and property; notes the price paid or consideration; the conditions if any; and, from the thirteenth century, the date of transaction.

With the growing complexity of the land law, legal men proliferated and deeds became complicated. Lawyers began to quote back to previous conveyances of the property in order to prove the purchaser's good title. This central section of a feoffment, following the word 'whereas,' may review the history of the estate for several centuries. It was the custom too in later centuries, especially if old bundles of deeds were not going to be handed over, to provide an abstract of title mentioning all possible deeds relating to the property one by one over at least a generation, but usually for a century, and occasionally for hundreds of years.

The ordinary medieval conveyance is a short document on parchment and in Latin, though paper and English are occasionally introduced in the fifteenth century. Written on one side of the parchment only and authenticated by the donor's seal, a gift names the various parties, describes the property shortly ('all my tenement in Holt'), and notes conditions in the *habendum* clause ('to have and to hold the aforesaid tenement to the said Robert . . . of the chief lord of that fee for the services thence due and accustomed for ever'). The deed is witnessed, and from about 1280, dated. There is often an endorsement about livery of seisin, that is, handing over a piece of the property prior to the indenture. The date may be expressed in the form: 'the day before the feast of St John the Baptist in the fifth year of the reign of king Edward the third'. If so, use C. R. Cheney, *Handbook of Dates* (1961), to work out the modern form.

A conveyance of the period after 1536 may well provide the information which appears in the following calendar. The language is usually English and several skins of parchment may be used.

Lease and release: for £40:
(1) James Smithson of Netherton, yeoman, to
(2) William Hicks of Manley, husbandman
—all that Messuage or Dwelling House scituate and being in Netherton aforesaid called or known by the name of Phillipsons tenement—15/16 May 1721.
Endorsed: Hannah Young & Richard Pitt witnesses
Seal. Signatures of parties

You should not be satisfied unless you extract at least as much from every modern deed as in this example.

Now take a lengthier deed that quotes back over several generations. The format is the same as before but tucked away below the names of the parties and above the description of the estate is the 'whereas' clause. Here is the deed itself in summary form.

> Lease and release: for £300:
> (1) Elizabeth widow of Philip Goughe of Stafford to
> (2) Nathaniel Baldock of Swynehead in Netherton, gentleman
> —all that freehold estate called Johnsons with the newly built farmhouse barn outhouses and land situate near the turnpike road to Stafford aforesaid formerly parcel of the manor or reputed manor of Netherton—5 Aug 1785

This deed quotes the following in chronological order. The originals of the first two documents are in Latin but the 1785 deed quotes the gist of them in English.

> 1521 Feoffment to create a tenant to the praecipe and exemplification of the recovery suffered by William Atkyneson of Nederton, gentleman—twelve messuages twelve gardens 400 acres of land 60 acres of meadow 80 acres of pasture 200 acres of wood and common of pasture for all manner of animals with the appurtenances in Nedertoun.
>
> 1521
>
> 1522 Feoffment: for £1,100:
> (1) William Atkynsonne of Nethertoun, gentleman, to
> (2) Henry Jeffereys of London, merchant—manor of Netherton with the mansion house two cottages freehold tenement and land appurtenant—16 Feb 1521/2
>
> 1597 Bargain and sale: for £750:
> (1) William Jefferies of Netherton, esquire, to
> (2) Thomas Johnson of Ambley, yeoman—freehold tenement called Swynesheved with the wood appleorchard and land adjoining the king's heigheway in Netherton—18 Apr 1597
>
> 1692 Mortgage: for £400:
> (1) Henry Johnson the younger of Swyenehed in Netherton, yeoman, to
> (2) William Goughe of Stafford, merchant—all that freehold estate known as Swynehed adjoining the Stafford road—3 May 1692

Medieval landowners regularly found feudal services burdensome to perform. They might lose all their property in some

political setback. They were not able until 1540 to devise real
estate by will. To find a way round these and other problems
lawyers worked out a document known as the feoffment to uses.
A conveyed his land to B to hold 'to the use of' A, or C a third
person, or X a body of people. B became owner at common law
liable to perform all services, while A no longer feared the loss of
his lands for rebellion. A's beneficial interest could be devised by
will. Yet A still enjoyed all profits of the property because Chancery protected his interests, insisting B remained merely nominal
owner on behalf of A (or C or X). B, of course, not actually being
in possession could not perform services due to the lords of the
fee and A, not being legal owner at all, equally escaped obligations.
Great landowners, and especially the king, therefore lost heavily.
Some religious communities and private individuals whom the
king had forbidden to own land contentedly profited from estates
held to their use by feoffees.

It was left to the Tudors to rescue royal authority and revenue.
In 1536 parliament passed the Statute of Uses which gave to the
person in whom the use or profit is vested (A, C or X in the above
cases) the legal estate. To transfer property, a deed called a bargain
and sale was employed. This is a contract to convey interests in
real estate following payment of an agreed price. A, the vendor,
bargains and sells land to B; A remaining seised to the use of B
as is implied in the terms of the agreement. But such a deed had to
be enrolled with the clerk of the peace or one of the courts at
Westminster from 1536. Publication by enrolment identifies B as
the person in whom the use is vested and, under the terms of the
Statute of Uses, he is vested immediately with the fee simple. The
bargain and sale is written out in duplicate on one piece of parchment that is later divided by an indented cut, so that both parties
to the agreement receive a copy.

The bargain and sale is often in English. It opens with details
of the parties and the date before stating the consideration (or cash
paid) and extent of property involved. The important formula
which distinguishes this deed from others is 'doth grant bargain
and sell'. The document is signed and sealed by both parties.

During the sixteenth and early seventeenth centuries, most people conveyed property by a contract executed in writing in the form of a bargain and sale, followed by a feoffment either recorded in the form of an endorsement or written as a separate document. Note the operative words: 'alien grant bargain sell enfeoff and confirm'.

The lease and release first appears in 1614. On one day the lessor A bargains and sells a lease to the lessee B who pays normally five shillings. A is seised of his property to the use of B for six months or a year, depending on the terms. The Statute of Uses causes the lease immediately to vest in B, however, and on the second day A releases the freehold reversion to B who is already in possession. B pays the full purchase price of the property under the terms of the release. The lease is a short document folded inside the more substantial release. The latter's distinguishing words are: 'granted bargained sold remised released quitclaimed and confirmed'. Historians write the dates of the two documents in the form 5/6 May. The lease and release ousted the bargain and sale as a means of conveyance after 1660 because no public livery of seisin or enrolment was involved. It had immediate effect wherever English law operated. It was eventually replaced in 1841 by a simple release and in 1845 by a deed of grant.

Many feoffments transferred land on certain conditions. In 1285, the feudal lords succeeded in having a statute passed concerning conditional grants, *de donis conditionalibus*, which protected the fee tail or estate in which the inheritance is limited. The original grant might specify that property should pass 'to A and the heirs of his body' for ever or through children of a particular spouse. This being so later owners could not deprive of their rights persons interested in the estate. Thus portions of land could not be sold to help pay for improvements to the remainder because this would deprive future generations of parts of their inheritance. The means by which landowners got round this problem will be discussed below. Estates in fee tail continued to be created, despite inconveniences, in order to protect family property from ill-considered sales or improvements. Medieval owners employed feoffees to uses. The 1536 statute rendered such conveyances useless for the purpose in mind. Consequently lawyers drew up the modern settlement protected by Chancery under which A enfeoffs B to hold to the use of B in trust for C or A or X. B must hold the common law estate for the benefit of C, A or X upon whose equitable (Chancery-protected) estate remainders may be limited. Settlements are complicated documents and must be read carefully. They usually take the form of a lease and release with a special *habendum* clause to limit uses and remainders.

Until 1856 settled land could not be sold without an act of parliament (which should be sought in the House of Lords Record Office). Because each generation was so restricted by law, the family found little scope for developing the land, building houses or factories, cutting down woodland or selling portions to raise capital. Not until the Settled Land Act of 1925, might the owner claim wide statutory powers to deal with the land for the benefit of those persons with an interest under the original settlement. Estate papers contain hundreds of settlements from medieval times to about 1914. Many documents after about 1700 onwards are exceptionally bulky and verbose.

Probably the most common type and easiest to follow is the settlement made prior to marriage usually, but not always, relating to ancient or prosperous families with complicated legal affairs. I consulted one medieval settlement produced by a couple of modest farming families. One father possessed but one daughter. He desired to be sure that his neighbour's son would marry the girl, take the girl's surname, and produce an heir; and he insisted that the settlement specify these conditions. If all conditions were not carried out, the other sons in turn were to marry the heiress. Marriage settlements name parents, children and relatives; describe estates often in minute detail; provide a family history; and lay out the conditions on which property and money are settled on the parties.

Medieval land law demanded conveyance of property by livery of seisin rather than by deed. But landowners felt the need for some permanent and sure record for future generations, something safer even than a deed of feoffment. Lawyers in the twelfth century devised a fictitious suit in the Common Pleas concluded by a final agreement or fine. A, the plaintiff and actual purchaser, commences a case against B the deforceant, or conusor, who is supposed to be wrongfully in possession of the property in question. The case is settled by an amicable agreement or final concord recorded in court rolls showing A's unimpeachable right to the land. The cash settlement is conventional and should be ignored.

Several owners might appear in one document having combined doubtless to avoid expense. In such cases their respective interests are defined in deeds either to lead or to declare uses of a fine. Written in Latin until 1733, a fine begins with an original writ of covenant out of the Court of Common Pleas. A royal licence for levying the fine is paid for in silver. Then follows the conusance or concord, expressing the terms of the assurance. This is equivalent to the conditions in a conveyance. The note of the fine is made, an abstract of the original concord. Finally, on a large membrane of parchment, the clerk engrosses three identical texts of the proceedings. He begins with the words: 'this is the final agreement' (*hec est finalis concordia*), and notes the names of parties and justices, location and approximate often exaggerated size of property, and date. The parchment is cut by indented line into three parts, the 'foot' remaining as court record, the 'indentures' travelling to family muniments as title deeds. The essential portion of a final concord can be calendared in the following way.

Plaintiff: Oswald Metecalff
Deforceant: Christopher and Ann Metecalff
Messuage called Tylehowse grange with lands in Tylehowse in the parish of Oldbyland.
                                        Michaelmas sessions 1562

To disentail land after the creation of a conditional estate landowners employed the common recovery, which was certainly in use by Edward IV's reign. The recovery is a strong assurance of title because founded on a judgment of court, rather than a mere agreement recorded under court auspices. Court action takes various forms depending on period and estate; but usually to begin the process the tenant in tail, A, conveyed his life estate to the tenant to the praecipe C, to allow the writ to be served on C. Some friendly plaintiff or demandant B then brought a collusive suit against C, alleging C's wrongful possession of the estate by virtue of a disseisin carried out by a third party, Hugh Hunt. But C responds that he had the estate from A whom he vouches to warranty, that is, calls on to support his title. But A vouches to warranty another person, D, usually called Edward Howse, the court crier. B, the demandant and Edward Howse appear in court but beg leave to confer outside the court. They withdraw and D disappears. By default, therefore, C, the tenant to the praecipe, loses his case. The property passes to the plaintiff B. The property in B's lands is freed from the estate tail and all remainders and reversions expectant on it. All B has to do is to convey back to A the estate in fee simple.

Recoveries were enrolled on court rolls in the public records and were also engrossed and sealed for the parties. They are complicated documents written in Latin till 1733, and in a difficult court hand, but usually exhibit a pleasing royal portrait within the initial letter of the deed. Much of the wording is common form; despite appearances there is no bitter quarrel between parties, not even a sale of lands. Hugh Hunt, Edward Howse and Richard Rowe who appear in recoveries are in fact fictitious names. In a recovery by double voucher, however, one of the vouchees will generally be the tenant in tail. Description of property is conventional. The historian therefore merely notes the name of the tenant in tail (who appears in the grant of the life estate to C prior to the exemplification of the recovery), location of lands and date of case. In 1833 fines and recoveries were replaced by a disentailing deed. In 1925, an act allowed the tenant in possession to disentail by deed and obtain a legal estate in fee simple, provided that any purchase money of a subsequent sale went to trustees for the benefit of persons entitled under the original settlement.

Plans of houses, streets, farms and estates accompany title deeds especially from 1800 onwards. Sometimes one plan is drawn on the deed itself rather than on a separate sheet. Occasionally old

deeds have been written out in chartularies. This was done usually
prior to destruction of the original documents as too bulky. The
chartulary version may well omit common form from each type
of deed, providing the gist only. One farmhouse whose history I
studied seemed to possess deeds no older than 1910. But a township survey and hearth tax list told me the names of the owners
in the seventeenth century. Descendants of these owners still
lived locally and among their family archive held a fine Stuart
chartulary recording deeds to my farm from 1483 to 1620.

Title deeds are by no means the simplest of documents to read.
Even if the language is neither Norman-French nor Latin, it may
be the equally abstruse legal English. Handwriting of all centuries
must be practised before reading becomes easy. Certain deeds
like fines and recoveries prove almost insuperable obstacles because of their language, palaeography and complicated legal form.
For a fuller guide see any law dictionary; W. S. Holdsworth's
History of English law; and Julian Cornwall's *How to Read Old
Title Deeds XVI–XIX Centuries* (Birmingham University Extra-
Mural Studies Department, 1964). Nearly every title deed follows
a set pattern. Much of the wording being common form may be
ignored. It is, of course, essential to note names and places which
change from deed to deed but, once you know what in general a
feoffment or recovery or lease and release achieves, its verbiage
can usually be safely left unread.

Title deeds were not produced with the historian's needs in
view, but they do provide a sound history of the property none
the less. They show how estates were built up or divided; names
of owners and occupiers; descriptions of buildings on the site
including notes of new erections; records of law cases, family
settlements, marriages, deaths, bankruptcies; plans of expansion
and improvement; even the laying of field drains, access roads,
electricity cables or fences.

I traced the history of one small freehold house and farmland
back to the fifteenth century using just one bundle of deeds to the
property in the Lancashire Record Office. I once wondered why
one house whose history I investigated fronts on to the Trent and

F

Mersey Canal and turns its back on a busy turnpike road. The
earliest deed dated 1844 describes 'all those two Messuages for-
merly one Messuage'. In the 'whereas' clause is quoted a mortgage
of 1817 concerning 'all that newly erected Messuage or Dwellinghouse Shop Oven and Buildings conveniences and erections . . .
the Shop and House also fronting to the Northwest and the
Towing Path . . .' A boatman built this shop to serve passing canal
people, his oven baking fresh bread for the hungry workers. The
deed thus tacitly explains why the place possessed such a large
front window and four good-sized rooms, so different from others
in the neighbourhood.

Deeds provide topographical details referring to layout of fields,
mills, saltings, paths, lanes, woods, ancient mounds, streams, new
hedges, moorland and waste, village greens, market houses and
crosses, crossroad gibbets. They refer often obliquely to manorial
rights, ferry services, fisheries and mineral rights. For genealogical
purposes deeds are essential sources. Settlement deeds certainly
prove family connections; and from documents of the period
1700–1900, a wide-spreading family tree is easily drawn. Medieval
title deeds are one of the few sources for genealogists working
backwards beyond the beginning of parish registers.

Manorial records

Manorial organisation was superimposed prior to the Conquest on
communities already divided into estates of varying size. Manor
courts regulated the responsibilities and interrelationship of
manorial lord, his steward, bailiff and reeve on one side and
village people on the other. Courts were held by the lord at
regular intervals, often fortnightly, to deal with every aspect of
village agriculture, industry and social life; with changes of tenure
and tenancy; with services, dues and rights. These ordinary courts
in later medieval times are often divided into courts leet and
baron, though the distinction is not very important to the layman.
Not many judicial cases come to the manor court, these being
dealt with in hundred, shire or royal courts, though by special
franchise some courts did undertake such work in the absence of

higher courts. The most usual addition is the view of frankpledge, of Saxon origin, to which tithings present cases of breach of law and order among their members. Manor courts functioned in some cases into Victorian times and were not abolished until 1926.

Manor court records themselves are usually on parchments (though paper is after 1660 common) stitched together to form long rolls four or five feet long. Not always in the best condition, court rolls are difficult to study, their extremely cursive crabbed handwriting, abbreviated Latin, and somewhat technical vocabulary, at least until 1660, proving too much for the lay researcher. It is advisable always to make sure a printed translation is available before you commence work on the manor records, though an archivist's typescript is of course an excellent substitute. There is a list of all court rolls in the Public Record Office (published 1896, though a more up-to-date list can be consulted at the PRO itself). The National Register of Archives issues a list of all known court rolls. This is available either at the NRA in London or in many libraries and county record offices. In his *Handlist of Record Publications* (1951), Sir Robert Somerville lists court records printed by local societies. For an introduction to court rolls, see F. W. Maitland, *Select Pleas in Manorial and Other Seignorial Courts* (1889). Court rolls are protected by the master of the rolls as public records. They may not be destroyed but are available for a fee (usually waived) for research purposes.

The record of the manor court, the court roll proper, begins with title of court and the date: 'court of Wenintun held on the Sunday next after the feast of St John the baptist in the eighth year of the reign of king Edward the third.' Then follow all the administrative problems of a manor: 'John Winton is accused of having cut turf from the lord's wasteland without permission, pays 2d . . . for removing one boundary stone between his own and widow Thorneleigh's strip . . . for licence to transfer his house to William Woodeson 6d . . . John atte Forde acknowledges he owes for his tenement the following services, that is to say, three days ploughing a year, 3 days harrowing after ploughing, 3 days harvesting, and 3s rent . . . for right to pasture his pigs in Westwood one pound of cumin . . . Juliana Brown for merchet 2s'. Merchet is a fine to the lord for permission to marry. A number of cases concern such offences as theft which by Elizabethan times would be dealt with at quarter or petty sessions: 'for stealing Richard Greene's horse 6d'. Many court rolls exhibit lists of jurors whose job it was to help the lord's steward reach a decision in court.

Manor custumals set out the customs of the manor, binding lord, officials and villagers to behave in certain ways at work and in public service. Formularies or treatises prepared by legal men tell stewards how to conduct courts, what formalities and forms to observe, what bounds there are to the lord's authority. Whenever a manorial tenant gave up his land or died, the property officially passed to the lord. However, on payment of a fine or relief, a new tenant named by the former tenant could take over. The transaction is recorded in the normal court roll. The steward then sees that a second record is written for the tenant's use showing the name of the person surrendering the land, the date and the reason; and the name of the person admitted, with the fine paid and the date. The property is shortly described. The new tenant is a copyholder, holding by copy of the court roll, and his title is as sound as any freeholder's because protected by ancient custom. These surrenders and admittances, usually on parchment and in Latin till 1733, are commonly found in family muniments. Even small cottagers might boast of such a bundle, though they had no other papers about the house. Such documents were supposed to be written out for copyhold property till 1926. I have certainly traced one small Lancashire farm by using surrenders back from 1910 to 1582.

Manorial extents provide the historian with the customs and topography of a manor. Produced for some special reason like the death of the lord, extents are found with manorial records in family muniments and also accompanying inquisitions *post mortem* in the Public Record Office. They are in Latin, in a very tiresome court hand, and abound in phrases that raise legal and technical problems calculated to trip up the unwary. They are generally on parchment. The opening words are *extenta manerii*, 'this is the extent of the manor'. Then follow name of manor, date of survey and names of jurors. The customs of the manor are recorded: allotment of commons, pannage of pigs, crop rotation, dues to lord and church, use of woodland, administration of meadows. To this is appended acreage of demesne, arable, woodland, pasture and meadow; lord's income from land, rents, aids and tenants' services; value and perquisites of the court; names and holdings of each tenant with rents and services owing by each, special mention being made of frequency and conditions of boon labour; details of church advowson, mill, fishponds, saltworks, dovecotes and deer park. Sometimes the bounds of the manor are beaten: 'from the highway to the oak tree at the corner of Westfield thence along the boundary of that field to Mill Brook and so south to . . .' Extents are unfortunately infrequently printed in full. Some are calendared by local societies, while Public Record Office extents are listed in the calendars of inquisitions *post mortem*.

Manor court records serve as diaries of local events and can be used as such: in May 1394 widow Sykes let her cow stray into the open field; John Fairchild neglected to scour a ditch; Matthew Peare's diseased sheep caused havoc on the high moor. But it is wise to read more into the wording of these presentments: 'breaking the Westfield with horses before the town consented' implies that the community possessed at least one open field on the west side (doubtless where West lane now runs) that was regulated by a town meeting; the field lay fallow as pasture until a meeting decided ploughing should begin (and incidentally agreed on what crop should be sown over the whole field); that horses not oxen were employed; not everyone including the culprit thought the town meeting should any longer be empowered to regulate the fields.

Take another example from the town of Whitby: 'for being wont to empty his chamberpot into the high street to the public detriment' indicates that the community believed in regulations serving toward the common good; but that, none the less, it was a habit of town dwellers to throw waste out of front doors or windows into the high street gutter. It is all too easy to misinterpret these

documents. Orders and byelaws of the court are essential sources
in proving the types of offence sufficiently common to warrant
regulation and in indicating the kind of community people aimed
to create. The strict regulation of the common would have been
unnecessary unless people were taking advantage of its previously
unregulated state.

Maps

Estate maps usually illustrate the property of one landowner
whether great magnate, industrial or railway company, grammar
school or parish church. Maps therefore show merely a couple of
fields belonging to the glebe, six cottages and gardens of a railway
company or the proprietary village of a peer of the realm. It was
only when interest in the techniques of land surveying revived,
after the renaissance of learning, that men began to produce
adequate and detailed maps. Early surveyors seem to have trained
themselves, and their books, chains and other equipment occasionally grace an unused space on a map. Professional surveyors
from 1700 draw most accurate and pleasing maps, that have never
been bettered. Estate maps therefore date from around 1570 to
about 1860. They may be huge rolls of parchment or small pieces
of paper; separate papers are regularly fastened together and given
a cloth or linen backing. Some surveyors prefer black ink sketches,
others use bright water colours. Some adopt the ground plan
approach as in modern ordnance surveys. Others prefer the pic-
torial bird's eye view, as if the estate were seen obliquely from the
air. The latter must therefore represent houses, people, hedges,
huntsmen, ploughteams, beasts of burden, and indeed everything
in the map as would be seen by an artist sitting on a neighbouring
high hill. Many surveys fall between these two groups.

The usual scale varies from three to six chains to an inch, or as
large as the great twenty-five-inch ordnance surveys or the tithe
maps. Because landowners commission these maps, surveyors are
encouraged to represent every feature of interest or use to the
proprietor. They therefore include every house, specifying number of bays of building, chimneys, storeys, building material,

every garden, orchard, fence and gate, every tree, hedge, dovecote, lane and stream, every waggon-way, mine, factory, toll-bar, place of worship and parsonage. Written on the map or in an accompanying schedule are names of tenants, house occupiers, fields, streets and workshops. Acreage, annual value, rents, purchase prices and crops are sometimes noted. Only when ordnance maps on a large scale superseded estate maps did these documents become rare.

Estate maps are pictures of towns or villages at one point in time. They may well come long before tithe, enclosure or ordnance maps and hence be the best source for judging the state of industry and agriculture. Strips in the open field, crops in enclosures, emerging manufactories and improved means of transport should therefore be sought on maps. You will not only see at a glance whether a particular building is in existence, but notice its physical features also. The person tracing the history of a house often learns the name of occupier as well as owner. This knowledge leads to other types of document. You see examples of eighteenth-century town planning as squares and terraces of uniform design march across the map. A series of town estate maps follows the progress of urban growth during the industrial revolution. The student of place-names (fields, streets, farms and similarly modest features) is usually well rewarded.

Various records

It is not easy to find worthwhile series of family and estate accounts before about 1570. The Elizabethan household entered into a volume details of expenditure and income for home, farm and business purposes. Later family records-keepers preserved tradesmen's bills, vouchers of payments to estate workers, books for rents, mining royalties and household expenses.

Estate and family letters are not usually separated until the eighteenth century. Letters together with diaries, journals, drawings, family Bible, genealogical notes, photographs and newspaper clippings are treasure trove for the historian. One of the best collections of estate correspondence was written by the Pastons of Norfolk between 1418 and 1506, all of which is now in print.

A survey is a word picture of an estate, usually dating from 1540–1720: 'mansion outhouse stables and garden 2r . . . one windemillne . . . William Horsfeldes close called saltersclose adjoynes north-Easte on the Common, south and west on Hall Fielde lac. 2r.'

Notices, conditions and particulars of sale or lease of houses, land and personal goods were often inserted in local newspapers or nailed on walls prior to disposal of property. Landowners kept several copies of these printed documents which sometimes describe property in useful detail. They date from 1700 to the present.

Rentals set out the names of tenants and properties against rent paid or due. Medieval documents are generally on parchment in a greatly abbreviated Latin and refer to borough or monastic property. Private estate and manorial rentals are not uncommon and of course appear in thousands by the sixteenth century. The size of these documents depends on the area of the estate. Rentals can be very detailed:

NAME OF TENANT	John Phillipson, yeoman
SITUATION	1. Mainwarings farm
	2. Long hey close
	3. High wood
	4. Cottage
TERMS	1. Lease for three lives of John Phillipson, decd, John Phillipson, present tenant (29), Mary his wife (26) at £40 rent
	2. By year £5
	3. By year £10
	4. At will 1s a week
RENT DUE 25 MAR	£28 16s
PAID	£26
ARREARS	£2 16s

Although no written deed was required for a demise or lease till 1677, landowners have leased property to tenants since medieval times. The Black Death of the fourteenth century encouraged proprietors to abandon customary husbandry with labour services in favour of wage labour and leasing out the estate for terms of years or lives at fixed rent. Gradually terms grew longer, often to twenty-one years. In a lease for three lives were written the names of the three people during whose lives the lease would continue. The rent was fixed, greatly benefiting the tenants if agricultural profits rose. (Many tenants, however, held at the will or pleasure of the landlord and could be turned out without warning.) The operative words of a lease are 'demise grant and to farm let . . . yielding and paying'. Rent was low until the eighteenth century, proprietors preferring to demand a high fine at the commencement of the lease.

A mortgage is the pledging of property in order to secure a loan. The usual form was a demise for five hundred years or some similarly long term which would be voided on repayment of the principal. Chancery protected the mortgagor's interests because the loan was rarely repaid within the one year stipulated in the demise. A mortgage might well be effected by lease and release, though such deeds are difficult to identify as mortgages. The mortgagee could of course assign his demise to another person if he became short of money before the mortgagor was ready to repay his debts. A mortgage is an excellent form of investment. A mortgaged estate need not imply the owner's bankruptcy. He might, for instance, need ready cash to build a factory or houses and prefer to use somebody else's capital rather than his own (which might have been earning good interest elsewhere). An assignment of a term in trust, to attend the freehold and inheritance, is employed when a mortgage is redeemed and property sold at the same time. It has four parties, but states nothing except the fact that the mortgage has been redeemed.

Chapter 4

CATHEDRAL

THE diocesan bishop's throne stands in the cathedral church, and this place is the administrative centre of the bishop's diocese. The bishop's fellow clergy at the cathedral, even before the Norman Conquest, formed a corporate body known as the chapter to govern the cathedral church, neighbouring parishes and the whole diocese. These men, living according to definite rules, were called canons and their leader the dean. They served as trustees of episcopal property, had a veto on financial matters, often acquired a peculiar jurisdiction in the cathedral city, were supreme governors of the cathedral itself, restricting the bishop's freedom of action in cathedral and estate matters almost entirely.

Some cathedrals, however, were the churches of monasteries. The prior and convent formed the chapter, and the cathedral is known as monastic or regular, the monks living according to regulations. These were given deans and chapters after the dissolution of the monasteries in 1536–9. Since 1836, new dioceses have been created at places like Truro and Liverpool, by carving areas from older dioceses. Records were not usually transferred when this happened.

Until the era of mid-Victorian reform, the bishop exercised wide powers as administrator and judge. He dealt with probate of wills and divorce cases, licensed schoolmasters and governed charities, visited every parish and supervised the career of every clergyman. He registered documents which people deposited in obedience to canon law or act of parliament, such as glebe terriers and transcripts of parish registers. But he did not interfere with the chapter's authority over the cathedral and capitular estates.

Capitular records

Capitular records include title deeds, leases, surveys, rentals, manor court rolls and correspondence—that is, a typical estate archive—from as early as the eleventh century onwards. Minutes of decisions of the dean and chapter, affecting cathedral estate matters and services, are written up in chapter act books. The York book begins in 1290.

Episcopal records

Bishops' registers are among the oldest records, beginning in 1209 at Lincoln and later in the same century at York, Winchester, Exeter, Canterbury and elsewhere. Contents include consecrations of churches, appropriations of benefices to religious houses, institutions to benefices, ordinations (admissions) to holy orders, visitation injunctions, notes about probate of wills and decisions arrived at in church courts; altogether a complete record of the bishop's daily business from the thirteenth to the sixteenth centuries.

Registers were presumably accompanied by hundreds of loose documents, which have not survived from before the late fifteenth century. At this date comprehensive registers are abandoned in favour of separate files and registers relating to different types of activity. Early registers, like all diocesan records, are almost entirely in Latin until about 1520 and then in an English-Latin mixture till 1733, so the non-medievalist should think twice before starting research on medieval church subjects. He should remember that ecclesiastical administration is not yet perfectly understood, and consequently entries in registers present some difficulties of interpretation. Historical societies have translated and published a few medieval registers, but even edited versions cannot save the unwary student from committing errors through lack of background knowledge.

After about 1490 records of institutions, collations, deprivations, resignations, as well as ordinations to holy orders gradually separate themselves from bishop's registers. Examinations, orders, letters and testimonials forming bulky files still, however, contain the same kind of information: name of ordinand and of bishop, date and place of ceremony, with miscellaneous supporting evidence like birth certificate. Documents sometimes date from Stuart times though most begin only after Archbishop Wake's official letter to his clergy of 1716 which regularised practices. Both Latin and English are encountered. Records of consecrations of new churches are not numerous till Georgian times, because most communities already possessed places of worship by 1300 before most registers begin. Petitions to build churches, title deeds of property, conveyances to trustees, narratives of the ceremony and other documents form files known as consecration papers, most of which are in English and concern industrial towns or new suburbs of old boroughs.

Licences

From Elizabeth I's reign onwards the bishop issued licences, dispensations and faculties concerning such matters as church repairs, marriage and administration of an intestate's goods. Documents themselves are partly in English (wholly after 1733) but were handed over to the interested parties, copies sometimes being preserved in diocesan archives. The bishop's actions were, however, usually chronologically noted in the bishop's register or in the diocesan chancellor's book. This record may well be in an abbreviated Latin following a set pattern which is not difficult to learn.

A faculty is a licence by the bishop allowing local church authorities to complete alterations to their buildings or confirming work already finished, to allot seats in church, reserve vaults and grave spaces or erect parsonages. First appearing in England about 1240 this licence often responds to a petition setting forth reasons for work to be done: 'sheweth that the west wall and tower being of wood . . . are so ruinous and decayed . . . your petitioners seek to rebuild . . .' Plans of alterations and counter-petitions accompany petitions. The licence or faculty on parchment (a copy of which remains in the diocesan or officials' registers) repeats the words of the petition and grants permission. The church, its roof, windows and balcony, pulpit, organ and pews, ornaments, goods, utensils, altar rails, vaults, monuments and glebe buildings appear in various faculty papers which generally are no older than about 1720.

Licences were issued by the bishop allowing schoolmasters to teach, incumbents to be non-resident, ministers to preach, laymen to eat meat in Lent or to marry in that season, priests to engage in trade, surgeons, midwives and parish clerks to function, un-beneficed clerks to serve the cure of souls in specified parishes and clergy to hold livings in plurality. Documents may be recorded in special registers before 1803 but after this certainly must be, following an act for the stricter control of ecclesiastical licences.

People applied for licences to marry in church from medieval times onwards. Some wanted to avoid the publicity inherent in publishing banns from the pulpit and the consequent expense of entertaining guests. Others like sailors or pregnant women sought speed: marriage could follow immediately on obtaining a licence. Then parsons did not marry in Lent or on fasting days except by licence. Though marriage was considered valid till 1754 without banns or licence, couples began to seek licences in growing numbers from Elizabethan days. In 1597 and 1604, church authorities tried to limit the power of granting licences to episcopal officials and to demand the binding of sureties to fulfil strict conditions. From this time licences were granted by the arch-bishops and bishops, certain archdeacons and clergy appointed as surrogates. Heads of peculiars were not supposed to issue licences but did. Marriage licences were not issued during the Common-wealth because there were no bishops to issue them. By Lord Hardwicke's Act of 1753, a marriage must be by banns or licence, and the latter could be granted only for a church or chapel in whose area one of the parties had resided for four weeks prior to the granting of the licence.

Every type of person applied for licences, not merely the rich or gentry. Firstly, the groom (usually) went to the diocesan registry and made an allegation or sworn statement concerning the lawfulness of the marriage. The groom is supposed to prove the parents' consent. Ages given are usually approximate only: 'both aged 21½ yeares' meant in one case thirty-five. The allegations are entered chronologically in books or on forms. Few registries possess complete series. Canterbury archbishopric holds a good collection from 1543 to 1869; York from 1567 onwards, Bristol only from 1746.

Then comes the marriage bond. Two sureties or bondsmen (one of whom is often the groom) bind themselves in a certain sum. Names, addresses, occupations and sum involved appear in this first part, which is normally in Latin till 1733. The sureties undertake to see that the couple (who are both named) shall 'lawfully marry together' in a specified church or chapel. This part of the bond is in English. The whole bond is written on one piece of paper, much of the wording being common form and printed. Bonds (often wrongly called licences) are at the registry in bundles arranged by the year, sometimes alphabetically, and rarely begin before 1600. They became unnecessary in 1823. The licence is now issued for conveyance to the specified church. Sometimes a choice is given of several churches. Here the parson holds the licence as authority or returns it to the couple for preservation in their own records, not at the registry. A note of the issuing of the licence appears in a special register. Indexes of bonds and allegations are printed by societies like the Lancashire and Cheshire Record Society, the Sussex Record Society, and the Harleian Society.

Marriage bonds seem to scotch a legend that, in olden times, couples married young. Where ages are given, it is clear that marriage was generally late, indeed comparatively much later than today, when the shorter life expectancy is considered. The Canterbury marriage licences 1619–60 show an average age of twenty-four for brides, twenty-eight for grooms. The only class capable financially and (probably) physically of earlier marriage was the gentry and nobility. But is this true for your district? Bonds of course show where a marriage was supposed to take place, though they are not evidence of marriage in themselves.

Terriers

A terrier (from the Latin *terra*, land) lists the possessions and rights of a church. Drawn up in obedience to a canon of 1571 for return to registries of dioceses and archdeaconries, it has rarely survived before 1604, when another canon made the return of terriers mandatory everywhere. Copies of terriers in parish chests usually date from after 1660. This document of parchment or paper is bundled by year of visitation, sometimes in alphabetical order of parishes. A typical terrier begins with an inventory of furnishings, books and other goods in the church, describes the church fabric, tower, roofing, bells, churchyard, parsonage and its grounds and customs concerning church repairs. Outbuildings and church cottages appear: 'a mere cottage built with clay walls and covered with thatch containing 3 rooms' (1604). Then the clerk names the glebe lands belonging to the benefice usually mentioning the exact locality of each strip, oxgang or enclosure. Allowances of meadow, woodland and grazing common are not forgotten, together with special customs about rotation and re-allotment. Then are recited the rights of the benefice like tithe revenue, Easter offerings, mortuaries, surplice fees. Finally comes a note on the upkeep of bells and clock and the payment of the parish clerk.

The student searches terriers for a description of church property especially in the period 1600–1820. Agricultural customs of pre-enclosure days are stated or at least hinted at. Apart from rare estate maps and more common surveys, there are no more useful documents for re-creating the village that has long since disappeared. The topographer notices the location of a forgotten windmill, charity land, peasant's cottage, coppice or track. Names of fields, lanes, enclosures, woods and strips in the open field

appear in a form closer to the original medieval spelling, and
suggest an interpretation to the experienced linguist. This last job
should be left to experts, for guesswork can yield ludicrous
answers. The genealogist notes local surnames. The architecture
student gets a conducted tour of typical parsonages and every type
of peasants' cottage. Since so many dwellings have disappeared
without trace, this document may give the only description now
available.

Subscriptions

Even in medieval days bishops acted on the government's behalf
in such matters as the return of royal writs concerning clergy,
levying clerical subsidies and punishment in church courts of
criminous clerks. Such work appears in the general registers. The
post-Reformation bishops were naturally more intimately concerned with secular matters, their duties being enforced by acts
of parliament as well as church canons. Thus from Elizabeth's
reign onwards, they had to ensure that all clergy, ordinands,
teachers and lecturers subscribed 'willingly and heartily' to the
three articles: royal supremacy in the church; use of the Book of
Common Prayer; and the thirty-nine articles agreed to in 1562.
Subscriptions are recorded on paper or in registers certainly from
the passing of the Act of Uniformity of 1662. In each case the
man's name is followed by his occupation or benefice, date of
subscription, and (possibly) date and place of birth. After 1688
diocesan registries were supposed to license dissenters' meeting
houses and records may be in consistory court act books, special
registers or loose files.

Census

In April 1676 every priest in the country was supposed to return
to the archbishop of either York or Canterbury a statement of the
number of persons 'by common estimation and account in your
parish inhabiting', those attending parish communion, and those
popish recusants and protestant dissenters absenting themselves.
Some incumbents, as at Clayworth, Nottinghamshire, made drafts

of the returns, which may well still lie in the parish chest. To the archbishops' records went in most cases merely a statement on paper from each parish of numbers of people in each of the categories. The returns are known as the Compton census after Henry Compton, bishop of London, and now are discovered among diocesan records. Carlisle diocesan returns are in the Bodleian Library, Oxford.

Bishop's transcripts

Bishop's transcripts are normally supposed to date from the provincial constitution of Canterbury of 1597. Churchwardens of each parish must, within a month of Easter, annually send to the diocesan registry a transcript of the parish register entries of the preceding year. Some parishes had already been ordered to return transcripts long before 1597. Transcripts for Lincoln archdeaconry start in 1561, for Canterbury diocese in 1558. Parishes lying in peculiars (areas exempt from the bishop's jurisdiction) returned transcripts only to the head of the peculiar, and these records will be sought nowadays in places like the county record office, British Museum and occasionally the diocesan registry.

Not all dioceses bothered with transcripts. In 1800, only nine or ten parishes out of 434, in Salisbury diocese, were in the habit of making returns. London's transcripts are almost non-existent. Regular collection of transcripts ceased with the passing of the Registration Act in 1836. It is evident that some transcripts are copied from the clerk's rough notebook, as were registers too. Others are taken from loose pieces of paper, whose entries never got into the registers. Indeed transcripts were, to some extent, regarded as more important than the merely parochial registers. Thus they are generally of parchment. They vary in size from handkerchief to tablecloth. Their present condition largely depends on the past state of the attic or cellar of the diocesan registry, while not a few transcripts have been destroyed by rats, fire and students. The writing on others is so encrusted with grime that long soaking in water and rubbing clean is essential. They are gathered sometimes by parishes, sometimes by year and deanery.

G

Most transcripts disagree at some points with the registers, omitting names, dates, memoranda, even whole entries. Some set out more information; for example, the parish register of Walton near Liverpool records the burial on 9 August 1729 of what appear to be two sisters:

Ellin & Anne Bridge of Walton

But the transcript says:

Ellin Bridge Sp. & Ann w. of Jo: Bridge husb.

Bishop's transcripts, not necessarily being copies of parish registers, serve as alternative sources of baptisms, marriages and burials. Older than registers in certain cases they are also used to detect forgeries and carelessly inscribed entries in the parish documents. Transcripts are generally in English at least from 1660. Nowadays they are arranged chronologically by parish.

Routine benefice papers

Bishops were further burdened from the eighteenth century by legislation affecting church affairs and particularly church property. Various types of documents are preserved in parochial bundles often known as routine benefice papers, and these may be summarised in registers. A number of diocesan registries have sorted into separate files the different kinds of documents, making all the more tiresome the job of finding information about a single parish. Among routine benefice papers are registers of appointments of commissioners to report on the condition of parsonages (from 1838); registers of surveyors' returns concerning church buildings during vacancies (under the Dilapidations Act 1871); files and registers about new parishes and unions or disunions of benefices (1840); registers and files of augmentation deeds relating to the increase in the value of livings through the action of private donors, Queen Anne's Bounty and the Church Commissioners; title and trust deeds of parochial schools, charities, playing fields and meeting rooms. In addition the bishop may hold records of church conferences, theological colleges, missionary societies, clergy pension funds, diocesan boards of education, boards of patronage and women's organisations.

Visitations

From the thirteenth century, the bishop began regularly to visit certain convenient points in his diocese in order to correct abuses and maintain ecclesiastical authority. The medieval bishop obviously concerned himself with monasteries to a large extent but also organised the visitation of secular clergy and laymen. This scheme of visitation every three or four years continued after the Reformation, though much of the tedious business of hearings and judging was left to diocesan officials. Laymen had been encouraged to make presentations of parochial abuses from about 1450 ('we present John Levett and Frances his wife, for antenuptial Fornication'). Anglican bishops later sent out articles of inquiry prior to visitation to direct the laymen's thoughts along useful channels: the state of church fabric and graveyard, conduct of priests and parishioners both at service and in daily life, quality of services, names of charities, extent of church lands, attendance at Sunday School, age and value of church goods, preservation of registers and presence of nonconformists or papists. Some fifteenth-century presentments survive. Articles of inquiry with answers, compulsory from the early seventeenth century, date mainly from 1660 onwards. From these returns some bishops compiled surveys or *specula* of the diocese listing parishes alphabetically and exhibiting names of clergy and patron, details of services, number of communicants, notes on charities and schools and so on.

To the visitation centres were then summoned by a general monition all clergy, teachers, preachers, farmers of tithes, lay officers of the churches, executors named in wills and delinquents. Any of the latter whose crimes seemed sufficiently serious were served with a special citation. The diocesan registrar normally prepared prior to visitation miscellaneous visitation books in which he could list clergy, churchwardens, documents, fees and judgments. Here may be recorded Elizabethan examinations of recusants and schoolmasters, serving as short biographies of these people. All these documents the registrar filed together as the record of a single visitation and this collection need be supplemented only with the bishop's official court books. The majority of post-1660 documents that prove of most use to the local historian are in English and clearly written. They can help the student fill some gaps in his knowledge of the church in the last three centuries but are by no means as intimate, spontaneous or explicit as court papers or diocesan files. Finally appear injunctions setting out one by one all the faults of commission or omission to be corrected; penances; certificates of performance of penances; and the act book of the visitor's court of audience recording judicial proceedings against scandalous offenders.

Episcopal courts

The bishop has since the earliest times regulated the affairs of the church—faith, religious practices, behaviour, patronage, wills, property, revenue—and until 1860 thus claimed jurisdiction over both clerics and laymen. He erected an apparatus of courts of record supervised by officials which were fully operative by the sixteenth century, and reserved to his own court of audience only the most flagrant cases of clerical immorality or high-society matrimonial disputes. The bishop's own cases are usually recorded in general registers, while the remainder of disputes appear in separate files or books. Each diocese worked out its own organisation which is reflected in the great variety of court records. This type of archive is therefore somewhat complicated to understand. Individual documents in abbreviated Latin and (often) in a most trying court hand are not to be tackled by any but the most dedicated and patient. In the consistory court, the bishop's official heard cases from the fourteenth century onwards.

On presentment or inquisition of an easily remedied abuse, the court of summary jurisdiction listened to the accused and various witnesses before orally pronouncing sentence. This was usually a penance (after the Reformation, a reading aloud at morning service of a confession). The act book sets out date and place of the hearing, name, parish and fault of the accused, and court proceedings: 'upon the Saboth day he did yoke a horse and drawe a boate upon a sled to the great offence of manye'.

For the more serious and doubtful cases brought on the promotion, perhaps, of a third party the procedure of plenary jurisdiction was followed. Such cases began with a statement of the problem and continued as defendant and prosecution propounded their positions. Each step of the way is fully described in documents which are filed together, leaving the act book to record merely dates of the various hearings and fees due. Most useful to local historians are individual documents called *responsa personalia*, articles or *materia*, allegations and depositions. All set out differing statements of the case (mostly in Latin with some English thrown in where the clerk's Latin failed).

Court causes concern and mention local customs, farming practices, parish bounds, deponents' birthplaces and ages, fornication, decrees of nullity of marriage, incest, marriage within prohibited degrees, adultery, slander, non-payment of tithes and Easter offerings and non-observance of holy days. Registries preserve annual bundles of all court papers usually entirely unindexed.

The local historian will want to know if any of the causes deal with people or subjects in his chosen district. Unless files are calendared or transcribed, it will be virtually impossible to satisfy this demand. There is a glimmer of hope in the fact that many records are now with the county archivist and he may, time permitting, be able to identify one or two relevant causes and to transcribe these for a serious and dedicated student. It is just as difficult for the church historian who is neither palaeographer nor Latinist to extract from administrative records all references to the church, clergy and parsonage, at least in the period prior to 1733.

Wills

A will is the instrument by which a person disposes of property upon or after his or her death. The document may attempt to bind an estate or family for generations, and regularly appoints guardians and a course of training for surviving children. Because a will becomes operative on man's passage out of this life the church, as most efficient, lettered, ever-present and trusted authority in medieval times, dealt with all probate matters from an early date. Many people never made a will, property passing by custom, unspoken understanding or word of mouth. It was also possible for a nuncupative will, a spoken testament made before witnesses just before death, to be recognised as valid. Even when people actually wrote out a will, the document was not always proved; that is taken for authentification, partly to save expense, partly because the heir's title was undisputed. So merely a minority of people, mostly adult males, asked church authorities to prove their wills. Only in 1858 did the state establish probate registries and abolish ecclesiastical control of wills.

The process of probate was, from medieval times till 1858, relatively simple. The testator writes his will usually in English on paper or parchment. He often asks a clerk for help in writing the document comprehensibly; the clerk often being at first the village cleric or parson, later usually a lawyer. Large fortunes, estates and families encouraged the writing of lengthy carefully-worded documents thirty or forty foolscap pages in bulk. Widows, spinsters and wealthy women wrote wills; the mass of women did not till after 1858. After the testator's death the will (often with a copy) is despatched to the registry of the archdeaconry or diocese where his property lay. If the man held property in several dioceses the will went to the court of the province (either York or Canterbury). Men of substance generally proved wills at Canterbury.

The registrar proves the will in due course by recording, in Latin until 1733, in the diocesan act book (the notebook so to speak of daily actions) the name of the deceased, his former residence and job, the names of executors, the date of will, of death, of probate. On the original signed will is noted date of death and probate, together with value of personalty. This is preserved among diocesan records and has usually survived to this day. Some registrars copied wills into large registers as a double precaution. A copy of the will produced by the testator, or for a fee by the diocesan authorities, is sealed and returned to the executors who take out a bond to administer the estate fairly. The family's copy of the will, if still in existence, lies among family and estate papers. Wills are sometimes filed in series known as 'supra' when the personalty is valued above £40, 'infra' when below £40, and 'diocesan' when the will has been subject to a dispute in court. An inventory of the deceased's personal goods, appraised soon after death, should accompany each will though surviving documents date usually from 1540 to 1740.

If the deceased produced no will, his representatives often signed a bond in double the value of the personalty to administer the property honestly. The administration bonds are preserved in chronological bundles and their contents noted in the act book under deceased's name, showing date of bond, value bound and administrators' names. Read Peter Walne's *English Wills* (1964) for more background information. Since most of the vital portions of probate records are in English, practice with handwriting will enable you to read all but the oldest of wills. For old-fashioned out-of-the-way words consult J. Wright's *The English Dialect Dictionary* (1898–1905) and specialised books on your own county's dialect.

A typical will after acknowledgement to the deity ('in the name of God, amen') records testator's name, residence, status or occupation. Then follow details of all real and personal estate, trading interests, shares in industry, cash, jewels, books, and so on to be left at death providing circumstances do not alter: 'my Dwelling House lately rebuilt with the old room adjoyneing occupied by James Fletcher Blacksmith . . . all my fifteen shares in the London and Birmingham railway company . . . my carridge and horses . . . ten thousand pounds . . . my silver tea service . . . my second best bed . . . all that my cotton mill outhouses steam-ingine and other appertenances'. The testator divides his property as he considers equitable, naming family, relations, servants, friends and charities: 'to my daughter Ann so long as she remains unmarried . . . my faithful servant-girl Mary Jenkyns . . . to the poor of Mellynge . . . to the churchwardens for erecting six almshouses to bear my name . . . to Thomas Dewhirst priest'. There are normally conditions to be fulfilled: 'and so on in the male line son to son . . .

until the age of one and twenty yeares . . . in tail male . . . as long as she continues to inhabit my said dwelling'. The testator often arranges his own funeral: 'six horses draped in black . . . one oak coffyn . . . one pint of best beere for each man'. He then dates his will and signs in the presence of two witnesses. A will in the archives may often be folded in a paper wrapper on which is endorsed date of death, date of probate and name of testator. A probate copy must be sealed with the diocesan seal.

An inventory on parchment or paper may well be an enormous document, twenty or thirty feet long when unrolled or unfolded. It is written by the appraisers in handwriting which varies according to the men's book-learning. They note the deceased's name, the date the inventory was taken of 'all the goodes and cattels'. Then they journey round the property supposedly noting and valuing everything though accuracy in monetary terms cannot be relied on. They name the rooms in the dwelling and their purpose: 'in the hawle . . . the chamber over the Parlour . . . the buttery . . . cheese chamber . . . in the seller . . . in the yellow Chamber of my cozen Mary'.

Inventories are one of the best sources for descriptions of Tudor and Stuart houses. The room by room progress of appraisers enables each house to be reconstructed in drawing even if the building itself has long since been altered or demolished. Ground plans and elevations of the period 1540–1740 follow certain patterns according to region, and the student of vernacular architecture can be reasonably sure that his reconstruction is approximately correct. In John West's *Village Records* (1962) an architect has drawn pictures of early Stuart houses from information about rooms in inventories. M. W. Barley has examined inventories from various parts of the country in order to work out the types of houses found in each region from 1500 to 1700. His book *The English Farmhouse and Cottage* (1961) with its skilfully-drawn pictures of houses provides a model for students of vernacular architecture (that is, everyday buildings rather than mansions or churches).

The appraisers describe the contents of each room: '2 bedsteads

2 flockbeds 4 featherbolsters 2 coverletts in the maydes chamber
£3 15s 6d . . . one joyned desk . . . 3 carpetts 7 quishions . . . 3
brasen candlesticks 3 coffers 1 cupborde 2 chayres 1 forme 1 stoole
1 planke 2 skeeles 32s 6¾d'. Kitchen utensils are numerous and
nearly always strange to post-Victorian housewives: spit, pothook,
posnett, skimmer, cresset, broche, andirons, wetting vat, salting
trough, hair sieve, all described in a good dictionary. Of course
some people possess much in the way of jewels and personal
fripperies: 'one jewell with a unicorn horne sett in gold with a
stone £10 . . . locket with pictures 7s'. Clothes are sorted through;
in the man's room they find 'one payre of blacke satin velvet
Venetian drawers . . . 15 pair of worsted stockings . . . payre of
lether hose layd on with lacynge . . . 3 velvet jerkins'. The woman
owns 'one white satin kirtle layde over with silver lace and fringed
with silke and silver lined with white sarsnett . . . three stayes . . .
2 payre of velvet shoos'.

The appraisers journey outdoors into farmyard, craftsman's
workshop, barn, fields and stable. They notice 'iii kyne vi sheepe
one wain one harrow a mattock ii plowbeames . . . barley & oats
on the ground in hey close £5 10s . . . peas in West feilde . . . fire
woode . . . all the shoppe tooles £9 17s . . . Taffity silk lace and
other items of trade . . . 1 whimble bitte and a nawger'. The last
two items are a drill and an auger for carpentry. People described
as yeoman often seem to work as shopkeepers too. One such
possessed Iceland cod and other fish in large quantities, sufficient
to supply a small town. Another stored masses of paper, parchment, quills, ink and leather about the 'chamber nexte the hawle'.
Men with specialised collections of personalty may not always be
in trade. There are detailed inventories of book collections which
seem to be as often private libraries as stationers' goods. Weapons
are generally held by substantial householders as a matter of
course, and in obedience to the law: 'a sworde dagger 2 rapiers
3 bucklers 2 sword girdles . . . 4 bowes of Ewe 9 score arrowes . . .
1 horne flaske boxe for powder'. And many inventories record
debts owing to and by the dead person: 'his purse £5 . . . value
in gold £40 . . . things forgot 15s'.

From these records one can study the possessions of various kinds of family. Was a yeoman seemingly more prosperous in 1750 than he had been a century before? How did a shoemaker's home compare with a husbandman's? Was the kitchen of a gentleman's mansion equipped with labour-saving devices or did the kitchen staff just use three times as many posnets and porringers as anyone else? Why was the kitchen filled with more goods than any other room? Did the materials from which bed-linen, spoons and tableware were made differ considerably from house to house in the village? And if so, is the variation significant? In the house too are spread out the family's clothes not only the Sunday best of portraits but working garments, underwear and nightgowns. A competent appraiser describes material, styling, colour as well as attachments like garters, laces and points, contributing to a history of clothing if not of high fashion in your own locality among every rank of inhabitant. The literate appraiser may well survey books in the house, and his lists add to our knowledge of the distribution of reading matter, the types of book most favoured, and the value of these early editions. Of course most people possess merely a Bible, perhaps a prayer book or devotional tome, while others own dozens of assorted volumes. Did these last-named people use their knowledge by teaching or lecturing in the town? Did professional men like doctors and parsons own books to aid them in their work? Did these men and their neighbours obey the law by keeping at home arms and armour for military defence purposes? If so, were the arms modern or merely converted farm tools? Were men in general prepared for foreign invasion or civil unrest? What classes were armed already on the eve of the Civil War and 1688 Revolution?

Wills and administration bonds are used for genealogical purposes. Indeed a will often proves as useful as a parish register in relating family ties. I examined one will which connected three branches of the family, in the West Indies, London and Yorkshire, with their common ancestor, a Midlands squire. In the chapter on research methods a genealogical abstract has been demonstrated, so it is only necessary to repeat here that every name in the record must be extracted and relationships noted. The bare bones of pedigrees so drawn up can be given dates from registers in due course.

Economic conditions figure largely in probate records, as is natural in documents by which men set their affairs straight. Wills and inventories recall the enclosure of commons, strips in open fields, crops grown and stored, animals working the land, implements, produce available for sale in the market, the number of labourers employed, servants in husbandry and other facts which by intimation and careful interpretation furnish a survey of local agricultural affairs. Trading activity figures in wills and inventories of merchants, factory owners, craftsmen, even farmers. To know the extent of the real and personal property of town and country people in the centuries prior to 1858 may help to explain the provenance of capital to finance industrial changes. Some very obscure farmers and craftsmen owned property in small amounts over a comparatively wide area. Their income lent out to enterprising but poor merchants and craftsmen may have aided industrial growth. Solicitors seem to have acted as middlemen in this transfer of capital before the Victorian era, though in some districts these men make a very late appearance. Who served in this position from 1500 to 1780 in your locality? Who was the wealthiest man as regards personalty? Was he in trade or on the land? What men kept most ready money about the house? Who had lent money to whom? It is a worthwhile task to list the jobs of men who left wills or inventories in order to gain an inkling of the pattern of jobs available in each century. Note all goods mentioned and the varying prices: 'pair of stockings (man) 1600 20d, 1621 16d, 1640 17d'. Prices so collected are useful as a contribution to cost of living tables, though you must remember that the stockings in 1600 may well have been a gentleman's and brand new; in 1621 a yeoman's and darned; and the appraisers were different each time and possibly ignorant of prices.

Wills themselves serve as title deeds and family settlements. A testator leaving his house to his son creates another deed to add to the bundle already safely preserved. An early will may well be the first title deed that has survived for a property. Thus its description of the estate, together with the inventory, prove invaluable to the householder researching into the history of the house. Wills sometimes mention just 'all my property real and personal', but regularly name every portion of the estate scattered as it could be across the country and abroad. They state the terms by which the estate ought to descend and not infrequently cause much family trouble as a result. They go further, and attempt to settle family affairs for a generation or so by leaving money or land on condition a daughter marry a certain man or a son-in-law's sons alter their surname and continue the family business. A man endows a school or charity by means of his will and the history of such an authority starts with the probate copy and the conditions proposed there. It is, of course, as well to make sure that the school or charity is not being merely re-founded despite what the testator asserts. Certainly, one old Cheshire grammar school, supposedly founded by will in 1557, was functioning earlier.

Wills and inventories, so often written by ordinary townsmen or villagers, are good examples of handwriting. Even those produced by scribes are signed by testators or appraisers. Genealogists find such examples fascinating not only as ancestors' own hands but as clues to character, for graphological purposes. You could devise a table counting the number of literates and illiterates in each decade for your parish. The process of proving wills leads to a discussion of church administrative history: functions of diocese, archdeaconry, peculiar. How did it come about that the prebend of Good Easter in Essex lay in the peculiar of Westminster? Why does a man reveal his political or religious interests by naming friends, charities or parties? Were these interests generally known during his lifetime?

Diocesan probate records survive from medieval times until 1858. Wills proved at Canterbury form a large collection from 1383 to 1858. Chester wills date from 1545–1858; archdeaconry of Middlesex, diocese of London, 1608–1794. Most but not all wills were proved at diocesan registries where they have remained unless transferred to county record offices or archives departments of libraries. Thus wills proved at the Chester registry came from Cheshire and southern Lancashire. They lay at Abbey Gateway, Chester, until divided geographically into two collections, one for the Cheshire, one for the Lancashire Record Office. Archdeaconry wills have generally been deposited in record offices. Wills proved in peculiar jurisdictions have sometimes been lost if there has been no convenient archives office. Wills proved at Canterbury are now at Somerset House, London, not a county record office.

Thus in order to find the present place of deposit of a will, first decide where the testator owned property or perhaps lived and died; then the approximate date of death: say Paddington, Middlesex, about 1670. Then turn to A. J. Camp, *Wills and Their Whereabouts* (1963), and look under LONDON AND MIDDLESEX. Here are listed the various church authorities that proved wills. Paddington in 1670 lay in the royal peculiar of the dean and chapter of Westminster. According to the book, the original wills are now with the City of Westminster Archives Department, Public Library, SW1. A. J. Camp mentions inventories and administration bonds as well as act books and will registers, with covering dates of each. He points out what records are in print. Printed indexes are available of Canterbury wills from 1383 to the eighteenth century and of Canterbury administrations from 1559 to the seventeenth century. The Stationery Office printed an index of Canterbury probate records of the years 1853–7.

Access to records

Access to all cathedral records has for long been both too easy and too difficult. It has obviously been too easy for rats, souvenir hunters and browsers to rummage through the records. Untidy bundles, damaged papers and missing documents testify to careless supervision over several centuries. It has equally been very difficult to consult diocesan and capitular records, many of which have been in the possession of church solicitors whose somewhat zealous attention to secrecy has all too often resulted in gross neglect of the oldest documents on the principle of 'out of sight, out of mind'. Capitular muniments were usually regarded as private estate deeds and consequently guarded by clergymen in cathedral precinct fastnesses, accessible only after long negotiations, but old documents are mostly now in record offices. Numerous archives were scattered at the dissolution of monasteries in 1536–9 and during the interregnum of 1649–60.

Diocesan records at the registry are usually available, after negotiation, by appointment for a fee, though historical researchers usually obtain freer access. Many documents no longer in current use will be found in private estate muniments, libraries and county record offices where they are properly stored, indexed and freely available to all historians. It is normally a good policy to address your first inquiry about diocesan records to your county archivist, rather than to the diocesan registry. Then before commencing actual research on documents read J. S. Purvis, *Introduction to Ecclesiastical Records* (1953), written for the non-specialist and containing transcripts in the original language (whether Latin or English) of most types of diocesan records. The concise but very complete survey by Dorothy M. Owen, *The Records of the Established Church in England Excluding Parochial Records* (1970), will introduce you to archidiaconal, provincial (archbishops') and national records of the Church of England in addition to diocesan documents.

Chapter 5

PARISH CHEST

THE English parish is a district in the pastoral care of a single priest, to whom accrue ecclesiastical dues like tithes. Parish organisation is supposed to date from the late seventh century when Theodore of Tarsus was archbishop of Canterbury, though his parishes correspond in area more to modern dioceses. From then until the fourteenth century, the church created some 9,500 parishes to serve thriving settlements or townships, especially in the southern part of the country. Large towns and boroughs were divided into several parishes each with its own church and clergy: York had forty, Stamford twenty. Parishes in sparsely populated areas like the eastern part of Lancashire usually embraced dozens of hamlets. Fourteenth-century pestilence and economic distress destroyed many settlements and weakened most, laying church buildings in ruins and undermining parochial organisation.

Parish boundaries altered little with the nineteenth century, despite the agitation of reformers. Additional churches did appear, of course, but these were generally chapels-of-ease to the mother church and known as chapels or chapelries. Thus the market town of Mountsorrel, Leicestershire, standing astride the boundary between two ancient parishes remained merely a chapel-of-ease. Industrial development from about 1780 and reform of church and state after 1832 led to the founding of new parishes in manufacturing areas. Evangelical zeal affected remote country districts, where large parishes were carved up and new livings created. The parish therefore as an ecclesiastical unit is often not as ancient as the settlement or township. It is entirely separate from the manor. Naturally in certain districts township, manor and parish boundaries coincide and the functions of each authority become confused.

The parish proper is organised under a priest and his assistants. The priest is in legal terms a corporation sole with perpetual succession in whom is vested the freehold of church property (including the parish chest and its contents) subject to parishioners' rights of user (for example the right of burial in the churchyard and of access to the registers). A priest who owns the tithes has in recent centuries been called a rector. He becomes a vicar when great tithes are impropriate, that is, devolved into someone else's hands. The incumbent is aided by two or more churchwardens, officials established by the fourteenth century who are appointed by the minister and parishioners. They are responsible for the upkeep of church property and the provision of utensils for services. The parish clerk is supposed to deal with all church records, the sexton with church property.

The vestry, a meeting of parishioners and officials in the church vestry originating in medieval times, raised rates to pay for the preservation of the church, chapelries and religious services. Frequently the vestry took over the civil authority of the old town assembly of freemen and of decaying manor courts, especially from Tudor times onwards; and its religious and civil functions are reflected in a variety of documents in its parish chest.

Church rates have been levied by the common law of the country since medieval times, though the duty of repairing the church should fall on the tithe owner. Rates were accepted as inevitable by most parishioners and their compulsory nature was not abolished till 1868.

A number of English parish meetings from the fifteenth century appointed the local constable, hayward, pinder, nightwatchman, assuming manorial powers. The parish school (grammar school) was often conducted by the priest or curate under the church balcony. Concern for pauper children, the unemployed, the invalid, the old and apprentices can also be traced to medieval times. In September 1538 Thomas Cromwell issued a mandate to every incumbent to enter in a book every wedding, christening and burial in the parish. The vestry was to provide a 'sure coffer' with two locks, the parson holding one key, the wardens the other. Most churches already possessed a parish chest, often of richly-carved oak with wooden or iron nails, strong locks and bolts. This chest was usually capacious enough to contain the new register books, though many chests do in fact date from Tudor times. An act of 1812 demanded an iron chest, and these are usually stamped with the date '1813'.

Between 1538 and 1834, a multitude of further duties was heaped on the parish. The vestry managed all highways (except those turnpiked) from 1555 till (in some cases) 1899. The Elizabethan poor law envisaged a stock of raw material belonging to the parish for paupers able profitably to labour, 'convenient houses of habitation' for the aged and impotent, the apprenticeship of pauper children, the relief of the sick and indigent and the punishment of incorrigible rogues and vagabonds. After the Restoration, the law of settlement and removal (1662) tried to regulate the movement of the poor. In 1722 an act for the provision of workhouses allowed parishes to combine to build one if necessary. The vestry meeting in the parish church became in fact the basic unit of local government. Its activities impinged on every household whether Anglican or dissenting, wealthy or poor. This explains why the parish chest is—or should be—a source of information second to none.

As the parish acquired civil responsibilities, the vestry assumed the right to appoint officers to look after specific fields of activity. Where the parish was composed of townships, each unit held its own meeting of ratepayers, the town meeting and nominated for appointment its own officers. The overseer of the poor appears in 1572 as an alms collector and supervisor of rogues and vagabonds. Most of his duties ceased in 1834. The supervisor of the highways or waywarden maintains parish roads and tracks according to an

H

act of 1555. He is appointed by the magistrates (after 1691) from a list submitted by the vestry. He gains more power under the Highway Act of 1835 but disappears between 1862 and 1899. The constable, probably originally a manorial official, is mentioned in the thirteenth century. His duties were clarified by the Parish Constables Act 1842. Other officers include pinder, hayward, hedge-looker and field reeve. All have left some trace of their activities in the parish chest.

Nineteenth-century reforms progressively diminished civil responsibilities of the parish, and parish records become less useful. In 1834 the Poor Law Amendment Act removed the poor from parochial control. Hence settlement certificates, bastardy cases, removal orders, overseers' accounts, with correspondence about the aged and sick, all disappear. Road works might be alternatively arranged under acts of 1862–94. Civil registration of births, marriages and deaths commenced in 1837. Local boards of health from 1848 and rural sanitary authorities (1872) dealt in broad terms with health matters. Then in 1889 county councils were established. By act of 1894 the civil parish was created, usually from the ancient township or settlement rather than from the ecclesiastical parish, having its own elected council, its own clerk, its own records. Under a Church Assembly measure of 1921 the parochial church council concerned itself entirely with church affairs.

Access

The parish chest contains documents that belong to the incumbent and vestry. Records are not public as long as they relate to entirely ecclesiastical matters. By the Local Government Act of 1894, however, purely civil records like the accounts of overseers or constables, settlement certificates and enclosure awards were vested in the new parish council and parish meeting. This meant that only the registers remained to the incumbent. In practice the parish councils were not interested in archives and left records in the parish chest at the church. In effect therefore the incumbent retains the freehold and no one should copy records without his consent. But he must by law allow access, even to the registers, at all reasonable times on payment of an agreed fee. There is a leaflet on *Parish Register Searching in England and Wales* published by the Institute of Heraldic and Genealogical Studies, Canterbury (1967), showing fees and rules of access. Leaflet *LF 7* by the Church Information Office is a guide for clergy on fees. Despite all rules, however, the student must work with the goodwill of the priest. He must accept a cold and cramped vestry and records in poor condition. He will discover many gaps in the records, so many documents having been treated like dogs, destroyed 'on account of their age'.

Churchwarden's records

The oldest records in the parish chest are likely to be church-wardens' account books and papers presented for approval to and preserved by the vestry meeting. These records in some town parishes start in the fourteenth century. Early pre-1550 accounts (unless translated and printed) should not be tackled by anyone save the good palaeographer and Latinist. Churchwardens' records deal with the business of the church: the bishop's visitation, collection of alms, repairs to the fabric (and obtaining of faculties for extensive alterations), provision of goods, utensils and ornaments, graveyard upkeep, tolling of the bell, decoration of the church at festival time; 'to Dorothy More for washing the Surplice 3s od . . . for Bread and wine at Easter 6s 5d . . . for making the alter 2s 4d.' Many of these duties have continued to the present day. Certain secular matters appear too; for instance because the wardens were always honorary overseers of the poor, they occasionally trespass on the province of these officers. Accounts are usually allowed by the vestry, and interspersed in the account book may be minutes of the vestry meeting concerning vestry policy.

Churchwardens' accounts prove the richness of medieval churches. Exquisite metal work, carved oak screens, rich hanging fabrics, paintings and inscriptions, jewelled cups and silver plates, colourful tombs, great chests, bells, clocks, flowers, rushes for the floor, illuminated service books, candles, all survive till the mid-sixteenth century. The church too is obviously a centre of village life, always active. Feasts and processions fill the year: May Day, Easter, Christmas, Plough Monday and many more. Several church ales give wardens the excuse to beg malt and brew ale. Mystery and miracle plays, games, dances, ceremonies of all kinds are mentioned. The records emphasise how the tone of church life changed from 1530 onwards. Usual comparisons can be drawn between medieval, Stuart, Puritan, Georgian and Victorian Anglicanism. Some aspects like the ringing of bells survived, others like the harvest festival had to be resurrected in Victorian times.

Church property itself may be studied in churchwardens' accounts. Although much of the architectural history of the church and parsonage should be written from an expert and careful examination of the buildings themselves, parish records fill in gaps and provide exact dates. Features like the fifteenth-century parsonage or Elizabethan nave roof may well have entirely disappeared, being re-created only from records. Church furnishings such as font, pews, chalice, rood screen and pulpit appear in churchwardens' accounts as fashions change. Notice how the altar is degraded and the pulpit upgraded after the Reformation, how pews are installed, leased, locked, made free according to local religious inclinations.

Vestry minutes

Vestry minutes record decisions of the inhabitants to regulate affairs of the parish. These may be recorded in a separate book or written up in churchwardens' account books. Minutes rarely date from before 1580. They concern church matters like services, burials, fabric repairs and appointment of new ministers. In the absence of manor or borough authority, minutes deal with secular affairs like rates, poor relief, settlement of paupers, schools, charities and prosecution of felons. And as the town grows this local parliament turns to housing, sanitation, water supply, lighting, paving, night watchmen, enclosure of commons and police. Because the well-to-do distrusted unpropertied vestrymen, minutes record the decision to invite to meetings only substantial ratepayers and in effect to create a select vestry.

Parish officers' records

Officers dealing with civil affairs generally possessed their own account books. Usually written on paper and bound in leather or parchment, accounts begin in Tudor times but mostly date from the period 1660–1834. In townships forming part of large parishes the officers' accounts are in individual town books signed by a town meeting. Where such books have not been deposited in the parish chest, they could be anywhere. Each officer puts down his expenditure. Thus the supervisor of the highways will claim for 'repaireing town causey £2 7s . . . gravel for lane in towne feilds 15s . . . building Winton brigde 116s . . . pd. to William Clarke 6 dayes worke in the highways 7s'. The constable seeks reimbursement 'for delivering the Traine Band armes and cloaths . . . repaireing the towne butts . . . for journeying to Liverpool conc. Hannah Westall's bastard dau. 95s . . . placeing Abraham Pytch in Stockes 6d . . . pounding cattle on Moore 6d'. The overseer of the poor claims 'pd. towards the cure of Robt. Gost £2 1s 6d . . . a pair of shows for Dor. Routh 2s 0d . . . 1724 For bread & beer at the children's breaking up at Christmas 9d'. He advances weekly pensions to paupers, in amount depending on size of families, and gives much relief in kind. Of course he finds little time for vagrants, 'common players of interludes', 'persons pretending to be Egyptians', pedlars and jugglers. He moves these people on, together with pregnant women having no legal settlement in his parish.

Expenditure has to be reimbursed and rate books list all sources of income. Some parishes kept a separate rate book though in most cases information is in the overseer's account book, clearly differentiated from expenses. Names of estates, farms, streets and houses; names of owners, leaseholders, tenants-at-will; value of property; amount of arrears; rent paid; even ages, size of families, parish of origin, religious denomination may appear in what are in certain cases house by house surveys of whole townships. Donations, bequests, income from town lands follow in the lists. Accounts of wardens, overseers, constables and supervisors provide the basis for a detailed sketch of a town's everyday life especially from 1600 to 1834.

The historian of roads studies records of village supervisors of the highways in order to learn the condition of both main and local roads from Elizabethan to Victorian days. How successful was the scheme of forcing every parishioner to labour four days a year? How many people paid to avoid labour? Did the hired labourers keep the roads in good repair? What qualifications had the supervisor? Is there evidence that the parish was often indicted for non-repair of roads? How far did state of roads hold back local economic development? What was the relationship between local vestry and county magistrates and how did this affect county help for local roads and bridges? Who paid for roads to local factories? Who supported the building of turnpikes, canals and railways and how did these affect local roads? These are some questions to bear in mind when studying highway documents.

From overseer's records make a graph of expenditure on relief if possible from 1600 to 1834. What pattern emerges? Did plague, high birth rates, poor harvests directly influence expenditure? Count the number of people relieved as a percentage of approximate total population at various dates. Population figures are worked out best from your card index of families (see chapter on research methods); the overseer mentions people whom he relieves, though you may have to check your card index or parish register to count the number of children relieved but not named in each family. Is there any significance in the pattern which emerges? Did industrialism bring poverty in its wake? What are the various proportions of parish money spent on pensions, clothing, legal expenses of removal, rent payments and setting the able-bodied to work? Notice how the old question comes up. Shall paupers be forced to work for their money or is it fairer and easier to hand out pensions? It is generally recognised that some people (children, aged, infirm) cannot work anyway. Many parishes find it costs more to organise work than to dole out cash or goods.

Workhouse records

Records of the parish workhouse are few partly because the 1601 act called for the provision of stocks of raw material for setting the able-bodied to work but not for a workhouse. Hardly any parishes provided a special building until the early eighteenth century, when acts allowed specific towns to erect a workhouse. Thaxted in Essex is one of the first rural parishes to follow suit (1711), and here the overseer's accounts yield the best information. Unions of parishes appear after acts of 1722 and 1782. Articles of association, lists of stock and rules may survive for these workhouses.

Charities

Parish charities are numerous. Benefactors leave money or land for parish use, perhaps fifty guineas to be invested in Consols for the apprenticing of one boy a year in perpetuity, perhaps a field whose rent might annually provide winter clothes for widows. In the parish chest should lie an original deed (often the probate copy of a will) which also is enrolled in Chancery; lists of benefactors and beneficiaries; leases of charity property; correspondence; and account books. Look for original question sheets with answers in connection with parliamentary investigations, like the returns concerning charitable donations of 1816 and the reports of the commissioners for inquiring concerning charities, 1819–37. The printed versions are accessible in the parliamentary papers section of a good reference library.

A brief is a royal mandate for the collection of money throughout a specified area for some good cause. Addressed to all ministers and churchwardens this informal parchment document was returned to the applicant endorsed with the amount collected. But parishes kept a brief book or noted details in the vestry minutes and registers. It is therefore possible to note names of churches needing repair, villages hit by floods, almshouses destroyed by fire. Briefs date mainly from the period 1540–1828, though they are also found before and after.

Settlement and removal records

'Recd. Abraham Ball's settlement certificate on his Comeing to the towne.' So reads one town book entry of 1740. A settlement certificate is a simple document by which one parish acknowledges responsibility for a person or family desiring to settle temporarily in another parish. In practice the emigrant stays in his new home as long as he does not claim relief from the rates. On his so claiming, he might be removed on a magistrate's order to his place of legal settlement, the name of which appears on the certificate. The 1662 Poor Relief Act allowed summary removal by justices, unless the person rented a tenement at £10 a year or found some good and sufficient security. If a man comes on a temporary visit, perhaps at harvest, he must bring a settlement certificate to discharge his adopted parish from all expense in relieving him. By an act of 1691, legal settlement could be obtained by serving a parish office, paying rates, being apprenticed or in service. From 1697 people could contemplate permanent settlement in a new home provided a certificate was brought from the place of former abode agreeing to accept them back at all times. (Abraham Ball's was of this type.) In 1743 it was decided that the bastard child of a vagrant did not achieve settlement in his place of birth. Prior to this, parish records are full of notes about pregnant paupers being hurried to a neighbouring town. Until 1795 people having no settlement could officially be moved on, whether they were chargeable or not.

Settlement certificates are, until about 1740, handwritten on small pieces of paper; printed forms appear after this. The certificate is signed by churchwardens and overseers of the poor of the parish who 'doe hereby acknowledge Abraham Ball and Sarah his Wife to be Inhabitants legally settled in our said Parish'. Northallerton has an eighteenth-century book with an alphabetical list of immigrants showing date of settlement certificate and original abode.

When parish officers request a removal order, local magistrates make an examination of the pauper's life history. The man will furnish his age and parentage, place of birth, first and subsequent jobs, various towns of residence, place of marriage, names and ages of children, supposed legal settlement. Examinations prior to removal may be preserved in the complaining parish's records and possibly deposited also with quarter sessions. They usually date from 1700 to 1834.

The magistrate's removal order granted and recorded at quarter sessions is addressed to and preserved by the churchwardens and overseers of the complaining parish. 'William Clarke and Mary his Wife and their three children namely William aged about eight years, Mary aged about six years and Ann aged about two years have come to inhabit in the said Parish . . . not having gained a legal settlement there . . . we the said Justices . . . do therefore require you . . . to convey the said William Clarke and Mary his Wife and their said three children . . . to the said Parish of . . .' Parish officers convey the family to their place of settlement, claiming reimbursement from the township for travel expenses. Sometimes the family are examined by justices on arrival in their supposed settlement to make sure of facts. Here then is a double chance of a life history. Not infrequently the order is suspended because the pauper is ill or great with child, but suspension is only temporary.

Vagrancy records concern a variety of people, from unemployed labourers, mariners joining ships, actors and beggars to thieves and escaped convicts. Documents usually date from 1660 to 1830. They include licences to mariners, soldiers and other poor but genuine travellers to pass unmolested despite their asking for relief.

Family migrations are traceable in these settlement and removal papers. Although papers may not be sufficiently complete by themselves to enable a statistical survey to be compiled, taken together with notes from parish registers, quarter-sessions records, wills, leases, title deeds and suchlike they may well yield significant results.

Indentures

Parish chests hold numerous apprenticeship indentures and registers. These deal mainly with paupers and orphans. An indenture is not usually earlier than the seventeenth century. It is
handwritten on paper, though printed forms and parchments are
not infrequently found. At least two copies are produced, one for
the master, the other for the parent, guardian or parish. These are
written head to head and the copies separated by cutting irregular,
wavy, indented or toothlike notches. The document expresses the
conditions on which an apprentice is to learn his trade; name,
parentage and (possibly) age of child; residence of child and
master; name and trade of master; and date of agreement.

Following the imposition of a tax on apprenticeship indentures
(except those for parish apprentices or where the fee was less than
one shilling), the government kept a register of agreements until
1802, now held at the Public Record Office. There is an index by
name for 1710–74 at the Society of Genealogists, London. Parish
apprenticeship consists of finding a suitable trade for poor boys
and girls. Officers sometimes travel widely and spend heavily to
fulfil these aims. More often children are consigned to Lancashire
cotton mills, to Newcastle collieries, to farmers 'to learn the art
and science of husbandry', to gentlemen 'to learn the art and
mystery of a housewife'. Masters within the parish could be com-
pelled to accept these apprentices on pain of fines. Lists of local
apprentices are recorded in vestry minutes or in special registers.
The performance of all conditions of an indenture is enforced by
executing a bond between the parties.

Several research projects emerge from a good collection of
apprenticeship bonds and indentures. What percentage of transactions represent genuine apprenticeship and what merely getting
rid of unwanted pauper children as household or farm servants?
What type of work is mentioned locally and which trades seem to
take most apprentices? What proportion of people are apprenticed
locally? How far afield are some children consigned? The indentures, admittedly reproducing somewhat archaic common form,

do none the less show a society dominated by the family. The master and his wife act as parents to their own children and to their workers and especially their apprentices. Generally, all live and work together under one roof. The master clothes and feeds his charges. His apprentices do not play 'cards, dice or other unlawful games', do not haunt taverns, do not get married. This pre-industrial unit as a family is large by later standards but as a factory or productive group is tiny. The home is the place for labour, and every member takes part in an enterprise whose beginning and end he sees and takes pride in.

Tithe records

Tithe documents were produced in the main when tithes in kind were commuted into money payments. Since Anglo-Saxon times one-tenth of the produce of land, stock or industry has been claimed by the church. Great tithes of corn, hay and wood sup-ported the rector (often an abbey, college or layman); small tithes from all other sources went to the resident vicar. All tithes proved a nuisance and burden to agriculture; and notes in parish registers, tithe account books and terriers as well as legal papers survive to testify to the friction between farmers and church. Local tithe customs are best studied in terriers and vestry minutes. Opposition to tithes is seen in vestry records, culminating in the demand for tithe commutation. This campaign sometimes succeeded and resultant records of agreements (usually to pay a corn rent) are in the parish chest. Finally, in 1836, the Tithe Commutation Act allowed the commutation (compulsory if necessary) of tithes into money payments.

A village meeting agreed on the value of tithes based on average corn prices for the past seven years. Commissioners then awarded a rent-charge to be shared among all proprietors of property. A land surveyor drew up a very large-scale and coloured plan of the village or town, detailing every parcel of land, every path, garden, shed, outhouse, stream and factory. The apportionment, provid-ing the key to the map, sets out, in columns, the names of owners and occupiers; description of each parcel of land ('Pew Moor',

'Quarry field', 'Church lane'); state of cultivation ('pasture', 'arable', 'woodland') and acreage; and tithe rent-charge. Award, map and apportionment are fastened together and sealed. Three copies are produced which today should be in the parish chest; diocesan registry or county record office; and Public Record Office. Each township in a large parish necessarily underwent its own process, but records passed to the parish chest not to the town meeting. In 1936 the rent-charge was abolished, a stock created to provide compensation, and the extinction of all payments envisaged in 1996.

Tithe apportionment records, late as they are, still often ante-date large-scale ordnance and estate maps. The patient worker can transfer all names from tithe maps on to the present-day large-scale ordnance surveys which invariably lack such details. This job will make access to field names easier to all, after the Ordnance Survey incorporates the information in new editions. Names like furlong, acre, selion, strip, headland, shot and flat appertain to land within the old open fields; hey, croft and yard lie outside. It is not impossible to discover from this the boundary of the open fields. Of course, the absence of open field names may indicate an anciently enclosed village or open up new avenues of research.

Tithe records of 1836–86 also allow research on landownership, state of cultivation, size of estates, routes of roads, tracks, railways and canals; number and location of demolished houses, farms and factories, traces of old earthworks and medieval cultivation, names of lanes, tracks, closes, commons and houses.

Church monuments

Monuments about the church and churchyard date from the thirteenth century onwards. Stone effigies include medieval knights and their dames, abbots, bishops, nobles, merchants, priests and burgesses. These people are usually recumbent, wearing everyday clothes reminiscent of their status. Inscriptions sometimes state the person's name and dates. Such effigies are rare after the Reformation, except for the really famous. Monumental brasses on floors and walls of parish churches appear in the thirteenth century, become numerous in the following centuries, and die out in the eighteenth century. The material is latten, a brass-like metal, and details are exceptionally fine at least until 1500. The lattener cut features that may well be true portraits, and every article of dress and adornment stands out sharply. Details of purses, ornaments, shoes, fur facings, sleeves, belts, even the hang of loose garments, can easily be recorded by the historian of dress. Heraldic items appear on all types of monument, and these can help in identifying anonymous portraits. There is often some symbol to indicate the man or woman's status and occupation. An inscription may well make this doubly apparent: 'pray for the souls of Thomas Forest, the park-keeper of Dunclent Park, and Margaret his wife'.

Stone monumental inscriptions in the church and on tombstones relate to even the poorest inhabitant from the sixteenth to the present century. Tombstone entries are usually fuller than parish registers and embrace several different members of a family. Thus two unrelated register entries are shown to be connected when you study the tombstone:

> John Wilson of Parkside died 20 April 1821 aged 81
> Also Janet daughter of Mary Armstrong widow
> sister to the above John died 25 May 1824 aged 44

Monuments with portraits or verbal character sketches may come in handy as evidence, provided the world's propensity to flattery or ambiguity is acknowledged. Look also for inscriptions mentioning local occupations, place-names and people's ages. These start to appear on gravestones in Elizabeth's reign but in most registers only in 1813. For an account of brasses read Mill Stephenson, *A List of Monumental Brasses in the British Isles* (1926, reprinted 1964). For monuments, see county and parish guides such as Nicholas Pevsner's *Buildings of England* series.

School records

School records are generally in the parish chest because for centuries the church organised local education. A small parochial school as well as the endowed grammar school might be held under the church gallery or in an adjoining building, the incumbent serving as master. Records will rarely be earlier than the sixteenth century and most will be merely Victorian. The foundation charter or title deed will say who established the school, for what reason, with what capital or land. Estate deeds of wealthier schools may run into hundreds and date from medieval times, long before the school itself started. School registers and correspondence sometimes from Tudor times provide lists of pupils, their achievements, problems and complaints. Log books, the school's daily diary of minor and important happenings usually begin around 1840. Most parochial schools, of course, were founded after 1811 by the National Society for Promoting the Education of the Poor in the Principles of the Established Church, as a result of Andrew Bell's pioneering work of the previous decade, and were aided by government grants only from 1833. Such schools possess a few log books and registers, often no earlier than 1870 when compulsory universal primary education was introduced. Their history is often best documented in *Minutes and Reports of the Committee of the Privy Council on Education*, 1839–99.

Parish lists

Lists of parish inhabitants are found in parish chests. These may well be names of householders for the purpose of rate collection or of men eligible to serve as parish officers or on the county grand jury. Some clerks counted men who should serve in the militia or the army of reserve. It is not impossible to work out approximate population figures from parish lists, though it must be kept in mind that paupers, large numbers of household and farm servants, most females and children, itinerant families and evaders of military service will not appear in these lists. Multiplication by five or six may be necessary. What purport to be full lists of inhabitants or alternatively parish population figures generally date from the eighteenth century onwards, though Ealing, Middlesex, has a census dated 1599, Stafford 1622, and Cogenhoe, Northamptonshire from 1618–28. April 1676 is the month of the Compton census of each parish, returns being made to the two archbishops;

and some lists of parishioners date from this time, for instance, the notable list of William Sampson, rector of Clayworth, Nottinghamshire.

In 1694 the act to tax births, marriages, burials, widowers and bachelors demanded an accurate annual list of all adult inhabitants and a note of their taxable activities and status. For the eleven years during which this tax was levied, many parish clerks probably drew up census lists of which a few survive locally. All the Exchequer returns have, however, disappeared. Fenny Compton, Warwickshire, and Melbourne, Derbyshire, possess lists dated 1698 and 1695 respectively. Inhabitants are listed one by one. Against the names are spaces for tax entries on burials, marriages and so on. These entries can be confirmed in parish registers. Other lists are often drafts for the national censuses of 1801, 1811, 1821 and 1831 since only figures of population had to be sent to London. The enumerator may well have deposited his drafts in the parish chest to be held for a short time in case of queries.

At the same period parish officers sometimes took the opportunity of getting information useful for local administration. Two Berkshire lists quoted in the *National Index of Parish Registers* may be taken as examples. One for Binfield, dated 1801, lists every parishioner, recently deceased family members, and people who have left the parish. Maiden names and places of origin of wives are given. The clerk adds notes like 'blind', 'ran away for stealing Cooper's geese', 'has burdened the Parish by a number of illegitimate children, and at length is obliged to seek relief from it himself'. The other, for Hungerford, was compiled on 1 January 1825. It gives names and ages of householders and children and ages of wives. It was updated between 1826 and 1835, and was obviously of use to check outdoor relief claimed according to size of families under the 1795 Speenhamland system.

Parish registers

In September 1538 Thomas Cromwell, Henry VIII's chief minister, issued his mandate to the clergy concerning the keeping of registers of christenings, marriages and burials. Medieval records of this type depended on personal decisions of the clergy, and few survive in parish chests. The 1538 mandate ordered every incumbent in the presence of one warden to enter in a book details of christenings, marriages and burials during the past week and then to lock the book away in a chest. Entries were generally on paper, and a few such registers survive, as at Staplehurst in Kent. On 25 October 1597, a provincial constitution of Canterbury (approved in 1598) ordered incumbents to make entries as before but on parchment and in the presence of both wardens. The parish chest acquired a third lock for the second warden's use. The older (usually paper) registers should be transcribed into new parchment books from 1538 'but especially since the first year of her majesty's reign' (1558). Because entries were made only once a week, in many cases the parish clerk or some other official often kept a rough notebook of parish events as a guide when writing up the register. In some cases the clerk's original entry is fuller than the register. At Cartmel according to the parish register was buried on 5 August 1769 Richard Maychell. But the notebook adds: 'lunatick; poison'd by eating nightshade berries'. Wherever comparison is possible between notes and register, discrepancies are seen to abound.

During the Commonwealth period from about 1645 till 1660, parish registers were neglected. Indeed, in 1653, custody of registers was removed from ministers and civil marriages were instituted. Dates of birth and of banns as well as, or in place of, dates of baptism and marriage appear in registers of this date. In 1666 and 1678, acts for burial of corpses only in woollen clothes were passed. A tax on marriages, births and burials was granted between 1694 and 1705. In 1753 Lord Hardwicke's Marriage Act provided that every marriage must be by banns or licence, that the ceremony should take place in one of the partners' own parish church, that the record be properly kept in a parchment or paper book and entries signed by parties and witnesses. Prior to this act, any marriage performed by a priest was legal without banns or licence.

Registers dating from 1538 to 1812 vary greatly in information.

Baptismal registers may well just say: 'John son of Thos Parkes 7 Sept'. Others provide detail. Parishes in the diocese of Durham between 1798 and 1812 exhibit particularly comprehensive entries as in this one from Newcastle-on-Tyne:

> July 15 1801   Edmund Reed born 10th June 2nd son of Edmund Reed miller native of Norfolk by his wife Hannah daughter of John Pile gardener of Norwich.

Marriage records ought always to give the full names of bride and groom and their home parish, though many do not: 'Matthew Tillot was married 14 Feb'. The Hardwicke registers from 1754 show on printed forms, four to a page, names and parishes of both parties, whether marriage is by banns or licence, date and place of the ceremony, whether with consent of parents or guardians, name of minister, and signatures (or marks) of parties, ministers and witnesses. Burial registers may merely state: 'widow Bell 14 June'. But they could say: 'Aug. 18. 1788 died at Bedhampton, of the small pox, Winifred Tucker widow, aged 63'.

Standard printed forms for registers were provided under Rose's Act of 1812. Baptism forms asked for date of baptism (date of birth was often written in as well), full names of child and parents, father's abode and profession and minister's name. Burial forms give name, abode, when buried, age and minister's name. Registers were to be held in a dry, iron chest. Parish registers did not cease after the institution in 1837 of civil registration, but become less useful for historical purposes.

The *National Index of Parish Registers* in course of publication by the Society of Genealogists, London, is a guide to genealogical sources and deals in detail with parish, Catholic and nonconformist records surviving in each parish of England and Wales. The first two volumes discuss various sources of births, marriages and deaths before 1837. Subsequent volumes supply individual parish information. A. M. Burke's *Key to the Ancient Parish Registers of England and Wales* (1908) lists all parishes alphabetically and supplies dates of earliest entries in the registers. Many registers are transcribed and published.

In 1878 the Harleian Society formed its register section and

I

later printed the registers of Canterbury Cathedral, 1564–1878, and of various London churches. The Parish Register Society came into being in 1895 to print registers through the efforts of G. W. Marshall, Rouge Croix Pursuivant of Arms. W. P. W. Phillimore went ahead with his idea of printing marriages up to 1812, to lighten the labour of transcribing whole registers. Local publishing societies were formed in the twentieth century in such counties as Buckinghamshire, Shropshire and Durham. But all societies felt the pinch when costs rose after 1914, and by 1970 few register societies survived.

Since 1911, the Society of Genealogists has transcribed registers and other records, and manuscripts are held in the society's library in London. The society supported the Pilgrim Trust's wartime work of microfilming some 1,500 registers. The Genealogical Society of the Church of Jesus Christ of Latter-Day Saints has also microfilmed registers, bishop's transcripts and much other material. Hundreds of thousands of frames of microfilm form part of the largest collection of genealogical material in the world and are stored in the society's vaults in Salt Lake City, USA. Copies of films are usually sent to owners of documents and to county archivists. Boyd's marriage index is a typescript index to marriages in printed parish registers, bishop's transcripts and marriage licences in the period 1538–1837. Compiled by the late Percival Boyd (1866–1955), the index contains seven million marriages arranged by counties, quarter century periods, and then men and women, usually separately alphabetically listed. Of course you must check the original record for the full entry. Thus Boyd's index says:

    1810   WYSALL Robert—Mary Stanley. Pentrich
    1810   STANLEY Mary—Robert Wysall. Pentrich

The printed marriage register records:

    12 Apl 1810   Robert Wysall age 18 years to Mary Stanley age 21.

Parochial records mention most types of work available in the district. Thus the register might note the burial in 1777 of Thomas Speakman, salt waller; an apprenticeship indenture, the craft of shoemaking; the 1735 overseer's accounts, the miller and farmer. The term 'yeoman' usually denotes a freehold farmer; 'husbandman' and 'farmer' a tenant occupying land for years or lives; 'clerk' means clergyman; 'Mr' a clergyman (1550–1700), professional man or squire; 'pauper' implies receipt of parish relief. The dual surname in the form of, for instance, 'Fisher alias Weaver' may record a recent change of family occupation. When writing a village history I drew up a table showing every year from 1550 to 1900. Against each year I wrote all occupations mentioned in records for that year, with numbers of men involved. A pattern of local employment, changing perceptibly, emerges. Farming often takes second place to handicrafts by 1800. Professional people like engineers and accountants appear around 1840. This table, of course, is most useful if results from other types of archive are added.

Marriage registers from 1754 are signed by both parties. Here is a means of testing parish literacy, making allowance for literate women who still used a mark in order to avoid embarrassing their illiterate husbands. Can conclusions be linked with the history of the parochial school, founding of Methodist Sunday schools, arrival of newspapers or lending library, and change of social composition of the community? Statistical work has been done on the registers of parishes showing the growth of literacy from 1754 to 1900, hinting at the importance of mid-Victorian schools as much as the 1871 Education Act. People able to read and write in a predominantly illiterate society were often politically and administratively active, because they alone could communicate with like-minded people over great distances and with the government in London. They received news and passed on views, considering themselves as naturally fit and able to think and act for the mass of the populace. Were the literate people in your parish voters in county or borough elections? Did this group owe allegiance to one religious sect or political faith? Who controlled the vestry meeting and village property?

The parish registers are probably the finest source for local surnames. When I studied the history of my own village I card-

indexed all names. These names I divided into four sections, using
P. H. Reaney, *Dictionary of British Surnames* (1958), and C. W.
Bardsley, *Dictionary of English and Welsh Surnames* (1901, reprinted 1967). Firstly, I listed names from localities like Houghton
or Sproston indicating that an ancestor had come from that place
or owned land there. Then there were occupational surnames like
Capper, Mather and Smith. Names originating as nicknames like
Lightfoot ('fleet of foot') and expressing relationship like Johnson
('son of John') came last. From what distance had my families
come? Was it possible to discover their route and the number of
centuries the journey lasted? How many families had not moved
at all—or just a few miles? Where had families originally carried
on the trade of their surname? Could there have been a local
industry now forgotten? A knowledge of surnames may lead to
suggestive conclusions and this study is just beginning to be
pursued. See R. A. McKinley, *Norfolk Surnames in the Sixteenth
Century* (1970), for a study of the distribution of Norfolk surnames
in Henry VIII's reign. With a core of characteristic local surnames,
he shows how the distribution of names can indicate movement
or stability of population and so pioneers a new field of study.

From noting the less standard parish Christian names, hints
about religious or political sympathies of parishioners are gained.
Puritan families (or parishioners of Puritan clergy) in the period
1580–1700 might choose Renatus, Donatus, Desire, Faith or even
Praise-God and Sorry-for-sin. Later nonconformists took scrip-
tural names like Elijah, Amos, Ebenezer and Caleb. These last
four are typical Methodist names of the period 1780–1880. Charles
or James might show Jacobite sympathies after 1688. When two
Christian names became fashionable (not before 1840) sympathies
are readily seen: John Wesley Harrison, George Washington
Cowper. Peregrine or Lazarus might be attached to children of
paupers or tramps.

Parish records—and especially registers—are used pre-
eminently by genealogists, people seeking out ancestors. Genealogists trace back generation by generation to discover the names,
occupations, social rank, dwelling places and education of an-

cestors. Genealogy may well in many cases be a time-consuming hobby, a nuisance to busy parish officials, but there is a serious educational aspect when devotees provide a careful portrait of past generations. Genealogical use of parish registers has been covered in such works as David E. Gardner and Frank Smith, *Genealogical Research in England and Wales* (1956–64), D. E. Gardner, D. Harland, F. Smith, *Basic Course in Genealogy* (1958), and David Iredale's pocket book, *Your Family Tree* (1970).

It is generally advisable to trace your family back to 1837 in civil registration certificates at Somerset House, before turning to parish registers. Suppose you know that William Lightfoot died 21 December 1889 aged sixty-four. He must have been born in 1824–5. Since he was married and worked in Barnton, he may well have been born in that neighbourhood. In 1825, Barnton lay in the chapelry of Little Leigh and parish of Great Budworth. Chapel and parish registers cover a number of townships and duly reveal William's baptism on 4 December 1825. Search in the baptisms for earlier children, and then in the marriage register prior to the earliest child's baptism for the parents' marriage. There it is: 'Ashton Lightfoot of Barnton and Martha Burgess of Anderton' married at Great Budworth 24 September 1822. Ashton claimed to be 'of full age' and was probably born before 1802. Search the parish baptisms for twenty years prior to 1802. Alternatively find Ashton's will which gives his date of death. Then obtain his death certificate from the parish register or registrar-general. This gives Ashton's age and by subtraction his birth date. There is no problem in finding 'Ashton son of James and Sarah Lightfoot' born 30 March 1798.

There exists no national index of surnames mentioned in registers. So when Ashton's father James disappears from Budworth registers prior to his marriage in 1797, you will have to commence a wide search. Take a county map showing ancient parish boundaries such as *A Genealogical Atlas of England and Wales* (1960) by D. E. Gardner, F. Smith and D. Harland and county maps sold by the Institute of Heraldic and Genealogical Studies, Northgate, Canterbury. Note all the parishes whose boundaries touch the parish where your ancestor is last known to have lived. Search the registers of these in turn for the entry under the relevant dates. If unsuccessful, widen the circle of parishes. By undertaking this protracted search, you eventually find James Lightfoot's baptism in 1772 at a parish church some twelve miles distant.

Historical demography

English historical demography means in effect the study of population of English communities mainly from the late sixteenth century onwards when parish records, the raw material of this science, become readily available. Individual and usually part-time historians work on the records of each of the ten thousand parishes because the study is too voluminous for all professional historians combined. The numerical study when finished for each parish need never be re-done. Once a majority of parishes are completed, information could be computerised and results printed in quite a small volume. A standard English textbook on this subject is edited by E. A. Wrigley, *An Introduction to English Historical Demography* (1966). See also T. H. Hollingsworth's *Historical Demography* (1970).

Demography is no mathematician's preserve and is not just collecting figures to please the statistician. Figures are collected to yield information about the family, individual men and village society that is essential to our understanding of the past, despite the fact that local historians still manage to ignore this approach. Thus the historian points out that London or Manchester or Puddlecombe expanded; the demographers seek to ascertain statistically why and how the change took place, both by aggregative analysis of registers and by family reconstitution. There is a most fascinating and balanced view of Stuart village society based on a demographic approach in Peter Laslett's *The World We Have Lost* (1965).

Aggregative analysis of parish registers seeks to produce, from a mass of individual figures, significant totals that help the historian to know more fully what English communities were like over the past four centuries. It is, of course, first essential to choose a register that is reasonably complete over at least fifty years and then to devise a simple form for recording numbers of christenings, marriages and burials. You should record totals month by month, then add up each year, and finally produce five-year accumulations. Note legitimate male and female and illegitimate male and female christenings separately before producing totals. For marriages, count numbers each month and then note whether bridegroom and bride were of the parish, from an adjoining parish, from the same county or from elsewhere. Record whether they had been widowed or widowered. Your burial form must show total burials, burials of all adults (eighteen years old and over) and all children, burials of a man, wife, widow, spinster and all women; burials of a son, daughter or infant under one year old; burial of male or female infants; burial of paupers or strangers. Such forms are reasonably swiftly filled out, especially if two people work together.

The exploitation of information consumes much more time. It is of course relatively simple to subtract all burials over ten years from all christenings to produce an indication of natural increase, or to multiply by thirty an averaged annual number of baptisms to learn the population; to divide all christenings by all marriages over a period to show the number of children per marriage (it is safest in this latter case to start a marriage period five years before a christening period: marriages 1701–20, christenings 1706–25); to divide infant burials by all burials, to indicate infant mortality at various dates.

Other calculations are more intricate, involving in not a few cases knowledge of approximate population figures, for example, by using the seventeenth-century hearth tax records, later parish census lists, or your card index of all inhabitants. Any list showing only numbers of households demands some doctoring in order to produce a population figure. Wherever proof has been available, demographers have found that the average country household held from 4·1 to 4·6 persons in the seventeenth and eighteenth centuries, the average urban household from 5·5 to 6·5. Of course in many farming villages perhaps the majority of persons lived in very large households, ten or twelve adults, children and servants, but, equally, dozens of households consisted of just one widow; parents and a couple of children; or a married childless couple, so bringing down the average to 4·5. If you multiply country households by 4·5 and town by 6 you should obtain an approximate population figure.

Your card index of persons ought to yield an accurate figure, too, especially if you work out four or five independent census lists (say for 1681, 1683, 1685 and 1687) and then take an average. You can plot on a graph census figures such as the Compton census of 1676, a parish rate list of 1735, and the national census of 1801. The line joining the three points shows an approximate population in any intermediate year ignoring temporary disasters like plague. Armed with population statistics and an aggregative analysis of the parish register you can work out crude (very crude, be it admitted) christening, marriage and burial rates by referring five-year averages of christenings, marriages and burials to population at those dates.

Therefore if the population of Puddlecombe around 1720–30 is about five hundred, and christenings number eighty-five in 1721–5, then the average annual number is seventeen. Thus $\frac{17}{500} \times \frac{1000}{1}$ shows a birth rate in excess of thirty-four per thousand. Birth rate will, of course, always be higher than christening rate because some children will die soon after birth, others will leave the community prior to christening, and an undefined group will not be christened in the parish church at all. Demographers no longer employ crude rates very much because these are too likely to mislead. But the rates can usefully set the situation in say 1660 against that prevailing in say 1860 in order to prove that the birth rate was about the same level in both years (though actual population growth differed considerably) and then to initiate a discussion on reasons for the two different situations.

That birth rates quite regularly fall behind death rates raises the problem of how population rose at all, except by immigration. Analysis reveals certain years indeed when deaths seem to wipe

Baptised	christian name	surname
13 Mar 1836 ~~born~~	JAMES Morriss	BLEE

<u>male</u> | female | unknown
bastard | twin
stillborn | abortion

Father

name ..... George

residence ..... Truro ..... t.p. ✓

occupation ..... Druggist

Mother	maiden name
name ..... Mary Ann	CUMMING

mother's father's name ..... John

residence ..... Truro ..... t.p. ✓

occupation ..... confectioner

Remarks

George born 22 Sep. 1810 at Truro

Parish St. Mary TRURO (Cornwall)

E.S. I   viii 64   No. ....

Form used to record details of baptism,
prior to family reconstitution

out whole families and decimate communities. Such periods of
wretched harvest, famine, economic distress or plague usually
caused an immediate spate of marriages and pregnancies when
children occupied their dead parents' homes and holdings. All
these rates do depend on a complete and accurate parish register
and a district where people attended the Anglican services. In one
country parish which I studied so many families attended nonconformist or Roman Catholic churches that the parish register
lacked something like 20 per cent of christenings. Town registers
by 1780 become unreliable for this reason, and by 1815 both urban
and country people in comparatively large numbers ceased to
attend any church especially for christening. About this demo-
grapher's nightmare see an article on 'The Changing adequacy of
English registration, 1690–1837' in *Population in History* (1965)
edited by D. V. Glass and D. E. C. Eversley. The journal *Population Studies* publishes the results of recent research on demography
and should not be neglected by local historians.

Family reconstruction

In reconstituting families, you draw together all references in
parish records to each family in such a way that significant
characteristics more readily appear. This is done for a whole
community over a stated period and is no different essentially from
tracing a family tree, save that in the latter case the genealogist
deals with one interrelated group over an unstated period. Reconstitution cannot begin before 1538 when registers commence.
It demands registers with long complete runs of at least one
century and sufficient detail to identify individuals and families.
It is almost impossible in large towns, on account of continual
migrations and the necessity of examining so many registers of
different parishes.

First developed in France the method has recently been adapted
for application to English parish registers. A separate slip is made
out for each family christening and burial; one slip also for each
partner in a marriage. A family reconstitution form, FRF for
short, is produced to show all the information from registers for

each family. Individual families can then be grouped by parishes, occupation, size, by century in which each flourished, by terms on which they held land. What is distinctive about each group, district or century? This comparative and cumulative work will eventually clarify the demography of England from Elizabethan times till 1837. Anyone who wishes to engage in family reconstitution can obtain the necessary FRF from the Cambridge Group for the History of Population and Social Structure, 20 Silver St, Cambridge. Read the statement of French technique in M. Fleury and L. Henry, *Nouveau manuel de dépouillement et d'exploitation de l'état civil ancien* (Paris, 1965), and chapter 4 of *An Introduction to English Historical Demography*.

The following is a summary of the work involved. Firstly, count the number of christenings, marriages and burials month by month and place results on a form. Then study the registers in depth, transferring to standard printed forms details of every christening, marriage and burial for your chosen period. As a safeguard check results against bishop's transcripts and chapelry registers, taking into account (if you so decide) nonconformist and Roman Catholic registers as well as other parish records. Then sort the slips alphabetically by surnames and within each surname chronologically, and fasten together with a slip knot the sets of forms of each surname. Make out marriage recall slips to show the wife's side of each marriage. Choose the christening, marriage and burial form for each surname in turn and fill in details on the FRF beginning with marriages. The FRF thus displays vital statistics of each parish family, for the whole period of study.

The FRF enables you to calculate the age at marriage of every inhabitant and to work out an average marriage age for each decade of a century. It is worth remembering that christening dates have (in the absence of birth dates) been employed on all forms. These are on average half a month after birth. Therefore calculations must take this $1/24$ of a year into account. To deduce the marriage age and age when couples conceive children is a most important calculation because a change in people's habits probably greatly affected population movement in the period 1650–1870. There may well be a direct connection between population increase and industrial growth too. Did people in the first half of the eighteenth century really marry at an average age of twenty-nine? Were wives generally a little older than their husbands in Stuart times? How many children might such a couple expect to produce before one partner died or the wife reached the end of child-bearing? Family reconstitution enables you to relate the total number of women in each five-year age group (say 20–24, 25–29 and so on) to the total number of legitimate children born to this group. The resulting figure indicates fertility, and a comparison of female fertility decade by decade is essential in any demographic study.

You may of course continue to work out the average length of marriages before death took one partner, the interval between death of spouse and subsequent remarriage, and the proportion of families that lost a parent before the end of child-bearing life. It is accepted that about one-third of people in Stuart times had been married more than once, mainly because death had snatched away a breadwinner or helpmeet. In what ways was your village life affected by the presence of step-mothers and step-children in so many homes? What was the average interval between conceptions? Does the interval grow longer with age? What evidence can be discovered of contraceptive practices? The picture of pre-Victorian family life may yield surprises. Do not therefore be amazed to see a high number of births, six being not uncommon, followed by the deaths of half the children in early childhood; to find half the population under the age of twenty-one; to discover that half the people getting married had already lost one or both parents (and had indeed got married only because that event released a home, job and land for the younger generation). Few grandparents lived with their children; two-thirds of Stuart households seem to hold the normal modern nuclear family of parents and children perhaps with a servant or two. But the pre-industrial and Victorian communities had at least one factor in common: a young population, energetic, noisy, quarrelsome, arrogant and impatient, a force (one might think) for radical change.

Family reconstitution follows the career of each individual. It therefore enables the historian to follow people's movements into and away from the community. Wherever it has been possible to study the question of mobility in pre-industrial decades, the answer has emerged that people were always on the move, despite economic and legal barriers. The population of townships altered from decade to decade by four means. Firstly births and deaths changed family composition. Then servants shifted jobs not only within the community but from village to village. Most servants were unmarried young people working as personal domestics, agricultural helpers, apprentices and industrial labourers, composing some 15 per cent of the population. Thirdly other individuals, and fourthly whole families, migrated. A 5 per cent annual turnover of population is nothing remarkable in the period 1600–1780. This your card index will show as you follow each departing individual to the graveyard and parish boundary, or visit the survivors and newcomers at home. Half the population has disappeared in ten years, then, in a period when (according to some writers) people rarely moved from their own hearths.

Reconstitution reveals the life span of individuals. Parish registers had until 1813 been somewhat reticent about people's ages, so the card index of christenings and burials alone proves age at death. To work out an average age of death for past generations is misleading, because of the high infant mortality rate, near 30 per cent in Stuart times in some places. The large number of infants dying at a few days old soon brings the average age at death down to a ludicrously low level. It is therefore essential to reject children aged four years old and under. Even with this deletion the average life span, until about 1880, remained low, as low as twenty-five years in some towns. Your local information should enable you to distinguish the different life spans of people from various social ranks. Did farmers and road labourers live any longer than miners, handloom weavers and factory hands? Was length of life dependent on district of habitation? Have women always outlived men? It should not be difficult to trace the effects of disasters like wretched weather, poor harvests, famine, civil unrest and plague.

A sharply rising death rate followed by a fall to normal conditions usually indicates some calamity. This parish register evidence might be supplemented with information from overseers' accounts, newspapers, diaries and correspondence, as well as from secondary sources like the *Gentleman's Magazine* and Lord Ernle's *English Farming Past and Present*, sixth edition (1961) where there are references to harvests and weather ('great heat of 1757', harvest 'of 1779 was long famous for its productiveness'). You can never be sure what particular conditions caused the increase in deaths. Sometimes all conditions combine to cause havoc. Parish records which purport to provide this information are seldom found before 1813. Most earlier documents are good in intention but too gossipy: 'died of plague', 'senile decay', and 'fell on a pitchfork which penetrated his fundament'. Even in nineteenth-century registers, clerks' statements must be taken with a pinch of salt; 'Consumption' is very popular with them; 'Lunatic' might conceal tumour on the brain. Be all this as it may, the essential point is to recognise periods of calamity and to calculate on which families the burden fell heaviest.

Family reconstitution is valuable because of its specificity. You might state that Puddlecombe's death rate rose rapidly in 1817–18. You could suggest the reasons: unemployment, wretched harvest, expensive food, plague, hunger, poor sanitation and so on. But only an examination one by one of every family that suffered death proves the real reason. Notice that people in the new middle-class section of town hardly felt any effects. The people that died were prospering factory workers on reasonable wages and fully employed. Their houses had just been built, but they drew water from wells in a limited district of the town, wells that encircled an old marsh on to whose boggy surface human excrement was habitually thrown. It is important to know exactly the reasons for all changes in this period in England and Wales, because it was in this country at that period that the modern industrial world began.

Chapter 6

MUNICIPAL MUNIMENT
ROOM

BOROUGHS, incorporated by charter of king or local magnate, were
self-governing enclaves almost independent of county authorities.
Usually of commercial or strategic importance, boroughs varied
in size and wealth. Their governments consisted of mayor and
corporation (aldermen and councillors), employing officers like
steward and clerk, though titles and functions differed from place
to place. Corporations exercised administrative, law-making and
judicial powers. Towns of the Industrial Revolution period usually
swallowed up dozens of parishes before being granted a charter
(Manchester, 1838). Modern county boroughs date from 1889.

The borough jealously guards its records, especially those proving privileges. A chest in the guildhall muniment room for long
secured this valuable archive, though the decay of boroughs into
mere villages or the adoption of new town constitutions necessarily
threatened the safety of older documents. During the last seventy
years or so boroughs have provided a strongroom in the town hall
or library, and this is known as the borough record office. The
Corporation of London Record Office is at the Guildhall.

Charters and letters patent together with custumals, laws and
ordinances sometimes date from the thirteenth century and mark
the stages by which the town's government developed or decayed.

Minutes and correspondence of the corporation do not usually
survive from before 1600, though Corporation of London letter
books begin in 1275 and journals of the Common Council in 1416.
Records of committees for paving, lighting and building have been
informative since about 1780. Thus the exact date at which all
houses in the borough were built or altered during the last hundred
years can be gained from housing committee records. You may
find enrolments of freemen and apprentices from about 1540 to
date.

Borough courts with names like Pie-Powder and Petty View
heard cases of assault, illegal trading, insanitary habits. Proceedings, minutes and orders for the better governance of the town are
found on loose parchments as well as in hefty volumes. In seacoast
towns, a court of admiralty would assemble. Special courts dealt
with markets and fairs, alehouses, enrolment of deeds. In London
an ancient Court of Husting functioned like a medieval county
court and a registry of deeds and wills. Courts of the mayor and
the sheriffs heard civil and commercial cases as well as problems
connected with apprentices and freemen. Documents exist from
the end of the thirteenth century. London had its own sessions
with the mayor and aldermen as magistrates. Records begin in
early Stuart times. Borough account books are among the earliest
surviving records. They may be termed steward's or chamberlain's
books. In Bristol the Mayor's Audit records start in 1532.

By an act of 1694, parliament taxed births, marriages, burials,
childless widowers and bachelors to provide war revenue. Local
assessors gave tax commissioners complete lists of people in their
area: name, estate, degree, title, tax liable; including servants,
lodgers and women. This tax was collected until 1706 but most
returns are lost, though some survive in borough muniments,
county records or solicitors' offices. The 1695 returns for London
are at the Corporation of London Record Office being indexed in
volume 2 (1966) of the *London Record Society* series. The lists
serve as early census returns.

Records of borough property within and without the boundaries
include millions of title deeds with leases, maps, surveys and

accounts from the Middle Ages to the present. London Bridge estate deeds relate to the City, Middlesex, Essex, Surrey and Kent from the twelfth century onwards. Boroughs owning ancient manors will thus possess manor court documents.

Tradesmen, merchants and craftsmen have since early Norman days formed within corporate towns an association called the guild merchant. To this most members of the burghal community could belong regardless of occupation. Members were free of local tolls and monopolised trading save in victuals. The guild provided money in times of sickness and adversity. Because the guild merchant and borough corporation were closely linked in personnel, policy and function, records of the two are often intermingled at the guildhall.

Improvement commissioners were appointed by parliament to develop town lighting, streets, paving and sewage during the early nineteenth century in unincorporated towns and in boroughs whose corporations were moribund. Most such places were given town councils later in the century, and records of the commissioners are usually found today in borough archives.

A rate is a tax raised on the annual value of property to pay for local services. Medieval rates were sought for specific purposes like bridge building. The 1601 Poor Law Act introduced the compulsory principle for poor-rates, and this policy was followed later for such purposes as highways (1662–91) and gaols (1700). All kinds of property might be rated, though in practice from the fourteenth century the burden fell on lands and buildings. Each parish collected its own rates, so records are in the parish chest as well as borough muniment room. An act of 1744 gave all residents the right to examine rate books and this may have encouraged parishes to keep adequate records. Only London, the central parishes of old boroughs and a few rural places possess documents dating back to medieval or Tudor times, most are no older than 1744. Early assessments are often on scraps of paper or in rough notebooks. From the eighteenth century, bound volumes sometimes bear printed headings and neatly ruled columns for names of all householders, description and annual

K

value of property, rates due and paid. The assessor normally wrote
down entries in house-by-house rotation, though a new man might
easily vary the route causing a change in the layout of the record.
Names of streets alter occasionally. House numbering was introduced into London only after 1767, elsewhere usually after the
Towns Improvement Act of 1847. Few rate books are in print. For
the metropolis see the corporation's catalogue of *London Rate
Assessments and Inhabitants Lists in Guildhall Library and the
Corporation of London Records Office*, second edition (1968).

   Municipal records are essential sources for town history, showing the struggles in medieval times against disease, hunger and
outside influence, in Victorian times against wretched industrial
housing conditions. Specific businesses and tradesmen are mentioned, buildings and churches surveyed. Court records chronicle
the fight to preserve law and order, illustrating the hard work of
magistrates, merchants and police. Estate plans and building committee minutes show the extension of towns into open country,
especially in Georgian and Victorian times. Compare the attitude
to town development and improvement of corporations in ancient
boroughs with vestry authorities in new communities. Estimate
the extent to which industrial growth was hindered or aided by
borough regulations and the guild merchant's inclinations.

   Rate books supply lists of householders, and are of some use to
people compiling parish census lists and to genealogists. The
proud house owner, too, occasionally wishes to know who lived
in his house before him. He can locate his house in modern rate
books, and then work back year by year, recording changes of
occupier, property description, rateable value and so on. He
extracts three or four entries each side of the relevant one to make
certain he is always dealing with the same block of land. It is
unlikely that householders and rateable values of seven adjoining
premises would all alter at once. If they appear to do so, then the
street has changed its name or house numbering. The researcher
arranges notes as follows taking a rate book every five years to save
labour. Supposing he is searching for the occupants of No 10
William Street.

	1835 *William Street*		*1830* *William Street*	*1825* *Old Hall Lane*
7	J. Ledward £10	4	J. Ledward £13	J. Ledward £10
8	W. Greene £12 10s	3	J. Smith £12 10s	H. Smith £11
9	M. Marshall £12 10s	2	N. Goodchild £12 10s	N. Goodchild £11
10	HENRY GRANGER £9	1	MATTHEW GRANGER £9	MARY SWIFT £8
			Market Place	*Market Place*
	Red Lion T. Lowes		Red Lion T. Lowes	Hannah Lowes £10
	£11 15s		£10	£10
12	Eliz Hand £6 2s		Shop & E. Hand £20 house	E. Hand £5 10s
	Shop in Eliz Hand the market £15 10s			H. Southey £14

Rate books help to determine when houses were first built, rebuilt, altered, divided into two dwellings, demolished or combined to form larger residences, all of which show in fluctuations of rateable value. The local historian sometimes wants to know in which house—or on what site—a famous person lived. He must begin in this case with a rate book which mentions the relevant person as householder. He then traces the particular parcel of land and house forward to the present day, taking care to note changes of street numbering or property description, rateable value and names of three neighbours either side. Rate books, finally, record old street and place-names with alterations over the years.

Chapter 7

COMPANY SAFE

THOUSANDS of business archives remain in private custody at workshop or factory. Even the modest self-employed craftsman has created some records like accounts and correspondence. The village inn and cornmill are likely places to find hidden documents. Records of most small businesses do not survive very long after the owner's death and only by chance can you expect to discover a carpenter's account book, for instance, that dates from before 1820. Larger enterprises were by no means rare even in the thirteenth century. In the sixteenth century people began to contribute to joint-stock groups which traded as companies using the services of paid officials. Sometimes these were incorporated by royal charter thus gaining perpetual existence and limited liability: until 1690 or so this applied mainly to trading firms like Hudson's Bay Company.

As an alternative to incorporation, companies concerned with public undertakings sought parliamentary sanction. These trusts, to develop roads, rivers, canals and railways, date from the late seventeenth century. Each separate undertaking created its own archive which remained in the care of the clerk or solicitor. The latter was nearly always in private practice: records are now in solicitors' accumulations, especially if the enterprise no longer functions. Turnpike trust records are all either destroyed or at the solicitor's, who may have passed documents to the county record office. River navigations still survive, and there is a central muniment room at headquarters. Canals were usually taken over by railway companies, so that British Rail Historical Record Offices at London and York are national repositories for such transport records.

Most enterprises could not afford a charter or act; yet the legislation of 1719 restricted severely their raising of capital and legal rights, the liability of each partner in a venture being unlimited. By acts of 1834–62, especially the Joint-Stock Company Act, 1844, company law was reformed. Incorporation was obtained by registration and liability of shareholders limited. Records were created and preserved by these public companies, partly because shareholders had to be informed of business progress. Additional archives come from businesses and estates taken over by the parent company. The nineteenth-century private company did not publicly sell shares. Its records are not always complete and many archives are inaccessible to students.

Minutes of meetings of partners, directors and shareholders describe the making and effects of company policy. In the correspondence, can be studied the day-by-day working out of this policy, relations with customers and efficiency of staff. Some firms preserve letters permanently. The keeping of copies of letters despatched was facilitated after the introduction of Watt's copying press (patented 1780) and Wedgwood's 'manifold writer' (patented 1806). Efficient typewriting and carbon copying came only in the last decade of the nineteenth century.

Accounts are usually the bulkiest of business records and the most difficult to interpret. Work involved in studying columns of figures in double-entry ledger books is not particularly productive, especially when minutes and abstracts of accounts survive. Annual reports when available are satisfactory condensations of and substitutes for account books. Many companies own property, and thus estate documents. The river navigation company can be expected to own land and houses adjoining its waterway. A firm like ICI possesses deeds to wide areas of the country including ancient estates. Such documents need not be concerned with business at all; for maps and plans can relate to all property owned or developed by the company. Most date from after the company's foundation, though a number will have descended from previous owners of the site. Drawings, specifications, submissions of tenders, bills of quantities and conditions of contract have accompanied the establishment of factories or undertaking of construction projects. They date from after 1760. Firms issued catalogues of products or services in order to attract customers. Pictures and descriptions are found in these documents that range from pamphlets to stout volumes. Look for drawings of the factory itself accompanied by a short history of the firm. Catalogues begin to appear about 1820.

Insurance records are particularly interesting for property histories. Company records show names of insurers and description of property over the period of insurance. It may be possible to read of 'one ancient dwelling house now rebuilt in brick and slate and used as an academy for the daughters of gentlefolk' (1810). This policy has a reference number which was embossed on a plaque called a fire-mark attached to the wall of the insured property, as a sign to the fire brigade. Insurance companies date from Stuart times and preserve their own records, though Sun Fire archives are at Guildhall Library, London.

Business archives are obviously of most use if you are writing a study of a particular firm, a biography of a partner, or the history of an industry of which the firm was part. But records mention old houses, waterways, stage-coach routes, strikes, wage rates, local elections and schools among other topics. Thus records of Samuel Courtauld & Company, textile manufacturers, deposited at Essex Record Office, can be used for studying local history in general. Access to company records is somewhat restricted. It is true that almost all documents are in a clearly written English script, not too complicated for the amateur to comprehend, with the exception of double-entry ledgers. But records are privately created and owned. Indeed some company archives are so confidential that they remain closed for a century or more. Most businesses do not feel their affairs should be scrutinised by all and sundry, even after the lapse of two or three generations. Others are proud of their history and hold on to all records in the clerk's department or company archives. Because records-keepers will mainly concern themselves with modern records in everyday use, historical research falls into a minor activity. A few firms, however, have equipped themselves with research centres; Messrs Pilkington's of St Helens is a case in point. Company papers in solicitor's hands are usually the most inaccessible of all archives. Of course every record office offers some business documents including very voluminous Victorian archives but these are generally still unlisted and uncalendared. Business history is therefore most rewarding on account of the pristine state of many archives, but not for the faint-hearted or unpersevering.

Chapter 8

SOLICITOR'S OFFICE

SOLICITORS' offices are repositories for estate, business, official and parochial documents. Archives proper, as well as artificial collections, are represented. Solicitors have always served as clerks or agents to landowners, statutory authorities and industries. Documents were created in and preserved at the office where they have remained in well-built strongroom, damp cellar or crumbling attic. Few solicitors know the extent of their document collections.

There is virtually no type of archive or document that cannot be found in a solicitor's muniment room. Even if the law business itself dates from only 1850, families may have deposited archives there dating back to the twelfth century. In one office I found several pre-Conquest charters; in another I came upon series of the now uncommon county coroners' records, 1806–88.

The law business itself may be old enough to possess its own old records, especially correspondence, accounts, diaries and drafts of deeds and cases. These reveal the widespread influence of attorneys in local affairs and the extent to which landowners relied on these men for financial support. A legal firm would make a worthwhile study. To discover which firm is old look at a local directory of, say, 1810 or watch which lawyers' names appear on pre-1800 deeds in your town.

The local solicitor served as clerk to such authorities as the board of guardians, canal or river navigation, railway or mining company and turnpike trust. In most cases he retained all records in his own office. Here they have remained unless (as is usual) they have been deposited in the county record office. Turnpike trust documents, to take just one example, follow the activity of the group of landowners and merchants that combined to obtain an act of parliament for the purpose of improving a specified stretch of main road. It had, since 1555, fallen to each parish to repair its own roads. Work was generally wretchedly inadequate, to the detriment of industry, trade and communications. Even the employment of free statute labour and magistrates' supervision made little improvement.

So from 1663 onwards interested people in each locality sought an act of parliament to enable them to take over a portion of road, erect toll-gates or turnpikes, appoint salaried officers, and improve the road by re-surfacing, drainage, bridge-building and straightening out bends. The turnpike act generally fixed charges for use of the road by horses, sheep, carriages and suchlike. The trust hired professional surveyors and bands of labourers. It either employed turnpike-keepers or let out gates on lease to the highest bidder. After a general turnpike act of 1773, the golden age of road travel saw royal mail and stagecoaches racing across country. After 1840 most roads felt the competition of railways, and trusts came to an end.

Turnpike records include the original act and extension acts which provide names of promoters, description of main road and position of gates, the trust's administrative organisation, and details of tolls on every type of traveller and vehicle (not forgetting 'steam-engines'). The minute book records discussions and decisions at meetings of the proprietors. In this book will also appear the trust's rules and amendments to rules together with orders to officials. Account books show income from gates and expenditure on wages and road materials. Trusts usually were enabled by act to take material from town quarries at no cost and to demand statute labour from parishes along the road. When gates were leased out to undertakers, there should survive counterparts of agreements to pay specific sums over periods of years. A few gate-keepers kept day-by-day records of receipts. Mortgages deal with the raising of capital on the security of future tolls, a risky business by 1840. Correspondence and agreements mention disputes with parish officers, cost of labour and material, tolls, and contributions from industry. Occasionally maps and plans of the road survive with plans and elevations of toll-houses, bridges and proposed improvements. These documents are not to be confused with plans deposited after 1794 with the clerk of the peace and with parliament prior to the passing of the original act.

Chapter 9

NEWSPAPER OFFICE

NEWSPAPERS in England and Wales began during the early seventeenth century. They are documents of the utmost importance for historical purposes, and newspaper offices are archive centres that must never be neglected by students. Although printed in large numbers, newspapers remain in every sense primary source material, equivalent to tithe maps or title deeds rather than books. Freedom of the early press was curtailed in 1655–95; licensed papers like the *Oxford Gazette* (later called the *London Gazette*) alone survived. This paper indeed continued as an official organ of government to print official news such as naturalisation certificates, bankruptcy notes and proclamations. With relaxation of licensing, London newspapers proliferated, some weekly, some daily, some evening. The *Daily Courant* came out from 1702 till 1735, the *London Evening Post*, 1727–1806. The *Gentleman's Magazine* or *Monthly Intelligencer* was from 1731 to 1883, an important (and indexed) source of scientific, geographical, genealogical, economic and social news. The most popular mid-eighteenth-century paper was the *London Daily Post and General Advertiser* (later the *Public Advertiser*) 1734–94 in which appeared, for instance, the 'Letters of Junius' lampooning the ministry of George III for its abuse of royal prerogative in denying John Wilkes his seat in parliament. The *Morning Chronicle* to which Charles Dickens contributed ran from 1769 to 1862; the *Morning Herald*, 1781–1869; the *Morning Post*, 1772–1937. The *Daily*

155

Universal Register began in 1785, becoming *The Times*, the famous 'thunderer', in 1788. The Sunday paper, the *Observer*, began publication in 1791.

Provincial papers started with the *Norwich Post* in 1701 and *Bristol Post Boy* in 1702. The *Worcester Post-Man*, later called *Berrow's Worcester Journal*, founded in 1709 is the oldest surviving English newspaper after the official *London Gazette*. Although earliest newspapers are southern, the expanding north began to catch up by 1770: Williamson's *Liverpool Advertiser* appeared in 1756. But even in 1800, only one hundred provincial newspapers existed. Until 1855–61 obnoxious duties on paper, advertisements and the sale of newspapers hampered the growth of the London and provincial press. As soon as duties were removed papers sprang up in uneconomic numbers. The majority of local papers therefore date from after 1855.

In order to use newspapers, the student must first become acquainted with a number of finding aids. For example, a *Handlist of English and Welsh Newspapers 1620–1920* explains when papers began, ended or merged. Similar information emerges from the *British Union Catalogue of Periodicals*. Willing's annual *Press Guide* provides details of newspapers still in existence. The *Newspaper Press Directory*, issued annually since 1846, describes the district in which each newspaper circulates. Most newspapers are not indexed, so it is necessary to plough through hundreds of issues and thousands of closely-printed pages. A single event that can be dated is easily found but for a town history there is no help save in searching the whole file. The *Gentleman's Magazine* is indexed and for *The Times* there is *Palmer's Index* running from 1790 to 1941 and the *Official index* beginning in 1907. *Palmer's* is arranged by subjects like deaths, bankruptcies, criminal trials not names. The official index, however, deals in names, places and subjects. The *Bury and Norfolk Post* is indexed for births, marriages and deaths from 1794 to 1830. Four manuscript volumes of this index are in the British Museum Newspaper Library at Colindale. York City Library has card indexed portions of the *York Courant* dating from 1725.

Newspapers are available to courteous inquirers in most newspaper offices. Papers that have merged with rivals usually deposit old files with their successors. For addresses consult Willing's *Press Guide*. The British Museum in London keeps pre-1800 London papers, *The Times*, and the *London Gazette*. All post-1800 London as well as provincial and foreign papers are in the Colindale repository. Local libraries possess some files. Northampton preserves the *Northampton Mercury* from 1720, Gloucester *The Gloucester Journal* from 1722. County record offices actively collect files too. Lancashire has the *Preston Chronicle* from 1812 to a century ago, and is acquiring one more volume each year from the *Lancashire Evening Post*.

Though newspapers appear as single issues they are usually fastened together and bound by the month, quarter or year for ready reference. Until the present century print is small and headlines restrained. Even advertisements do not obtrude. Indeed when an advertiser paid for six inches of column his notice was not usually enlarged, merely reproduced two or three times. Newspaper columns date from the earliest days, small crude drawings in advertisements from the eighteenth century, sketches of people and events from around 1840 (the *Illustrated London News* commenced in 1842). Photographs gradually replace engravings as illustrative material between 1880 and 1905.

Newspapers have, since about 1720, displayed a panorama of events sufficiently varied to arouse the enthusiasm of most historians. Thus news of property deals, especially the notices of sale and lease, supplement title deeds and land tax lists. One advertisement of 1832 describes 'all those seven cottages in Lydiart Lane lately converted from one messuage then used as a farmhouse and barn'; another of 1790 describes the 'new, and substantial built DWELLING HOUSE for a genteel family' in Somerset Street, Bristol, in nice detail. Acreage, field names, value, occupiers' names, lost place-names, vanished houses, rooms, furnishings, even a history of the property, are all noted in advertisements. If therefore you have any suspicion that property was leased or sold at any period, check local newspapers carefully.

Criminal trials are reported at length. The more evil the criminal, the more sensational the murder or robbery, the longer the report becomes. It is not impossible to discover a criminal's family background in this way and to follow his movements to prison, gallows or plantations overseas. Were crimes punished as savagely as legends assert? What proportion of sentences of death were commuted? How were minors treated? More often than not the paper prints a full calendar of prisoners awaiting trial at quarter sessions or assizes.

Prisoner	Henry Binham
Offence	on 8th of February charged with feloniously stealing at Newington one leg of pork
Age	16 (can neither read nor write)
Sentence	14 days solitary confinement & privately whipped

Details of the sentence are generally added. All too frequently it is 'Found guilty. Transported 14 years'.

Industry, agriculture and trade figure prominently. Useful tables showing weather, cotton prices at Liverpool, corn market prices, stocks and shares, bank rates, foreign currency exchange, costs of fruit and vegetables, of coal, timber, bread and suchlike have been used by historians. Lord Beveridge drew on this material for his monumental work on wages and prices in England. Reports on the economic state of nation and locality are voluminous during the booming nineteenth century. The *Manchester Guardian* is an excellent source in this field, discussing as it does cotton trade, strikes, lock-outs, railway investment, collieries, canals, wages, prices, customs duties, government borrowing and farming prosperity quite smoothly in one issue. It is not unknown for a historian to get much of his needs for economic studies from the local paper. Bankruptcies, to take one example, are listed in national and provincial papers, with names of defaulting men or firms, address, amount involved, type of trade and date. A high number of bankrupts may indicate local depression but can also appear in boom periods like the canal and the railway manias. I found my first mention of canal tunnel building in my village while looking through newspaper files. I noticed reports of patented inventions, some of which may have been put into action locally. On 30 September 1793, the *Gloucester Journal* mentions the patent machine 'for expediting the formation of Canals' invented by Mr Carne of St Austell, Cornwall. Did this really work? Was its use economical, with labour so cheap?

Biographers and genealogists seek information on people's careers. Obviously news of births, marriages and deaths for every class of society—a service dating mainly from 1750—is much appreciated. The *Gentleman's Magazine* is most easily used because indexed, mentioning as it does industrialists, solicitors and traders as well as gentlemen. But local newspapers are interested in an even wider variety of people. Birth notices name the father, often the mother and child too, note the parent's residence and father's job, and may well say 'second son', 'fifth child'. Marriage entries are usually in the following form, quoted from the *Gloucester Journal* 17 May 1813:

> On Tuesday the 4th inst at Horsham, Sussex, Charles Greenaway, Esq, son of Giles Greenaway, Esq, of this city, to Charlotte, youngest daughter of Robert Hurst, Esq, MP of Horsham Park.

Notice how useful this entry is in pursuing a marriage that took place outside the county. How difficult it would be to find the entry in parish registers. Death notices are at first short:

> Died 3rd inst at Camp hill in this town Robert Dodd, grocer, aged 49.

These notices blossom in Victorian times into obituaries that serve as short biographies, provided the reporter does not allow his paragraphs of encomium to strangle his factual writings. Of course all obituaries must be treated carefully. The writer is unlikely to mention a dead man's homosexuality, conviction for fraud, violent temper (except as 'good-humoured irascibility'), or death from gout through too much imbibing of port; and he may well repeat legend. None the less it is evident from every good modern biography that a close study of every section of newspapers, including advertisements, alone can fill in biographical details, at least of nineteenth-century people.

The *London Gazette* and other London newspapers provide

information on changes of surnames and naturalisation of aliens. Not a few foreign names are jettisoned for very English-sounding surnames. Newspapers too discuss the arts, the stage, sport, outdoor living, travel and other leisure activities. Papers are generally the only source in the eighteenth century for the history of the stage. Except for correspondence and diaries, no better source exists for fox hunting, horse racing, boxing, agricultural shows, fairs, cricket, cock-fighting and bear-baiting.

Illustrations must be carefully treated. Some pictures are used time and again very obviously. In shipping notices the small picture of a ship is not intended to be a true sketch of the *Danzig* bound for the Baltic with salt and passengers; the same picture represents the *Maria*, the *Duke of York* and others. Similarly the gruesome pictures of gibbeted bodies are common form to all execution stories. Even pictures of supposedly real events of the period after 1840 may well be imagined or at least imaginatively drawn. Certainly some of the industrial views may have been outlined on the spot but detailed in the studio. Of course the artist's difficulties in speedily capturing a changing scene were enormous. He is likely to be most accurate when drawing new churches or town halls, machinery or civil engineering feats.

Chapter 10

VARIOUS REPOSITORIES

Almshouse

LOCAL charities to aid orphans, the aged, the poor and the sick; to educate; and to undertake works of public service have been established since medieval times. Records have remained in charge of the charity trustees sometimes at the solicitor's or church, but often at the charity almshouse or headquarters. Warwick Hospital (1571) was established to help twelve poor men; Trinity House, Deptford (1514), distressed mariners; and Chelsea Hospital, invalid soldiers.

Documents belonging to such charities include the foundation deed (enrolled also in Chancery), minutes of trustees' meetings, accounts, correspondence, applications for in- and out-door relief and registers of applicants and inmates. The latter may outline a whole life story. Charity papers are thus useful for genealogical purposes, for the history of poor relief and education, and for sidelights on the particular trade or service that the trust helped.

Roman Catholic presbytery

Roman Catholic archives are usually held in the local presbytery though some are deposited in record offices. Documents include registers of baptism, marriage and burial; records of itinerant priests; accounts; school log books and reports; diaries of the

161

local congregation. Most documents are no older than about 1778, when the first Catholic Relief Act was passed.

Methodist Manse

Methodist collections begin as early as 1760. There are registers of baptism and burial from about 1800; minutes of society meetings; preaching plans; Sunday School log books; day school accounts and logs; correspondence. Minutes of society meetings include poor relief expenditure, education proposals and charity disbursements. Circuit plans and minutes of local preachers' meetings name leading members and usually indicate the earliest beginnings of a local society. Trust deeds of chapels describe land purchases and name trustees. All these documents are in the central safe of each circuit rather than in local chapels.

Independent or Congregational chapel

Religious societies independent of the established church appeared during Elizabeth I's reign though it was not until Charles I's reign that independents became a power in the land. Each church regarded itself as an entity, paid its own minister and formulated its own rules. The Congregational Union was established in 1832. Archives are generally held by each church itself and include trust deeds of chapel, minister's house and burial ground, original covenants of the congregations, church minutes, minutes of trustees' meetings, church accounts and papers relating to charities. Registers of baptism, marriage and burial generally begin in 1837, earlier volumes being deposited at the Public Record Office. Many documents of old churches do date back to the seventeenth century.

Baptist manse

Baptist societies were formed in England after English exiles returned to London in 1612 and founded the General Baptist Church in Spitalfields. Particular (Calvinistic) Baptists appear in 1633. Both sects spread rapidly in the Commonwealth period; and Baptists also expanded during the industrial period after 1780, though many societies of General Baptists became Unitarians in the eighteenth and nineteenth centuries. Each society attempts to govern itself; though even in the seventeenth century, district associations were formed for the sake of efficiency. Baptist records are generally held by local societies but some archives are now with district associations; at Baptist Church House, London SW1; and at Dr Williams's Library, London. Documents are virtually of the same types as found in Congregational collections. Unitarian records may concern the administration of libraries and academies (schools) in the eighteenth and nineteenth centuries, the denomination leading the way in organising educational work at this period.

Quaker meeting house

The Society of Friends has preserved records since 1650. Monthly Meetings preserve original registers of births, marryings and deaths; minutes of meetings; registers of sufferings; accounts; title deeds; correspondence; charity papers. Documents are very explicit, illuminating the history of obscure parishes and the origins of some of the Victorian era's most influential families. The clerk of records of each meeting acts as archivist, though sometimes he hands over archives to the county record office. Friends House in London usually helps to locate archives.

Craft guild hall

Craft guilds sought to protect the interests of individual trades from as early as the twelfth century. Based in towns where sufficient numbers of fishmongers, cutlers, pinners and so forth lived and worked, guilds often organised themselves in opposition to borough corporation and guild merchant. Comparatively few guilds outside London became sufficiently prosperous and powerful in the middle ages to build a guild hall, obtain a charter, and create an archive. Records, for the most part preserved by the guilds or companies themselves, have therefore often disappeared, though some public-spirited bodies have placed muniments in borough or county record offices. The majority of London city companies have now deposited their documents in Guildhall Library. Craft guilds were most active in the five centuries prior to industrialisation and records date from about 1450 to 1750 (though London companies functioned much later and of course still survive).

Documents may be in a chest in the craft's hall, and the historian first seeks instruments of incorporation, constitution and privilege. Royal charters with confirmations and inspeximuses will bear the Great Seal. Ordinances, grants of arms and byelaws usually date from Tudor times. Because the guild acquired real property by gift or as investment, craft muniments will include grants, maps, rentals, leases, manor court rolls, probate records and mortgages relating to land not only in town but scattered across several counties. The importance of deeds has already been stressed in the chapter on estate records. Accounts are sometimes found from the early fourteenth century. These show expenditure of the guild in protecting members' interests as well as income from lands and buildings, membership dues, payments for admission to freedom and apprenticeship and fines for breaking of rules. Account books take over from parchment rolls about 1400. Ledgers do not appear till about 1750. Quarterage books show the dues paid every three months by court members, liverymen and yeomen (members on probation, not yet in the livery) and record movement of members and changes of address. One of the earliest such books is that of the Coopers dating from 1440. Minutes of craft guild meetings begin much later than accounts and show the varied work of the company in protecting or possibly hindering trade, admitting members, binding apprentices, fining bad workmen.

Informative registers (rather than calendars) of people admitted as freemen or bound as apprentices generally date from William and Mary's reign and later. At that time a stamp duty was placed on every freedom admittance and, in London, a tax laid on apprenticeship too. Details of earlier freemen or apprentices must be sought in minute books. Quest and search books accompanied by registers of fines summarise action taken against poor craftsmanship and misbehaviour. London companies sometimes conducted countrywide searches. The Pewterers did so from 1635 to 1723, surveying pewter manufacturing in England. Equally useful are mark books of guilds like the Cutlers and Coopers of London which authenticate individual craftsmen's monograms and ciphers. Calendars and lists of guild records may often be found in record offices and libraries even where documents themselves remain in the borough strongroom or guild hall. Craft muniments are essential if you are studying the development of a particular town or craft from medieval times until 1750. Biographies of specific members are incomplete without an examination of minutes to reveal the man's activities. For identifying antique articles like silver spoons or guns, registers of marks and ciphers are invaluable. If your house or land formed part of a guild estate its history may be traceable in the company's muniments of title.

Deeds registries

In Middlesex and the Ridings of Yorkshire, four deeds registries were established between 1704 and 1736. Every deed concerning the transfer of land together with enclosure awards and plans relating to the four counties has been copied into registers. All essential facts are noted: type of conveyance, names, addresses, occupations of parties, description (sometimes with plan) of property, conditions of sale and date. A small fee is charged to researchers. Registries are in London, Beverley, Wakefield and Northallerton.

Charity commissioners

In 1853, the Board of Charity Commissioners was established as a permanent authority to administer charitable trusts. From 1860, the board could order charities to improve their organisation. Educational charities were removed from the commission's control after 1899. Records include original documents accumulated by the former commissioners for inquiring into charities, 1817–50, as well as accounts of all charities in operation since 1853. Documents are open without restriction. The commissioners' headquarters is in Ryder Street, St James's, London SW1.

HM Customs and Excise

From the reign of Edward I until that of Charles II, Exchequer
administered the customs system, levying duties on imports and
exports according to rates determined by the government. In 1671
six commissioners for managing the duties in England and Wales
were appointed. This Board of Customs established London and
provincial (or outport) customs houses with salaried officers.
Excise duties have been levied on the manufacture, sale or consumption of goods inside the country since 1642 when parliament
raised the first excise to pay its army. Commissioners were appointed at the Restoration, and the hated excise officers appeared
throughout the country. Administration of the excise was transferred to customs in 1909. Customs records of the post-1671
period are held in London. Fire at the London Customs House
in 1814 destroyed most headquarters records but outport records
fortunately survive and are preserved with what remains of London's archive at HM Customs and Excise, King's Beam House,
Mark Lane, London EC3.

At the Public Record Office are ledgers of imports and exports
from the eighteenth century onwards setting out quantities, types
and value of British and foreign goods. These hundreds of volumes
prove of most use to the historian of British trade. Records at
King's Beam House are of more general interest. The earliest
documents date only from the late seventeenth century and relate,
of course, to provincial ports. The principal records are collectors'
letter books which deal with every aspect of port business and
incidentally with the affairs of the town or borough too. Much of
the correspondence contains recommendations, adverse reports,
baptismal certificates, notes on sickness and death concerning
government staff: 'complaining of the Conduct of Henry Comper,
a Boatman in absenting himself without leave from the said Boat
through Drunkenness' (1813) and 'in consequence of the insanity
of Mr. Richard Chiverton Coastwaiter at Ryde within the limits
of your Port you directed James Sammes a competent Tidewaiter
to act during the vacancy' (1813). Each officer taken on the

payroll is named in a book together with his age and capacity or capability to do his job. Local excise records are almost non-existent but indexed minute books of the Excise Board from 1695 to 1867 in 749 volumes contain appointments, complaints, promotions, memorials, suspensions, dismissals, notes on superannuation and records of excise cases. For the local historian and genealogist interested in any port, documents at King's Beam House are essential sources. Records are available to authenticated researchers and other students during normal office hours only.

Church Commissioners

In 1948 the Church Commissioners replaced both the Ecclesiastical Commissioners and the Governors of Queen Anne's Bounty for the augmentation of the poor clergy's incomes. Queen Anne's Bounty, chartered in 1704, accumulated minute books, files of requests for grants, plans of new parsonages (1803–1948), and title deeds to the property from which arose the clergy's incomes. The Ecclesiastical Commissioners (1836–1948) carried out church reforms, shaped and endowed new parishes, and acquired most estates of bishops, deans and chapters, and other cathedral officers (including large plots on which Victorian suburbs were erected). Although older capitular records are now mainly in local record offices, nineteenth-century estate documents remain with the commissioners. Also in the latter's care are minute books, surveyors' reports and letters of the Church Building Commissioners (1818–56) who negotiated the conveyance of sites for churches, parsonages and related property in addition to erecting churches. The Church Commissioners administer church property and hold in their headquarters at Millbank, London, over three miles of files and 400,000 deeds. Students genuinely interested in the history of churches, parsonages and any church estates may gain admission to most records, though it is advisable to negotiate by letter first.

Chapter 11

COUNTY RECORD OFFICE

ENGLISH and Welsh county record offices were established to preserve the great heritage of manuscript material scattered through every shire. Obviously many repositories in the country are not readily accessible to the majority of researchers; the solicitor does not allow strangers to sift through archives in his keeping; the factory owner cannot spare time from his production line to serve every historian; charitable societies need money for their good works rather than archives; the great landowner could not cope with crowds of students at his hall.

Most county offices developed out of the department of the clerk of the peace, the officer in charge of quarter sessions records, and it is with the county record office that we will deal from now on. The clerk of the peace has for centuries created and preserved court records, sometimes taking over a room in a permanent county building like shirehall or court house. Often old records were stored in sacks 'mixed together'. Suffolk records lay for years in a wooden press at the *Fountain Inn* in Bury St Edmunds.

The first county record office was set up in 1924 by the Bedfordshire County Council through the influence of Dr G. H. Fowler, chairman of the council's Records Committee. Dr Fowler became county archivist, the officer to whose care was entrusted all official county archives. There had been earlier full-time archivists in England and Wales employed by municipal corporations and city libraries, but the job of county archivist demanded many additional and differing skills and functions. After World War II, county record offices were established in all counties. Many establishments share responsibilities with city or borough record offices especially in populous counties like Lancashire. Other counties, like Sussex, have two archives centres for the two county councils. In a few cases the county council and county town joined to set up one record office: Norwich and Norfolk Record Office is an instance. Cumberland, Westmorland and Carlisle united to establish one service for the Lake District. The Greater London Record Office covers the heavily populated areas of the former London County Council and Middlesex. Some buildings (as at Durham) are new, others old (like Chester Castle).

Each record office exists to preserve county records. The oldest documents are from quarter sessions, dating from Elizabethan times, and these may be exceedingly voluminous. Large numbers of documents are being created by the sessions every year now. In addition, the archivist takes records of the county council itself beginning after the Act of 1888. These take up much room too. Then came the archives of bodies whose functions the council has assumed, such as local boards of health.

It would be hardly surprising if the archivist confined himself to sorting and calendaring these records alone. But it is his duty and aim to care for all manuscript material in his area whether archives proper or just single documents.

The county archivist thus inquires about the location of manuscripts in the county, investigating by letter, personal call or agent all sources discussed in previous chapters. This work demands tact and persistence. The archivist follows up all clues concerning collections, provides free advice on repairs and storage facilities, and even calendars archives in private custody. Eventually when owners trust the archivist and his record office, they will agree to deposit records on terms of permanent loan.

The county archivist visits factories, churches, mansions, schools and private homes. He investigates waterlogged cellars under solicitors' offices and rat-infested attics of council chambers.

He collects small bundles of deeds from the widow's sideboard, and chests of documents from the lord lieutenant's stables. He discovers manuscripts damp, mice-eaten, congealed by fire, rotten from silverfish, brittle, musty-smelling and layered with grime. With the owner's consent he piles the whole lot in boxes or sacks and transports the archive back to his county record office.

In no matter what condition new accessions arrive, the documents are unloaded into a sorting room where preliminary cleaning and accessioning take place. In the accessions register appears a one-line description of the archive with name and address of owner or depositor. Then damp documents are spread out to dry naturally and slowly in a current of air blowing from window to window across the room. Documents afflicted by mildew are fumigated. Thymol crystals are vaporised over electric lamps for a couple of hours in a cabinet. The lamps are then switched off, and the mildewed manuscripts placed in the cabinet and fumigated for twenty-four hours. Insects and silverfish are usually destroyed after treating documents carefully with DDT powder. Dust is removed with a duster or vacuum cleaner and dirt with a Hardmuth grey rubber or artist's gum eraser.

Next the preliminary rough sort is completed so that the collection may be put into boxes labelled 'title deeds', 'letters', 'official records', 'account books' and 'maps'; or 'medieval' and 'modern'; or 'Winslow', 'Brill', 'Waddesdon'. Cleaning and sorting must be swift to allow the archive to be put, for the time being, either in the main strongroom or in a special strongroom for uncalendared material. Because the archivist has assumed official custody of the documents, he does not want any to be lying around unguarded in his daytime sorting room. In this way they could, for example, be tampered with and become valueless in court. It is at this point that the boxes are also given the archive's accession number which serves to identify the collection until classification and calendaring are completed.

Repairs
The skilled repairs technician with correct and delicate tools and

materials can deal with paper and parchment documents. His laboratory is an essential and interesting part of the record office. The following account describes old and tested methods but intends no criticism of solvent lamination technique, lamination under heat and pressure in a machine, and use of cellulose acetate film.

To repair a paper document that has writing on just one side clean with rubber, damp with sponge and warm water, and place between sheets of waxed tissue. Take new hand-made repair paper, damp it and stretch it flat on a sheet of glass that is lighted from below. Paste repair paper evenly with a glue prepared previously, as follows. Boil half a pint of water in a double saucepan. Cream four ounces of best Canadian red wheat plain flour in cold water and add to the boiling water, stirring continuously for twenty-five minutes. Add a piece of thymol. This paste acquires a pearly sheen when ready.

Place the document face up on the pasted paper, ensuring that wire lines in both papers run the same way, so that stretching and shrinking are in identical directions. Any loose pieces of the document can be put in position with tweezers. To fill remaining holes or tears in the manuscript, add pieces of repair paper torn (not cut) to the correct shape. Rub the document gently with a bone folder to remove all creases. Place waxed tissue over the whole and bone down thoroughly to ensure old and new papers adhere together. The document is now adequately backed.

When a paper document has writing on both sides, sponge out new repair paper on lighted glass, damp a piece of silk gauze of the same size on to this, and paste both. Bone the damaged document flat on the gauze and add loose pieces of the manuscript in correct positions. Turn the whole over and lay down on a piece of waxed tissue. Damp again. The writing on the dorse of the document shows through gauze and repair paper. Take a bodkin and score a frame of new paper round the writing. Tear away all paper that covers the writing. Leave the new paper as a strong frame round the written area. The gauze strengthens, covers and protects the writing. Repeat this job on the other side of a very fragile document.

With a finger-tip dipped in paste press down the frame's edge. Then bone down the document so that old and new papers adhere together. Place document in waxed tissue and cartridge paper under light weights for a day to dry. Then press hard in a mechanical press. To strengthen the original document, add size with a camel-hair brush. Size is made by simmering parchment scraps in a little water for three hours, draining and adding thymol. Finally hang the document from wires to dry thoroughly and then press in a specially designed mechanical press.

To repair parchment, ensure that you have a good supply of new buffed parchments. New parchment is buffed or roughened with a half-round file or glass paper so that it will adhere to another parchment surface. Then damp the damaged document thoroughly. Paste down some sheets of waxed tissue on a piece of hardboard surfaced with plastic. Paste the document face down on the tissue and add loose fragments in their correct place.

Cut to shape some new parchment and pare the edges with a bevelled-edge knife. The chamfered edge can be boned into the old document. If there is any writing on the back of the document, gauze is to be placed over that area and corresponding windows cut in the new parchment. Paste this new parchment thickly and place correctly over the damaged document. Bone down the pared edges. Leave on the board under cartridge paper to dry. Later, turn the document over and fill in any holes through which the repair parchment shows with pieces of new skin cut and pared to shape. Bone down, and press hard for at least two days.

The excellent inks of earlier days have bitten into the surface of paper and parchment. Therefore damping, even immersion, cannot make the ink run or fade.

Remember, too, that the repairer must 'leave the nature and extent of his repair unmistakably evident'. He does not fill in missing words on documents and seals. Nor does he treat his new paper and parchment to make these look old. A repaired manuscript looks as though it has been repaired.

Classifying

In order to make any collection accessible to students, it must be
arranged in orderly fashion. The first step is usually obvious and
without problem: placing the entire collection in its proper class.
There are three broad divisions:

1. Official, such as county council, quarter sessions, parish council, urban district council
2. Semi-official, such as board of guardians, turnpike trust, river
   navigation
3. Non-official such as family archives

The archivist asks who created this archive? The depositor
could be an army colonel. But the documents are not his or his
family's. They were created, and for long preserved, by the village
vestry meeting. Hence they are parish records and are given the
class letters PR.

Each class of records has its own code letters which vary somewhat from place to place. You will know that any archive whose
code begins with PR is a parish collection. Other important codes
are:

CC   County Council
Q   Quarter Sessions
PC   Parish Council
PU   Poor Law Union
BC   Borough Council
DD   Documents deposited by families or businesses
DR   Diocesan records

The detailed sorting and arranging is skilled. Some collections
are nicely arranged into sections by owners: 'title deeds', 'maps',
'leases', 'correspondence'. Since these divisions may well be
almost as old as the archive itself, a product possibly of hard
thinking on the part of a long dead estate agent, it is dangerous
for the archivist to rearrange the collection. Indeed archivists
never disturb the arrangement of an archive without positive
reasoning. Whenever a bundle is broken up or a document transferred from one section to another or strays collected to form a new

section, a clear note is made in the calendar of what has been decided and why.

It is therefore essential that the archivist learn as much background information about the collection as possible: families and estates represented, business interests, offices held, various places where the archive has been stored, previous attempts at sorting and calendaring.

So the collection is further divided up, documents being placed in boxes labelled with class and section:

Q   Quarter Sessions records
QS   Court in session
QA   Administration

Each section is divided further, if necessary, to record the archive's growth.

QSR   Rolled files of documents received or created by the court, 1574–1642
QSB   Bundles of original petitions, recognisances and orders, 1610–1737
QSP   Petitions to court, 1660–1840
QSO   Order books of the magistrates, 1687 to date

Family documents are usually divided into:

1   Manorial: court rolls, extents, surveys
2   Deeds of title: conveyances, wills, settlements
3   Estate papers: surveys, leases, rentals
4   Accounts
5   Correspondence
6   Legal papers
7   Tithe
8   Enclosure
9   Official papers and public office
10 Business
11 Charity papers
12 Ecclesiastical papers
13 Maps and plans
14 Family (purely personal): pedigrees, settlements

Each family archive has its own code letters following DD. Thus the archive of Molyneux, earls of Sefton is DDM.

The collection now lies in the accession strongroom in cardboard boxes neatly labelled with section names or numbers. One box at a time can be removed to the sorting room for treatment in detail, depending on time available, the likely use of documents by researchers, and the importance of individual documents or the archive as a whole.

An entry in an archivist's preliminary listing appears as:
DDX/28: Manorial: Wiswell court verdicts 1732–1735
         Deeds: Clitheroe 1676–1859
         Misc: Agreement concerning Read moor 1600; diary
              of John Ward, cotton weaver, 1860–1864

The list forms a basis for a summary catalogue or descriptive list, manuscript by manuscript.

Manor of Berry in White Waltham

1	Court book	1 vol	1684–1875
2	Court book	1 vol	1875–1932
3–4	Minute books	2 vols	1865–77
5	Analytical index to estates held of the manor of Berry		
		1 vol	1858–1926

A record office calendar is more detailed still, exhibiting a full description of the document, full date, all personal and place-names, notes of covenants or provisions. The calendar ought to provide so much information that few researchers need consult the original document. This therefore aids the student and preserves the manuscript. Here is an example. 'Gift: for one pound of pepper yearly paid on the vigil of St John the Baptist to the church of St John in Ginges: Margaret of Munfichet to Fulk—5 acres of land which Godfrey le Fuchel held and 5 acres which Roger son of Aldiva held in my vill of Ginges—witnesses, Warren of Bassingbourne; Alexander his brother; William, chaplain of Ginges; William of the chamber.' nd c1170.

Certain documents obviously need special treatment. The seal and witnesses of a medieval charter must be recorded. A full précis of a letter from a government agent in Leeds to Whitehall about riots is called for. The Public Record Office calendars of state papers contain numerous examples of this very detailed approach to manuscripts.

Documents are usually arranged chronologically within each section: hence the word 'calendar'. The list of documents is typed and possibly duplicated or printed for use in the students' search room. Documents are themselves numbered in accordance with the list, sometimes in pencil, sometimes in Indian ink. A record office stamp is often also employed, especially on official records.

Strongroom

Boxes are removed to the main strongroom when all stages of accessioning, classification and cataloguing are completed. The archivist uses good uniform-sized boxes ventilated with holes, the holes themselves plugged with muslin to exclude dust. Boxes are stored singly or one on top of the other on shelves not more than six or seven feet high for sake of convenience.

The strongroom is securely built of permanent material with no outside walls, affording protection against fire, bombs, strong sunlight and damp. There are no water pipes; wires are encased in steel tubes; lights are of the hurricane type. Temperature and humidity must be controlled: air is circulated artificially, heat is provided through vents in the walls. Across the ceiling run pipes containing chemicals which can smother fires. Sprinkler heads capped with metal of a low melting point automatically spray the chemical when the room temperature rises ominously. A bell rings in the fire station at the same time.

Search room

Students work in the search room, where are lists and calendars of many collections, possibly a guide to the record office, and a card index of persons, places and subjects occurring in documents. An archivist is always at hand to help students and supervise the proper use of archives.

The small library contains most relevant local histories as well as the *Victoria County History* for the shire. There are books on national history, palaeography, archives, dating of documents, diplomatic and law. Look for the *New English Dictionary* ('Oxford Dictionary'), Wright's *Dialect Dictionary* and the revised guide to the Public Record Office published in 1963. Whenever the student visits the search room, he must write his name, address and purpose of visit in a register. On the first visit he reads the office rules carefully. He chooses from the list, index or calendar the documents he requires, asking for no more than three at a time. A requisition is filled in with document number, searcher's name and the date. Part of this is left on the strongroom shelf from which the document is taken. It is reunited with the other portion on return of the document. This gives the archivist a perpetual record of documents read by each student. Documents can never be borrowed because all manuscripts are unique and priceless. The student does not smoke in the search room. He always uses pencil. He may even place over fragile or exceptionally precious documents a sheet of clear cellulose acetate with some yellow Kodagraph to keep manuscripts clean and to filter bright light.

The archivist will always help you choose a subject for study. He points out significant documents, deciphers difficult handwriting and translates from Latin or French. He welcomes everyone to the office, both county ratepayers and visitors from outside. But he cannot undertake to complete research for you except to answer specific questions and solve problems that crop up during work. Nor can he take the place of university professor or teacher and lecture on the background of your chosen subject. One young man intent on examining quarter sessions records, with a view to writing the history of county administration prior to 1889, did not even know what quarter sessions was. Recusancy, enclosure, manor and parish are similarly popular topics of research but few are the students that have read the essential background history before embarking on the perilous seas of documents relating to those subjects.

Never ask the archivist for 'everything available' on your chosen topic unless it is a very limited field: 'the construction of the Trent and Mersey Canal in Little Leigh 1775–6'. Once an over-ambi-

M

tious and overbearing schoolteacher asked for 'everything available' on farming in the county. I happened to have at hand seven or eight boxes holding several thousand farm leases of the nineteenth century. The leases provided tenants' names, rentals, size of farm, conditions and length of lease with accompanying notes on farm improvements like drainage and new cottages. There was at least three weeks of full-time worthwhile study in those documents. But the teacher was dissatisfied.

'Oh, no,' he said impatiently. 'Haven't you anything more general?'

'Of course. What you really want is one document that on one page tells the history of farming in the county. And in English.'

'Yes. I haven't much time. I see you close in half an hour.'

I gave the teacher a photocopy of the article in *Chambers's Encyclopaedia* on agriculture. That is just what he wanted.

The archivist usually arranges to copy documents in the record office collection though he cannot undertake to do the same for material in other repositories. Occasionally the record will be photographed by expert county council or police photographers. Although very expensive in materials, and labour costs, the result is outstandingly clear. Small documents can be enlarged, extensive documents reduced, to suit the convenience of the student. Indeed the finished print often seems sharper than the original document. This print in matt finish is used for making a printer's block prior to publication. Commercial photographers, if brought into the record office, charge very high prices. You should explore the possibility of taking coloured slides of documents. When projected these are useful for lecture purposes, and can even serve for research projects in place of photographs. It is no trouble to sit in front of a projected slide taking notes of details, and a slide is certainly cheaper than a coloured print. And if the worst comes to the worst you can always have a slide printed.

Most record offices, however, provide photostat copies, negative or positive, at modest cost. A camera photographs a document on to sensitive paper. The result is as clear as you would wish, though possibly not quite good enough if you need a printer's block making for publication purposes. The cheapest method is the contact reflex method often called 'copycat' or 'xerox'. The process is satisfactory for copying most documents. Some machines, however, swallow documents and then regurgitate: account books and tithe maps will not therefore fit. Most machines copy only twenty inches by twelve inches at a time on the glass plate. Prints are not as clear as photostats and tend to fade or discolour with time, but for use as ready reference within a year or so cannot be criticised when costs are considered. For duplicating large numbers of a given print firms like Messrs Roneo and Messrs Gestetner produce an electronic duplicating stencil. The initial cost is high but dozens of copies can be cheaply run off thereafter.

But suppose you have the rules of your vestry meeting or manor court in secretary hand, dated 1597, and in Latin. Even the clearest police photograph is no use if you do not read Latin or secretary hand. What can be done? If your research project is genuine and worthwhile, if you have shown by your previous efforts that you yourself are dedicated and perfectly capable of using other documents—which are in English and more legible— to bring the project to fruition, the archivist is always more than willing to transcribe and translate for you. Of course the amount of work he can complete in the time available is limited but a ten-page document should not be too burdensome. He will generally provide you with a typescript. This helps the record office too, because a copy goes in the files for future reference and lecture purposes. It is not wise to consult professional records searchers unless these people have been recommended personally for the specific task by the county archivist.

Chapter 12

SOME RECORDS IN THE COUNTY RECORD OFFICE

IN the following paragraphs are mentioned some of the collections usually found in a county record office.

Quarter sessions

The archives of county quarter sessions dating usually from the sixteenth century onwards are readily available. Medieval guardians of the peace were appointed by the monarch to maintain internal order in each county. Known from the fourteenth century as justices of the peace, these unpaid local gentry found themselves loaded with many additional burdens. The magistrates met four times annually in quarter sessions, held at convenient county centres. They summoned a grand jury of the county, a twelve-man jury and many county or parish officers. The justices' clerk of the peace advised about points of law and took minutes of proceedings. In between sessions were held petty sessions. Any JP could deal with minor problems summarily in his own home.

The magistrate preserves the peace by suppressing riots, catching and sentencing criminals, and taking recognisances for good behaviour. All felonies and trespasses lay originally within the JP's jurisdiction, though some offences like murder and bigamy were by the nineteenth century removed to assizes. Constables are under the justice's control.

During the sixteenth century, the magistrate was given administrative duties such as highway maintenance and poor relief. He registered and preserved certain important series of documents. County finance and buildings became his province. Not until the nineteenth century were duties of JPs lightened. The Poor Law Act of 1834 and County Councils Act of 1888 removed most administrative duties while other acts defined and restricted judicial authority.

Records of quarter sessions were held by the clerk of the peace either at the county seat or in the clerk's own law office. Many sessions records begin only about 1590, and there has generally been no attempt at arranging and calendaring documents until the county record office took over custody.

Judicial records consist of petitions relating to such matters as poor relief, roads, schoolmasters and militiamen; recognisances or bonds to appear and answer charges or to prosecute; indictments; estreats (notes) of fines; appeals; witnesses' depositions; and presentments. Presentments by village constables are supposed to inform the magistrates of the state of local affairs: 'our alehouses are all Licensed . . . our poore are sufficiently provided for . . . Richard Miller and Mary Lee recusants do absent themselves from the church . . . that Lodge bridge is in dire need of repair . . . of riots and Routs we know None . . . one vagrant put in Stocks and whipped till his body be bloodied'. Men are indicted 'for assault on the body of Thomas Leycocke . . . keeping a common tippling-house . . . for stealing four loaves . . . for debt . . . for erecting a cottage on the waste of the said towne without laying foure acers thereto'. Whole townships are indicted for neglecting roads and bridges, ignoring vagrants and criminals, sheltering recusants. Articles concerning the misbehaviour and misdemeanour of specified persons provide reasons why matters have been brought to court: 'because she is a common scold . . . misbehaving her tongue against her mother-in-law . . . a peace-breaker . . . a teller of slanders . . . a contentious man'. Not infrequently women are accused of witchcraft, casting spells or giving the evil eye. They are not often executed but generally suffer imprisonment, flogging or a ducking in the fishpond. Petitioners seek money 'for Releif in Hard times . . . being maimed in the service of the parlement at Naseby . . . for five children orfaned . . . to rebuild their house destroyed by fyer'. During the hearing of all these cases the clerk kept rough notes of proceedings which he wrote up in a minute book or sessions roll. The final record of the court is in the order book. Calendars of prisoners sometimes give place and date of session; name, age and state of education of the accused; the offence and the sentence. There may also exist riot depositions especially in industrial areas, as well as insolvent debtors' papers. Many of these papers may be intermingled in files known as sessions bundles. Indexes of earlier records, up to say 1700, are available in record offices while counties like Buckingham and Hertford have published detailed calendars.

Administrative duties of JPs concerned gaols, houses of correction, lunatic asylums and other county buildings which magistrates built and superintended; the building and repair of highways and bridges especially between 1710 and 1889; diseases of animals in mid-Victorian days. Justices provided all stores for the Victorian militia and supervised village constables and county police. They therefore raised a county rate, ordered constables to collect this, and controlled the treasurer's expenditure. Their labour in administration often overshadowed judicial work: the various poor-law acts passed since Elizabethan times almost crippled the activity of some justices.

But the quarter sessions became the place for deposit, enrolment and registration of records. In 1786 parish authorities sent returns of charities to the clerk of the peace for transmission to parliament. Friendly societies deposited various documents from 1793 while rules of savings banks were deposited from 1817. Returns of men enlisted for army and navy service in Napoleonic times; lists of men aged twenty-one to seventy qualified to serve on juries, 1696–1832, showing ages, occupations and places of abode; registers of gamekeepers from 1710; registers of forty shilling freeholders, 1788–9; letters and lists relating to transportation of convicts mainly between 1790 and 1867; records of convictions under summary jurisdiction concerning beggars, tanners not paying duty, and juvenile offenders; all these indicate the extent of sessions records. Magistrates licensed badgers (itinerant sellers of corn, fish, cheese or butter) from 1563, and victuallers from 1552. The latter entered into a bond to be of good behaviour. Up to 1780 only names of alehousekeeper, his sureties and the inn itself survive; though from about 1780 to 1830 original bonds are found showing in full all conditions the justices specified before granting the licence. From 1832 the clerk of the peace received electoral lists showing the names of people qualified to vote in local and parliamentary elections. Usually printed, these documents provide information as follows:

ELECTORAL REGISTER OF BARNTON

Name	Qualification for Voting	Where Property Situated	Residence
Thomas Cross	occupier, leasehold land	Rays Brow lane	Church Hulme
	owner, freehold houses	Tunnel Road	

Note that Cross claimed a vote in Barnton but actually lived miles away in Church Hulme; such a fact is useful to the genealogist. Remember too that voting depended on ownership of property or payment of rent until 1885.

The clerk of the peace preserves hundreds of miscellaneous deeds and other documents concerning property. Under an act passed in 1536, deeds of bargain and sale were to be enrolled at Westminster or with the clerk of the peace of the appropriate county. People avoided obeying this act and comparatively few deeds were in fact enrolled. Then from 1718 for a century, wills of Roman Catholics and deeds of their property were enrolled. Various local acts allowed awards of corn rents in ecclesiastical parishes. Awards with detailed plans of parishes are in sessions records.

From 1711 pollbooks in disputed elections were to be preserved among sessions records. These have now joined other pollbooks from family muniments and solicitors' accumulations in the record office. Pollbooks provide lists of men voting at elections

together with an indication of the candidate they supported. Until
1872 men voted in public, normally for two out of four candidates.
They appeared before the returning officer and told him how they
wanted to vote. Their choice was recorded on the draft pollbook
which sometimes survives. Immediately after each election, a
commercial printer generally published the pollbook for his own
profit. Some books are mere pamphlets, others for populous
districts are weighty volumes. A large district is divided into
parishes or wards and people appear alphabetically or in order of
voting. Then under the name of the candidate or candidates is a
mark to show how each elector voted. Addresses and occupations
of voters occasionally appear. Pollbooks date from 1694 to 1872.
The History of Parliament Trust's draft register of pollbooks in
1953 recorded 1,750 surviving books. The Guildhall Library in
1970 published a handlist of pollbooks in its possession relating
to London.

From 1780 land tax assessments were deposited with the
magistrates. Parliament granted the first modern land tax in 1692
on real estate, tithes, public offices, shops, carriages and other
personal items in order to provide William III with money to make
war on Louis XIV. Commissioners surveyed and valued all property in town and village. Then the government took a varying
rate, from year to year, depending on need. The tax came more
and more from the annual value of land, was fixed usually at four
shillings in the pound, and was made perpetual in 1797. Landowners might for a lump sum redeem their tax and such redeemed
land never paid land tax again. Every year returns were compiled
by local assessors for commissioners who in turn sent abstracts and
money to London. Commissioners often retained land tax lists in
their own records from 1692 to 1780. But in that year no man could
qualify to vote unless he were assessed to the land tax. Lists were
therefore deposited with the clerk of the peace from 1780 until
1832 when electoral rolls appear. They therefore remain in quarter
sessions records to this day. Since a parish's quota to the county
total remained fixed, assessors decided each estate's liability and
this varied little subsequently despite changes in property values.

In 1949 compulsory redemption of land tax was envisaged at the death of the owner or transfer of his land by sale.

Assessors' lists vary in size according to the area and importance of the town or village. Some are mere scraps of paper, others bulky booklets stitched with thread and backed with cardboard. Petitions in quarter sessions records are generally arranged in alphabetical order of parishes, within each hundred of the county. Earlier lists from 1692 to 1779 in family muniments may often not be arranged at all. Sometimes returns have been entered into a ledger parish by parish with landowners' names alphabetically ordered. Land taxes give information in the following form:

Owner	Occupier	Description	Sum Assessed
Thomas HAYHURST	Messrs T. & C. CHANTLER	Salt-works and cottage	3s 7d
William DEAN	Self	Red Lion Inn	2s 4d

There are of course many variations especially in the period 1692–1797. Estates continue to be recorded even when their tax has been redeemed. A separate column of sums exonerated then appears to the right of the sums assessed.

Enclosure documents concern the enclosing of common land in England and Wales. Open fields, moorland and meadow being at one time common land have been enclosed for sake of efficient and individual farming since time out of mind. Medieval enclosures were sometimes effected by local agreement between lord of manor and other interested parties, but just as often by stealth or brute force. In the sixteenth and early seventeenth centuries, the courts of Exchequer and Chancery regularly supervised intending enclosures. Later still, and especially after 1750, people secured private acts of parliament. General enclosure acts have been passed since 1801 to facilitate enclosure.

Enclosure documents that are most accessible (being in the county record office) date only from around 1740. These include the agreement of inhabitants, landholders, lord of the manor and others to enclose certain common lands; copies of the relevant act of parliament (there is a printed index of local and personal acts, 1801–1947); and a minute book of the enclosure commissioners.

The award itself on parchment or paper, sometimes rolled, sometimes bound like a book, records the terms of enclosure and the disposition of all affected common. A map may accompany the award on which surveyors delineate the common as divided and, possibly, the entire village in order to mark the property in respect of which allotments are claimed. Examples of all can be found in the county record office though many documents lie elsewhere.

Records of medieval enclosures are usually in estate and manorial records. Tudor and Stuart documents ought to be in the Public Record Office (not easily accessible unless you know a date and names of parties). For parliamentary enclosures consult the return of inclosure acts in *House of Commons Sessional Papers*, 1914 (399), lxvii. Then the act itself will indicate where relevant documents were to be deposited: if with the clerk of the peace these should be in the county archives now. Awards (possibly with maps) dated 1801–45 were deposited either with the clerk of the peace or with a court of record at Westminster (in which latter case documents are at the Public Record Office). Awards dated from 1845 onwards are in the PRO and copies are with the clerk of the peace and in the parish chest. Most record offices prepare lists of all local awards and maps. There is also a return of awards in *House of Commons Sessional Papers*, 1904 (50), lxxviii. In Yorkshire and Middlesex, awards have been enrolled in county registries of deeds since the early eighteenth century.

Under standing orders of the Commons, first made in 1792, whenever an authority planned public works the project was to be surveyed and a plan deposited with the clerk of the peace. These documents are discussed in the section on House of Lords records above. From 1795 to 1871, all boats and barges exceeding thirteen tons burden used on inland navigations were registered. The owner's and master's names and the usual trade route of the vessel are noted. From 1822 annual accounts of turnpike trusts were sent to the justices. Road diversion and closure records since 1697 and plans since 1773 have at times been deposited. Accompanying these are landowners' depositions and magistrates' orders concerning the project.

Between 1673 and 1829, parliament required office holders to receive the sacrament in the parish church, to abjure the Stuarts, and to support the 1688 Settlement. Officials deposited with the sessions a certificate of having obeyed the acts. From 1715 papist property was registered at the sessions. From 1689 dissenters were allowed freedom of worship, provided places were recorded with the clerk of the peace or church authorities. A parliamentary survey of dissenting meeting-places was completed in 1829, naming sects and counting members. Original returns for each parish are with the clerk of the peace.

Taxation records are numerous. Look for hearth tax returns from 1662 to about 1674. These show each house in a village, numbering its hearths and naming its occupier. Land taxes have already been mentioned, but you may find early taxes from 1692 to 1780 in the clerk's records if previous clerks or justices themselves preserved the forms after sending abstracts to London. There was of course no legal need for preservation prior to 1780. A short-lived hairpowder duty was imposed in 1795. The latter tax helped change men's fashions swiftly.

Sessions records can be used to illustrate almost every aspect of local history. In the court bundles or rolls you will meet thieves and parsons, unmarried mothers, vagrants, bridge-builders, schoolmasters and witches, rich merchants and proud squires. You will find material relating to roads, open fields, commons, houses of correction and cottage industries. No history of the police force, crime and punishment could be completed without consulting sessions documents. For the genealogist nearly every document might yield a vital name and date. Calendars of prisoners showing sentences, ages and jobs; records of transportation to America and Australia; militia lists; electoral lists; land taxes are among documents which the researcher into family history usually consults. Lists of gamekeepers reveal names of lords of manors at various dates. Alehouse recognisances tell names of inns and innkeepers. The history of every charity, savings bank, local military force and bridge, to take just four examples, is illuminated by sessions records.

Pollbooks from 1694 to 1872 are used to show voting patterns. J. R. Vincent in his *Pollbooks; How Victorians Voted* (1967) has produced dozens of tables of voting habits from 1830–68. His introduction explains how these documents may be analysed to produce significant historical facts. He points out that the two Victorian parties received support from every class of society. Businessmen and factory workers were as often Tory as Liberal even in the great period of Liberal free trade and prosperity. But it is quite another question, and very important, whether the wealthy and the educated normally supported reform candidates. The answer in each locality ought to be deducible from poll-books.

It is worthwhile following the voting habits of men in specific trades and occupations. Catholic priests and, surprisingly, Wesleyan ministers usually voted Liberal while shopkeepers followed the preferences of their prosperous customers. The liquor trade formed a pressure group against Liberalism's temperance leanings. Thus fifty-five publicans and dealers voted Tory, twelve Liberal at Rochdale in 1857 when a Liberal temperance candidate stood. In some places people might vote as the squire did, in others workers voted against their employer. The reform acts of 1832 and 1867 and immigration of Irishmen and country families upset some borough patterns, while the conflict of church against chapel cut across class barriers. But the researcher need not deal with pollbooks in bulk. He can take those for his own locality and follow the voting pattern of men he already knows from other documents. The genealogist too learns something of an ancestor's character by knowing how he voted and, more important, what class and type of person voted for the same candidates. Did an ancestor vote differently from others of his occupation, social class or neighbourhood and if so why?

One village I know consists nowadays of several dozen scattered farmhouses set amidst walled fields with a church almost alone near a wide piece of waste. For a thousand years prior to enclosure this community packed itself tightly round the village green and church, all surrounded by three extensive open fields. Enclosure has frequently resulted in private enclosures, especially of former town moors, suitable for housing development. The enclosure award indicates distribution of land in the village before and after enclosure. Identity of owners and occupiers is specified. You should not find it difficult to decide whether prosperous land-owners got the largest and best-situated allotments and on balance what class of people (if any) lost by the process. Consider too the identity of the enclosure commissioners themselves. Incidentally there emerges a list of different types of tenure as well as the names of many parishioners, this latter useful for genealogists. Some families left the community for ever after receiving a raw deal at enclosure time.

Documents show the allotments of schools, charities and the poor. They are the ultimate title deeds to much property especially in southern and central England. They trace the course and width —and provide statutory authority for—hundreds of roads laid down at enclosure time as well as ditches, field drains, bridges, walls and hedges. Very important too is the emerging picture of pre-enclosure agriculture. Occasionally a map or award indicates this ancient system but more often the historian must strip away for himself the new pattern imposed by enclosure commission-ers.

Land tax returns may be used to trace the history of every parcel of land and all buildings in the township from 1692 to 1831, or for whatever dates returns survive. Names of owners and occupiers as well as approximate size of properties, changes of tenancy and ownership, dates of building new houses and demo-lishing old dwellings, appearance of factories and public works, these and similar facts emerge from a scientific year-by-year perusal of the records. I have copied all surviving land taxes for my village from 1731 to 1831, put results side by side, and have an excellent chart of property history. The process must be undertaken in stages.

1. Start with the latest land tax available, say 1831
2. Write down each estate in turn on long narrow cards and arrange the cards under one another

Owner	Occupier	Tax
Henry Thompson	John Page	2s

3. Take the tithe or estate map of the village. Use the schedule accompanying the map to write down the names of owners and occupiers of each property on long narrow cards. Place these cards alongside the first set. From the tithe or estate map you know exactly the location of each property and this in turn fixes each property named in the 1831 land tax.

TITHE MAP & APPORTIONMENT 1847			LAND TAX 1831		
Owner	Occupier	Tithe Description Number	Owner	Occupier	Tax
William Thompson Alice Ashley	11	cottage	Henry Thompson John Page	2s	
Henry King Hunslet	14–20 Self 27–62	hall & land	William King John & Thomas Hill	13s 8d	
William Fisher John Baldock	26, 97 121	factory & houses	Thomas Jenks Self	6s 8d	
Sarah Priest John Wauchope	134– 156	farm	John Wauchope senior Self	6s 4d	

4. Now take the next to latest land tax, 1830, and write down each estate on cards as before. Even in a small village there may be sixty different properties. Place the 1830 cards alongside the 1831 cards. If an 1831 property had been formed through the joining together of several 1830 estates, there will be more cards for 1830 than 1831. The 1831 series can be moved apart upwards or downwards to cater for this problem. The process

also works the other way if an 1830 estate is divided. It is very rare for name of owner and occupier, tax paid and description of estate (if given) all to alter so much from year to year that identification is rendered impossible. Remember too that the general rate of land tax is 4s in the £. Thus Henry Thompson's cottage always pays 2s. But if the rate varies, as it does in the early eighteenth century, say to 2s in the £ then the cottage will pay one shilling. All this helps in pinpointing properties.

5. Now take 1829 and repeat the process. Work back as far as you are able, taking a tax every five years if the village changes slowly, arranging cards with 1831 on the left, 1692 on the extreme right.

6. When all the cards are spread out backwards from 1831, information ought to be transferred to a long ruled piece of paper with the earliest land tax list this time on the left hand side. This list (mine stretched fifteen feet) shows changes of landownership very clearly.

The land tax lists at stage 5 look like this:

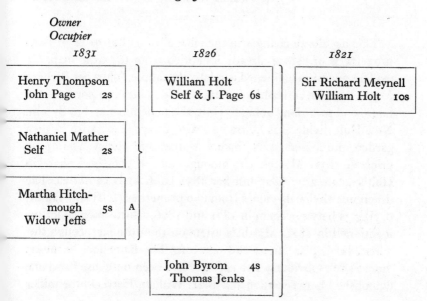

Owner
Occupier

1831	*1826*	*1821*
Henry Thompson John Page 2s	William Holt Self & J. Page 6s	Sir Richard Meynell William Holt 10s
Nathaniel Mather Self 2s		
Martha Hitch- mough 5s A Widow Jeffs		
	John Byrom 4s Thomas Jenks	

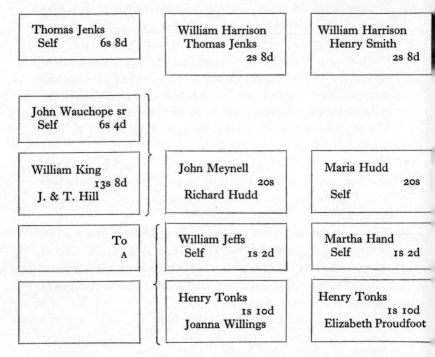

This list shows changes in the village from 1821 to 1831. Each
property is of course already identified from the tithe map. To
explain what has happened is relatively simple. Thus Sir Richard
Meynell's farm and land (of 1821) is divided into two portions, the
house and some land going to Holt, the remaining land to Byrom.
Now Holt divided his house into two cottages each with its own
garden, purchased by Nathaniel Mather and Henry Thompson
prior to 1831. Martha Hitchmough took a one-third share in
Holt's estate after 1826 but her 1831 land tax is 5s not 2s. The
difference obviously comes from two properties (Jeffs and Tonks)
paying 3s between them in 1821 and 1826, which were no longer
mentioned in 1831. Martha's estate on the tithe map consists of
house, land, plantations and one toft. The latter locally means
'house site'. Obviously two cottages had been purchased and one
demolished between 1826 and 1831. William Harrison the miller

in 1821 and 1826 sells his property to Thomas Jenks. The latter also purchases John Byrom's share of the Meynell estate to erect a factory and workers' dwellings. The Hudd family's ancestral home and parkland was sold after 1821 on account of industrialisation, a cousin becoming tenant to John Meynell for a few years until the division of the property in 1826–31. William King took the hall (a son-in-law owning it in 1847) and John Wauchope carving himself a farm from the remaining arable. Obviously the connection between changes in some cases is apparent only by taking taxes year by year. Even this does not always work and title deeds, wills and estate papers must be consulted for the vital clue.

County council

The modern county council and county borough were set up by act of 1888 to take over most of the justices' administrative duties. Since 1888 many further functions have been added. County council minute books, bye-laws, orders and year books since 1889 provide a general political background for county history. Records of various committees of the council are more specific, dealing with topics like agriculture, children's welfare, county finance, health, highways, education, planning of development in housing, land, ports and industry. The council owns thousands of deeds, some dating back several centuries. County council records can usually be consulted by serious students certainly up to 1920, often until 1939.

Many researchers are turning to modern administrative history because it is interesting, presents no palaeographical difficulties, and deals with problems that still beset us. By understanding recent developments, how we got where we are today, we are better equipped to make plans for reforms.

Guardians of the poor

The 1834 Poor Law Amendment Act established boards of guardians of the poor to deal with poverty in the districts or unions

N

into which the county was divided. The new law thus took away
from parish overseers, justices of the peace and local Gilbert
unions most poor relief work. The guardians built workhouses
where old, infirm, unemployed and children might seek food and
lodging, work, education and hospital treatment. Outdoor relief
was discouraged. The scheme, financed by local rates and controlled from London rather than quarter sessions, survived till
1929.

Records were usually stored where meetings took place, at the
workhouse. Local solicitors acted as clerks so many archives have
been preserved in solicitors' accumulations. Local district councils
took over other collections. In most cases nowadays the county
record office possesses whatever survives.

Minutes of meetings outline union policy and much that went
on in workhouses. Thus Helmsley Union minutes record the
drunken behaviour of the workhouse master and the machinations
attending the selection of a successor. John Wilson, a local farmer,
eventually got the job. His career is significant because his great-
grandson became prime minister of England. General ledgers,
returns of guardians and officials, lists of paupers with dates of
admission and discharge, school attendance registers, parochial
accounts, infirmary records, letter books, removal orders, accounts
from suppliers of food and clothing and rate books add to the bulk
of guardians' documents.

Union records can be used for family histories because so many
thousands of people passed through workhouses. Rate books
sometimes name individual householders in each parish. There is
much for the student of wages and prices, of clothing materials and
kitchen menus, of education practices in Victorian times, and of
course of Victorian poor-law policy.

Ordnance survey

Ordnance survey maps are among record office collections. The
one-inch to the mile survey began to appear in 1801, covering the
whole country south of a line from Preston to Hull by 1840.
Surveyors' drawings from this one-inch survey of 1795–1873,

showing great detail, are in manuscript form at the British Museum map room. A six-inch survey was started in 1840, and a twenty-five-inch in 1853. Towns are drawn at about five to ten feet to the mile, beginning with St Helens in 1843–4. London was completed in 1847–52 and 1862–71.

Large-scale plans mark every road, fence, field, stream, shed, house; names of many woods, lanes, dwellings and districts; use of industrial and commercial premises. From 1855 to 1886 maps are accompanied by reference books concerning area and land use. Maps show what nineteenth-century England looked like. They give clues about medieval open fields, farm sites, castles and landscape in general. There is a *Historian's Guide to Ordnance Survey maps* published by the National Council of Social Service (1965).

County maps

County maps and atlases were privately produced and printed from about 1570. Early surveyors like Christopher Saxton (1574–9) and John Speed (1611) drew small-scale, black and white or hand-coloured maps suitable for reproduction by the printing press. These mark cities, towns and villages by some symbol like a church tower; gentlemen's residences and parks; waterways, hills, forests, bridges and watermills. They have only limited uses because so many other types of document provide as clear a picture of the countryside, but they do emphasise the rural nature of the economy at this period, the smallness of settlements, the expanse of open land. Later surveyors increased the size of their maps and added many more features: roads, canals, factories, waggon-ways, collieries, historic monuments and parish boundaries. By 1780–1840, maps are almost as perfect as ordnance surveys though the scale is rarely more than one inch to the mile. But notice how accurate is every bend in the road, the position of farms, the site of mills. Maps available for each county are generally listed in a published book. Maps themselves can be studied in libraries and record offices or bought at enormous cost in antiquarian bookshops. Facsimiles of some maps are being produced commercially to a very high standard and at reasonable cost.

Directories

From about 1780 commercial directories are printed as contemporary guides to places, trades and people. Although printed in hundreds, these documents are primary source material of some importance to any local study. The most thorough and accurate directories, because based on a certain amount of original inquiry in the neighbourhood, are those by Pigot & Co, Slater, White, and Kelly or the Post Office directory. Directories are found in libraries and record offices today. Their layout is simple. Under the heading of each parish is a note of adjoining towns with distances, a history of the parish and description of the church, mention of coach, river or railway services, trades, post office, lord of the manor, charities, endowments and population. All this is useful to have in the one reference book though information is biased towards trade, church and charities while history is woefully inaccurate. Then follow lists of inhabitants showing their hamlet or other place of residence and their occupation. By no means all heads of household appear, even quite prosperous folk being absent, so the entries are no substitute for census lists. Occasionally all people are recorded alphabetically but usually there are occupational sub-headings like blacksmiths, carpenters, farmers, taverns, schools, gentry, attorneys, engineers. People are listed alphabetically according to occupation. There is generally a leaning to crafts and trades as is natural since these are commercial directories.

Most places in the country are surveyed, however, and directories are listed in Jane E. Norton, *Guide to the National and Provincial Directories of England and Wales, Excluding London, Published Before 1856* (1950), and C. W. F. Goss, *The London Directories 1677–1855* (1932). In addition there are specialised lists for medical, law, army, navy and clergy personnel that are not mentioned in the above guides. Directories provide a reasonable indication of social composition and economic activity in your locality, especially for the period 1780–1914. Genealogists occasionally discover people for whom they are searching, though it must be remembered that the books are not indexed by personal names.

Chapter 13

PALAEOGRAPHY

'IT's all Greek to me,' joked the young veterinary surgeon as he handed me the marriage settlement of one of his ancestors. 'No, I know it's medieval Latin but I need someone to translate.'

I looked at the document. 'A few hours each day to study handwriting and you'll be able to read this yourself,' I replied.

'I'll never learn a foreign language.'

The deed was, however, quite clearly written in English and dated 1494. Six weeks later after following my instructions, as outlined in this book, this keen local historian was himself deciphering the manuscript. The following chapter deals with styles of writing found in manuscripts in the Public Record Office, county record offices and parish chests. Examples have been taken from all sorts of written documents. Anglo-Saxon diplomas, English vernacular works of Henry III's reign, illuminated psalters and all printed books do not really come within our subject because handwriting is usually far removed from book hands. You can obtain transcripts, translations and reproductions of the most famous, formal or artistic works like *Canterbury Tales*, *Ayenbite of Inwyt*, *Anglo-Saxon Chronicle* and *Luttrell Psalter*, so there is little need for the busy local historian to specialise in those book hands. But not even one per cent of everyday documents, like letters or parish registers, is in print. If you are looking up your ancestry or composing a village history, you must be prepared to consult and read original documents after studying palaeography.

Palaeography is a branch of the science of documentary criticism. It concerns reading and interpreting old documents, the influence of handwriting and illumination schools, rules of calligraphy and scribal conventions, dating and origin of literary and ecclesiastical texts and distribution of styles. The word itself literally means 'old writing'.

Jean Mabillon (1622–1707), a Benedictine monk of the congregation of St Maur near Saumur, wrote *De re diplomatica* (published 1681), the first scientific study of palaeography and diplomatic. Then in 1703–5 the leading librarian and palaeographer in England, Bodley's librarian, Humfrey Wanley contributed a descriptive catalogue of all known Anglo-Saxon manuscripts to the learned treatise on northern languages written by his teacher George Hickes and called *Linguarum veterum septentrionalium thesaurus*. Wanley's catalogue of the British Museum's Harleian manuscripts, that treasury of local history material, is in large part still in use. Diplomatic was separated from palaeography with the work of Thomas Madox entitled *Formulare Anglicanum* (1702), an introduction to the forms used in royal and private charters. The study of writing languished until stimulated, after 1873, by publications of the Palaeographical Society.

There are several ways of studying old writing. You may by dint of hard work learn by heart the shapes of all letters of the alphabet as used in each century. With a good memory and keen eye you will recognise, for instance, a fifteenth-century *a*, a secretary *b* and a Chancery *c*. The letters so interpreted soon form words and sentences.

You may study the characteristics of various scripts in order to know what is medieval pipe roll hand, what is Elizabethan italic and what is English round hand. Learn the description, for example, of King's Remembrancer's script given in L. C. Hector's *The Handwriting of English Documents* (1958): 'slight departures from the generally vertical towards right or left, together with a

certain squatness in the minuscules, producing a sprawling appearance. There is no avoidance of links between letters . . .' and
so on. But even this precise description is difficult to comprehend
unless you have a clear sample of the script before you. It becomes
almost impossible to learn twenty or thirty such word-pictures and
to use the knowledge to read documents.

Learn palaeography by regular practice with documents, at first
under guidance, then by yourself. There are many advantages in
beginning with the latest documents, say from the Victorian
period, mastering these and working backwards in time. This
certainly shows stage by stage how individual letters developed.
But Victorian correspondence can prove a hindrance. Even expert
archivists stumble over the slovenly style of some missives. It is
not worth waiting till you can master all documents of one period
before embarking on earlier scripts. The sixteenth-century italic
is usually as easy to read as Victorian round hand.

Adopt the following plan:

1. Take a clear photocopy of the document you would like to read.
   Make sure there is an accurate transcript with translation if
   need be. You may hold or even mark the photocopy and have
   it with you at home. An original document is too precious to
   treat in this way.

2. Read letter by letter. Abandon without reservation your habit
   of taking in whole words or phrases at a glance and of guessing
   what is to come next. Take the first letter of your document and
   find it in one of the model alphabets printed in palaeographical
   works. There is a 'secretarie alphabete' of 1571 and various
   'old law Hands' of Tudor and Stuart times in H. E. P. Grieve's
   Examples of English Handwriting 1150–1750 with transcripts
   and translations (1959). See also the alphabets in Andrew
   Wright's *Court Hand Restored* (1776); C. Johnson and H.
   Jenkinson, *English Court Hand, 1066–1500* (1915); and H.
   Jenkinson, *The Later Court Hands in England* (1927). N.
   Denholm-Young, *Handwriting in England and Wales* (1954), is
   clear and concise.

3. Write down each letter you decipher. Some will always be

easier to recognise than others. Leave spaces where the reading is beyond your power.

4. Learn the most common letters like *a, e, r, h* as a start in reading documents of all centuries. The letter *e* is most important and provides a good start in deciphering a manuscript.

5. Fill in gaps as you learn more letters. Never guess because at first this will lead to errors; though intelligent deductions are allowed. When a medieval priest of good repute leaves a bequest to his

<h1 style="text-align:center">amira</h1>

it is safe to interpret this as *amita* (aunt) rather than *amica* (girl-friend).

6. Examine with magnifying glass an example of each letter to see the scribe's pen movements and peculiar habits. When you can understand how a letter is formed you recognise it more readily even in its badly scrawled versions. Loops, hair-strokes and bows show up clearly under the glass.

7. Complete three or four lines as far as you are able. Work these out from the first letter onwards some eight or nine times before taking the transcript to fill in missing letters. Now you will see that the letter which descends and curls so distinctively is an *h*. This you will not easily forget. That is another letter learned for that particular period.

8. Now try to decipher three or four more lines. It will be surprisingly clear this time.

Languages

The knowledge of Latin and French is indispensable for the reading of many documents. You can learn the handwriting of manuscripts by practice but to read other languages needs formal training. If important documents are in medieval Latin or French, you can either set about learning the languages or ask your county archivist for assistance.

o

Latin, the language of the Church, was known to all clerks both in holy orders and in government service. It became the written language of business and administration, the sole language till about 1280 and still important when abandoned in 1733. Medieval Latin is not very different from classical Latin except that the grammatical constructions of the former are less complicated. Differences are soon learned. The accusative and infinitive of classical Latin turns into *quod* meaning 'that' and the indicative. 'Dicit quod Robertus fecit purpresturam' means 'he says that Robert has made an encroachment'. And the gerund is employed as present participle: *cognoscendo* means 'knowing'.

Norman-French or Anglo-Norman, spoken by polite society since the Conquest, became the language of law courts and of documents less ceremonious than charters or letters patent. It is most usually found between 1310 and 1390. In 1487 it ceased to be used as the language of parliamentary statutes, surviving only in a few phrases like *le roy le veult* meaning 'the king consents to the act'.

English never disappeared despite the use of Latin and French. Most people spoke it in medieval times, and in the fifteenth century people wrote English in correspondence, account books and business minutes. By 1500 English had supplanted Latin in many informal documents. In 1650 English became the sole language of government though Latin was restored for the period 1660–1733.

It is evident that many writers are finding Latin and French beyond their powers. As time goes by, scribes either make up their own Latin words and endings or insert English phrases. There is a mixture of three tongues describing a law case in 1631 when a prisoner 'ject un Brickbat a le dit Justice que narrowly mist, & pur ceo immediately fuit Indictment drawn . . . & son dexter manus ampute & fix al Gibbet'. The two most useful dictionaries are R. E. Latham's *Revised Medieval Latin Word-List* (1965) and R. Kelham, *Anglo-Norman Dictionary* (1779). See also E. A. Gooder, *Latin for Local History* (1961).

Writing materials

People in past centuries wrote reasonably swiftly, considering their materials. Quill pens that must be continually dipped in ink do not allow breakneck speed, yet the huge number of manuscripts produced from 1280 onwards indicates a certain briskness. Monks and priests moreover were not the only scribes. Professional writers or scriveners produced letters, accounts, deeds and petitions for a fee from as early as 1150. Some were attached as lay brothers to monastic scriptoria or writing-rooms. Others served as parish clerks or manorial stewards to supplement earnings from writing. By 1350 both civil service and monasteries relied on professional scriveners who were only nominally clerks in holy orders. These men began to specialise in conveyancing and probate work. Their descendants in Elizabethan times were attorneys or lawyers, stationers and government clerks.

Medieval scribes wrote on parchment, a material supposedly perfected at and deriving its name from Pergamum in Asia Minor. Parchment superseded papyrus about AD 250. Skins of goats, sheep or calves are scraped free of hair and reduced in thickness, soaked, stretched, smoothed and dried. This produces at best a thin, smooth, white parchment, the flesh side being whiter and shinier than the hair side or dorse. Fine vellum is strictly 'veal-parchment'. Parchment began to lose ground to paper after 1500, though conservative government departments held on till Victorian times.

Paper is used in fourteenth-century England. Its successful manufacture in this country dates from only the seventeenth century. The watermark in paper is an excellent way to date documents very closely. Check the mark by holding the paper up to the light and find its date of manufacture in C. M. Briquet, *Les Filigranes* (1907, facsimile edition 1966).

The quill pen governed writing styles until about 1850, though use of the reed pen may account for the stiffness of some early scripts. Taking goose, swan or crow quills, the scribe cut an oblique edge. By holding the pen at an unchanging angle to the

surface he produced thick and thin strokes according to the angle
the nib made with the surface. Quills needed constant attention.
For later round hands the quill was cut to a fine point. Fine steel
pens after 1830–1 were sufficiently flexible for swift neat writing
but could produce thick strokes only when the pen was brought
towards the scribe. Up-strokes are therefore always thin.

. Good medieval ink contains iron salts and lasts for centuries.
The recipe demands galls (oak-apples) produced on the oak-tree
by the parasitic gall-fly and therefore acidic; gum; and copperas
(vitriol) or proto-sulphate of iron. Here is a fifteenth-century
recipe: 'To make hynke take galles and coporos or vitrial (quod
idem est) and gumme, of everyche a quartryn other helf quartryn,
and a halfe quartryn of galles more; and breke the galles a ij other
a iij and put ham togedere everyche on in a pot and stere hyt ofte;
and wythinne ij wykys after ye mow wryte therwyth' (PRO
C47/34/1/3). Other recipes have called for blood, urine and even
beer.

The mixing of acidic galls and iron salt produced a purplish-
black liquid which grows black with age. This burns into parchment and paper to such an extent that even wetting does not
remove the ink. Most ink-makers diluted their product with
water. Till 1400 ink looks reddish-brown, then becomes greenish-
black till 1520. After about 1500 a suspension of carbon (usually
lamp-black) in gum-water produces really black ink which, however, does not bite into the material and is not waterproof. When
the gum rots, the ink scrapes off. Writing that is faded can be to
some extent made legible by using an ultra-violet lamp to cause
a visible glow. Never under any circumstances use chemical
reagents applied directly to the writing, because eventually these
give an ineradicable stain.

Format

Formal documents like charters are written on the flesh side or
recto only. Endorsements are on the hair side or dorse or verso.
A seal is attached by cords to the doubled-up foot of the parchment. When writing continues from sheet to sheet—and this

applies also to Exchequer and common law court records—the
sheets are piled one on top of the other, flesh side uppermost, and
secured together by cord at the head. This pad or roll is easy to
consult by leafing through the bundle. Chancery sewed mem-
branes of parchment together head to tail and rolled them like a
cylinder, flesh side or face innermost. Both recto and dorse are
written on. In references 'm2' means membrane 2 face and 'm2d',
membrane 2 dorse. The whole roll must be unwound to read the
parchment at the centre.

Seals

The use of seals to authenticate or to secure documents was known
to antiquity. The popes employed a seal in the early seventh
century, and European kings followed suit. The practice spread
to bishops and great nobles, cities and corporations, merchants
and gentry by 1300 and to guilds in the following century. From
the sixteenth century, the signature replaced the seal as a means
of authentication, though papers were still secured by a seal.

The stamp or matrix which produced the impression was
usually of latten, silver or lead. This was pressed on wax which
either lay on the face of the document or hung by parchment tag,
twisted silk or cord from the bottom of the record. Many pendent
seals had an impression on both sides to foil forgers. Thus the
great seals of England showed the king in majesty one side and his
equestrian figure on the other. Most seals are circular, though
clergy and noblewomen preferred the pointed oval.

Ecclesiastical seals showed a conventional view of a church and
patron saint. Universities and colleges displayed the chancellor
and masters in convocation while towns preferred a view of the
guildhall, city gate or harbour. Equestrian figures suit knights'
seals but merchants and landowners put up with flowers, beasts
and trees. The lower clergy used a virgin and child. Many people
adopted a legend round their seals if merely the simple SIGILLUM
HENRICI meaning 'Henry's seal'. The script varied: Roman capitals
prior to 1150 (and after 1500), Lombardic 1150–1370 and 'black
letter' 1370–1470.

ERA   ERA   era
Roman   *Lombardic*   *Black letter*

King John adopted a privy seal, held by a clerk of the king's
chamber, for work not requiring the great seal. The officer gradually acquired a department of state and as Lord Privy Seal still
survives. Edward III began to use his signet ring to by-pass privy
seal but the king's secretary also assumed wide powers, fore-
shadowing the office of secretary of state. Read A. B. Wyon, *The
Great Seals of England* (1887), and the PRO's *A Guide to Seals in
the Public Record Office* (1954).

Chapter 14

HANDWRITING IN ENGLAND

In majuscule writing all letters are more or less of the same height. Square and rustic capitals as well as uncial letters are majuscule or two-line as it is often called. Minuscule is four-line: some letters descend below, some ascend above the main line of writing.

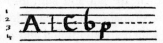

Roman A   Rustic E   Uncial E   Carolingian b p

By 'text' or 'book' hand is meant a script whose letters are written separately. The overall appearance is one of great clarity and formality. Thus the Romans carve inscriptions in square capitals, the medieval monks write psalters in Gothic script based on the Carolingian minuscule, and the printers produce this book in separated letters of roman type. But not everyone can afford to wait for such productions. By joining letters together the scribe speeds up his output of title deeds, accounts and court rolls. He is thus writing 'cursively' or 'currently'—'at running pace'—and his attached rounded letters may often lose beauty and clarity. Confusion results as one or two dashes represent two or three letters at a time. Of course cursive writing need not be illegible.

English cursive or current writing is often known as 'court' hand
to distinguish it from text or book hand. The court in question
is the royal court, the centre of administration and justice and the
largest producer of documents in England. Court hand becomes
noticeably distinct from book hand around 1200. Distinctive 'set'
hands for such departments as Exchequer and Chancery appear
about 1490. Alongside these hands were 'free' hands, the ordinary
businessman's script, used for deeds, letters and accounts.

The Egyptians probably first thought of an alphabet to represent sounds. But Semitic people like the Phoenicians perfected the
actual letter-forms which in a modified shape are still used today.
The Greeks adopted this alphabet about 850 BC and then introduced vowels on the same level as consonants. This alphabet was
again altered by the Romans whose square capitals are identified
with our own. Early lettering whether on stone, papyrus (an
Egyptian form of paper) or parchment is known as majuscule
because letters are roughly the same size, never rise above or drop
below the line of writing and are unjoined.

Roman scribes using papyrus or parchment soon developed
'rustic capitals' which are tall and slim and somewhat curved.
Meanwhile writers, probably in Africa, adopted the 'uncial' or
'inch-high' letters which are simplified and rounded. Then from

$$a \; \delta \; \epsilon \; \omega$$

Uncial a d e m

around AD 500 a half-uncial script appears in southern Europe, a
four-line or minuscule writing with parts of letters ascending
above and descending below the main line of writing.

$$de \, pᚱu$$

English half-uncial c750 d e p r n

Because none of these hands helped scribes write swiftly, the

Romans developed a cursive script whose letters can 'run on' from each other as in modern handwriting. From AD 350 cursive script influenced the growth of uncials and therefore of such national hands as Beneventan. It also produced new book hands. From Merovingian cursive came the Carolingian script, whose clear rounded upright and usually isolated letters are ancestors of modern roman printing types.

Handwriting in England owes much to the half-uncial round hand of Irish missionaries at Iona and Lindisfarne as well as to continental missionaries who used capitals and uncials. From about AD 650 to AD 850 Saxon half-uncial flourished, and was used for the Lindisfarne Gospels (AD c700). Then emerged a pointed minuscule script written cursively with special Saxon letter-forms and abbreviations and pointed descenders. The period 960–1020

ᵖ r ʒ ð

Pointed minuscule r s g d

is the golden age of Anglo-Saxon art especially in the illuminated service-books produced at Winchester.

The characteristics of Anglo-Saxon script continued to be evident till 1200: long *r* with shoulder dropping right down to the line of writing, *g*, long *f*, *s*; Saxon *th*. Then book hand and current business or court hand begin to influence scribes, and documents written in the English language from 1200 to 1480 acquire a distinctive appearance. This script is important because so many works are written in it: Chaucer's *Canterbury Tales*, Langland's *Vision of Piers Plowman*, and the *Chronicle of Robert of Gloucester*.

From the scripts in use in north-east France during the eighth century, monastic scribes developed the Carolingian minuscule. Adapting Merovingian cursive under uncial influence, the monks at Tours, with their English abbot Alcuin, and at Luxeuil and Corbie produced a clear hand which greatly interested Charlemagne, hence the term 'Carolingian' or 'Caroline'. This legible minuscule had been perfected by 830.

Carolingian minuscule reached England about 960 and was used by scribes from that date. Certain national peculiarities of treat-

r ſ g d

Carolingian minuscule in England 1058 r s g d

ment can be seen like the long *r* and flat-topped *g*. By 1100, book hands written by scribes began to look different from administrative hands. The latter exhibit notching of ascenders of *l*, *b*, *h* as well as some new abbreviations and the long *r*.

Book hand (1150–1500) may also be termed 'text' or 'Gothic' script. Curves of Carolingian letters are turned into angles. There

doτe   ote

Carolingian 1058   Book hand 1340

is a very distinct difference between light and heavy pen-strokes, the lightest obliques being by 1220 only hair-lines. The bow at the top of *a* closes down. From 1300 the script is hardly four-line but two-line, because ascenders and descenders of letters like *l* and *p* are shortened drastically. Look especially for curved letters which become fused as in *do*. The script is seen in headings of manuscripts, monumental brasses and document seals. It was employed by early printers in England in Tudor times.

Cursive scripts employed by government, courts, businessmen and private individuals emerge in the twelfth century. Book hand could not suit the needs of everyday life. The Court of Exchequer in London was the first to adopt a new hand (around 1125), followed by Chancery (1180), and the courts of law at Westminster. This type of everyday cursive script is often called 'court hand' because of its connection with the administrative organs of the royal court and with law courts. The writing of these offices became set by the fifteenth century. The pipe rolls are thus in a set hand which hardly altered between 1131 and 1832.

Court hand 1280

During the twelfth century, professional scribes ensured some uniformity and legibility of scripts. Notice the break-up of Roman capitals, cursive *e*, exaggeration of ascenders and descenders, slight bending forward and notching of ascenders, and the vertical stroke through some capital letters. The last feature makes currently-written capitals very obscure. Then after 1200 the influence of universities, business, and royal administration created much written material. Scribes tend to produce a small, current and compact script. They thicken horizontal and to some extent diagonal strokes from left to right. This produces beaver-tailed letters like *g* and capital *S* (1240–1320). Between 1220 and 1290 letters are floreated, ascenders and descenders are looped and notched.

From 1300 writing grows larger, possibly because parchment is plentiful. Floreation and loops give way to plain hooks on ascenders after 1320. The *e* turns over in 1330. Towards the last years of the century, a spiky angular script is popular. Fifteenth-century hands are vertical and angular, typically Gothic, with upright down-strokes and fine connecting strokes. The *e* is now entirely upside down; round letters have angular backs. Later fifteenth-century free hands become coarse, very cursive and difficult to decipher.

From about 1390 scribes mixed court and book hands to produce 'bastard script' for business, ecclesiastical and private purposes. Notice long tapering descenders, angularity of rounded

English vernacular 1450

letters and shouldered *r*. Bastard is a set hand. Departments
adopted bastard before developing their own set scripts. Chancery
set hand can hardly be recognised before 1450, common law court
hands before 1490.

From fifteenth-century set hands like bastard, writers under
free hand influence developed 'secretary', a current script for
everyday needs used mainly between 1525 and 1660. This hand
must not be neglected because many important types of documents—parish registers of christenings, marriages and burials,
quarter sessions petitions, wills and inventories, household accounts, diocesan act books—are in secretary. From about 1590
people began to mix italic with secretary eventually producing,
around 1660, a hybrid.

Secretary hand looks confusing but with perseverance you can
work out three-quarters of the letters. Indeed it is essential to

Secretary hand: preaches 1580

practise hard if you wish to study English manuscripts of this
period. Learn carefully the few characteristics of the hand: the
diagonal strokes attached to *a*, *c* and *i*; the *h* which sinks further
and further below the main line of writing; the *r* which takes
several shapes but never the long shoulderless form of court
hands; the *p* which resembles *x*; two-stroke and reversed *e*; long
s with descender as initial and medial; and final round *s*. Sixteenth-
century secretary looks flamboyant with thick descenders sweep-
ing down into lines below; bold and looped tall letters; a drastically
rightward leaning *t*; and generally large spreading letter-forms.
Writers obey few rules about capital and small letters or about
punctuation. Compared with court hand, secretary has few abbreviations. After 1600 scribes restrain themselves, shortening descenders, reducing the boldness of loops and flourishes, and (under
influence of italic) clarifying letter-forms.

Humanist writing attempted to re-create Carolingian minuscule of the tenth and eleventh centuries. First produced in Italy about 1400 this graceful, clear, legible script with letters standing apart from each other was taken over by continental printers being forerunner of the modern roman type (as in this book). When written cursively with letters joined and sloping to the right, the hand is known as 'italic'. Henry VIII's children learned italic, Elizabeth, taught by Roger Ascham, being able to write both secretary and italic at will. Italic print was first employed in England in 1524 and its use for emphasis dates from about 1545. Often the text of a document is in secretary while headings and quotations are in italic.

Writing-masters like John Baildon (who produced a copy-book in 1571) could teach distinct styles like secretary, italic and court hand, but the man in the study usually mixed these up. Indeed by 1610, it is almost impossible to classify a document as italic, secretary or legal. But italic forms gradually win general acceptance. Although secretary *d* and *e* survive into the eighteenth century, a new form of writing influenced by italic and Dutch script emerged in the period 1660–1700. In this way the cursive 'round' hand became the script of English people and followed English trade round the world. This medium-sized, sloping 'copperplate' script survived into the age of the typewriter. The change from court hand and secretary to italic and Italian-influenced round hand between 1600 and 1700 is the most drastic handwriting development that English people have experienced. Handwriting virtually makes a fresh start around 1600–50. Round hand forms are still with us and therefore call for little description letter by letter; difficulties in reading come from carelessness in writing. Some Victorian and modern hands, swiftly produced by a pen that followed the line of the fore-arm, must be deciphered merely by guesswork.

Set hands

Many documents commonly occurring in national and local archives are written in the special set hands that developed in the fifteenth century. Letter forms are not very different from examples already learned but scribes gave scripts distinctive and seemingly outlandish appearances that terrify the new student. First therefore, it is essential to master ordinary hands of the period 1400–1700, and then turn to special hands.

Chancery hand appears out of bastard around 1450, improves in the next century, and reaches an accomplished and graceful excellence by 1600. It is used in letters patent under the great seal, in writs, and in all enrolments of such documents as trust deeds and lists of bankrupts' estates. The hand has short ascenders and descenders. Thus lines of writing are close together and letters spread sideways. Connecting strokes, especially between minims, are almost eliminated. Letters are rounded.

1620 Chancery	*1590 Exchequer*	*1664 Legal*

Exchequer hand has several versions. Pipe roll hand developed as early as the twelfth century but is unlikely to be of much use to the student. The King's and Lord Treasurer's Remembrancers' hands appear between 1480 and 1550. Ascenders and descenders are long and angles abound. The KR scribe sprawls his words whereas the LTR exhibits exaggerated narrowness. Look for examples of this script in Public Record Office accounts and vouchers, memoranda rolls, and recusant rolls.

Legal hands can be recognised from around 1480. Documents passing through law courts like King's Bench and Common Pleas are in 'legal' script. Marriage settlements, judicial writs, fines and recoveries, to mention four types of records seen in county record offices, exhibit this backward sloping, angular hand. Vertical strokes called 'pigs' ribs' should be parallel; long descenders are given large angular bows; straight lines replace curves.

Engrossing hands
Engrossing hand appears in title deeds, enclosure agreements and

marriage settlements, among others, from around 1580 till the nineteenth century. Letters are at first secretary in style. The distinguishing feature is the contrast between thick and thin strokes, and especially the incredibly faint hair-strokes. Italic influence on letters like *h* is marked after 1640, producing the engrossing hand of 1640–1900. Some government departments as well as lawyers employed this hand in preference to common law court script.

1670

The Alphabet

The development of the alphabet in the period 1150–1700 is sketched below. Letter forms help to date a document. An unfamiliar letter in a manuscript may be recognised in the following examples. Only the few letters that alter significantly are described in words, the rest being drawn.

Both *a* and *A* present little difficulty (1–14), though secretary *a*, often open, is drawn with two pen strokes (6) and sometimes an attaching line (8).

1: 1210   *2:* 1285   *3:* 1380   *4:* 1440

5: 1450   *6:* 1570   *7:* 1610   *8:* 1611   *9:* 1700

10: 1235   *11:* 1400   *12:* 1430

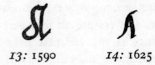

13: 1590   14: 1625

B and *b* change little (15–30). Loops and notches are noticed in the thirteenth century (17).

15: 1170   16: 1200   17: 1240   18: 1380

19: 1470   20: 1570   21: 1610   22: 1695

23: 1180   24: 1215   25: 1230   26: 1240

27: 1420   28: 1510   29: 1580   30: 1625

c (31–7) trips up the unwary when it is combined with a *t* (32–3) or when currently written (34). Secretary *c* with attaching stroke (35) and *C* lying on its back (42) should be carefully studied. *C* (38–44) is often confused with *D* or *E*.

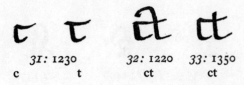

31: 1230   32: 1220   33: 1350
c   t   ct   ct

34: 1440   35: 1590   36: 1610   37: 1700

38: 1240   39: 1290   40: 1390   41: 1500

42: 1590   43: 1600   44: 1627

D and *d* (45–59) are usually currently written.

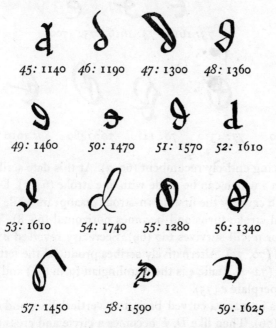

45: 1140   46: 1190   47: 1300   48: 1360

49: 1460   50: 1470   51: 1570   52: 1610

53: 1610   54: 1740   55: 1280   56: 1340

57: 1450   58: 1590   59: 1625

Use *e* as a means of dating documents because its form changes from century to century very distinctively. Notice how the letter seems to fall over backwards during the thirteenth century, by

P

ℰ   *e*   *e*   *e*

60: 1190   61: 1260   62: 1290   63: 1330

ᴐ   *ᴐ*   *ᴈ*   *ᴈ*

64: 1330   65: 1390   66: 1430   67: 1500

ᴈ   *e*   *ᴈ*   *e*   *e*

68: 1446   69: 1460   70: 1570   71: 1610   72: 1610

e   *ᴈ*   *e*

73: 1610   74: 1616   75: 1700

ℰ   ⊕   ℛ   ⊕   ℰ   ℰ

76: 1200   77: 1310   78: 1410   79: 1480   80: 1610   81: 1325

1330 being entirely recumbent (60–3). At this date scribes introduce an *e* which can be made with one stroke (64–5). During the
fifteenth century the first down-stroke disappears while the vertical final stroke turns and becomes horizontal (66–8). The book
hand form still survives too (69). Secretary reversed *e* is swiftly
written (70, 74). Alternatively scribes produced the letter in two
strokes (72–3). Italic *e* is the Carolingian form (71) and is copied
by copperplate *e* (75).

E has by 1200 a curved back, two vertical lines and one horizontal (76). Then like *D*, *E* becomes a circle and cross (77). The
letter is angular after 1400 (78) and very current from 1450 (79).
Secretary *E* (80) resembles the earlier form in (76). The italic
letter is round, not square like the Roman *E* (81).

82: 1150 *83:* 1180 *84:* 1280 *85:* 1300

86: 1380 *87:* 1380 *88:* 1495

89: 1590 *90:* 1612 *91:* 1740

The development of *f* is straightforward (82–91). There is no capital *F* till the eighteenth century.

Notice three-stroke medieval *g* (93–100), differing from Saxon (92) and italic (101–2). *G* appears in several bewildering shapes (103–5).

92: 1210 *93:* 1212 *94:* 1215 *95:* 1315

96: 1320 *97:* 1430 *98:* 1470 *99:* 1500

100: 1570 *101:* 1615 *102:* 1720

103: 1210   104: 1440   105: 1590

106: 1180   107: 1270   108: 1380   109: 1330

110: 1410   111: 1460   112: 1450   113: 1508

114: 1570   115: 1610   116: 1610   117: 1710

118: 1220   119: 1300   120: 1600

The *h* like *b* and *l* has a tendency to be notched (106) and around 1250–80 floreated (107). Floreations give way to loops or hooks from 1310 (109), producing triangular loops by 1390 (108). In the next century *h* is more speedily produced and its bow nearly disappears by 1490 (111–13). Secretary *h*, certainly after 1600, boasts a descender that sweeps down into the line below (114–15). Italic and round hand *h* contrast startlingly with secretary *h* (116–17).

H is not often written, the small letter taking its place even in proper names (118–20).

The *i* and *j* are two forms of one letter till 1700 (121–2) and the capitals are rare (123–4).

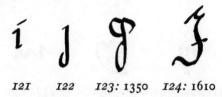

121   122   123: 1350   124: 1610

k and *K* (125–32) and *l* and *L* (133–40) to some extent resemble *b* in their development.

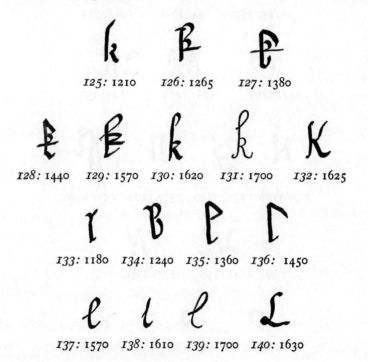

125: 1210   126: 1265   127: 1380

128: 1440   129: 1570   130: 1620   131: 1700   132: 1625

133: 1180   134: 1240   135: 1360   136: 1450

137: 1570   138: 1610   139: 1700   140: 1630

Both *m* and *n*, composed of short downstrokes known as minims, develop together (141–6). The uncial form governs medieval *M* (147–9). *N* is usually most perplexing because of the position of its cross-stroke (150–5). Some forms even look like long *s* (153). Scribes cannot vary *o* much (156–60).

P and *p* present few problems (161–76) save when *p* is combined with another *p* or an *o* (165–7) or is swiftly drawn to resemble an *x* (171, 173).

141: 1220   *142:* 1250   *143:* 1460

144: 1570 *145:* 1610 *146:* 1755

147: 1195   *148:* 1250   *149:* 1590

150: 1150 *151:* 1190 *152:* 1200 *153:* 1310

154: 1590   *155:* 1600

156: 1190   *157:* 1380   *158:* 1610

159: 1470   *160:* 1590

q may look like *g* (177–83). *Q* resembles *O* (184–8). Some forms show how the question mark originated (187–8).

The *r* is a most important means of dating documents. From two early forms spring all subsequent letters: one has a definite shoulder and its slightly curving stem may until about 1190 fall below the line of writing (189–91); the other at first is used only

161: 1140   *162:* 1200   *163:* 1250   *164:* 1340

165: 1250   *166:* 1295   *167:* 1340

168: 1460   *169:* 1470   *170:* 1570
xp

171: 1620   *172:* 1620   *173:* 1620   *174:* 1725

175: 1220   *176:* 1570

177: 1150   178: 1270   179: 1370   180: 1500

181: 1610   182: 1610   183: 1710

184: 1120   185: 1170   186: 1390

187: 1590   188: 1625

in the ligature *or* (192). In the thirteenth century scribes wrote the
first *r* without raising their pens and about 1225 lowered the point
from which the shoulder springs (193) and abandoned the shoulder
itself about 1260 (194). The second form of *r* is employed after

189: 890   190: 1150   191: 1150   192: 1160

193: 1240   194: 1290   195: 1310

196: 1420   197: 1450   198: 1550   199: 1570   200: 1610

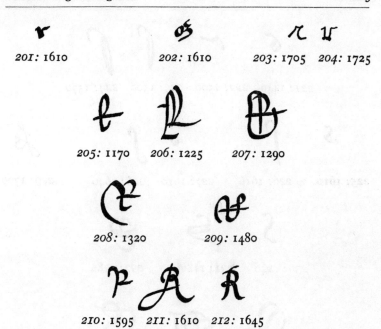

201: 1610   202: 1610   203: 1705 204: 1725

205: 1170   206: 1225   207: 1290

208: 1320   209: 1480

210: 1595   211: 1610   212: 1645

rounded letters *w, h, y, p, b, o, d* (195). These two forms persisted in the fourteenth and fifteenth centuries, the long *r* without shoulder being most common (196) though the round *r* may appear in almost any position (195, 197). Secretary *r* develops from bastard shouldered (190) and round (192) *r*, and exhibits several distinct shapes (198, 199, 201). Notice the curious initial *r* which

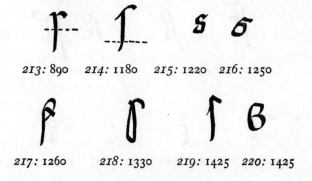

213: 890   214: 1180   215: 1220   216: 1250

217: 1260   218: 1330   219: 1425 220: 1425

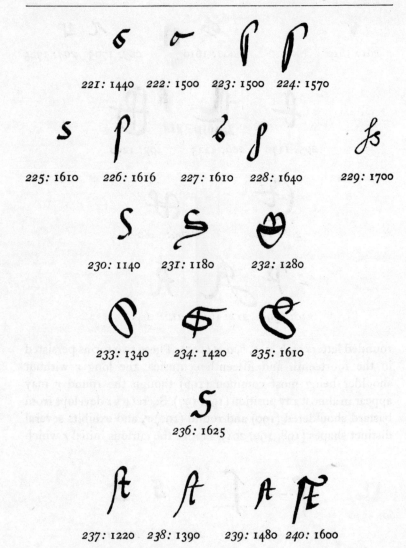

221: 1440   222: 1500   223: 1500   224: 1570

225: 1610   226: 1616   227: 1610   228: 1640   229: 1700

230: 1140   231: 1180   232: 1280

233: 1340   234: 1420   235: 1610

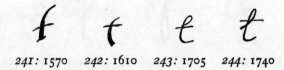

236: 1625

237: 1220   238: 1390   239: 1480   240: 1600

241: 1570   242: 1610   243: 1705   244: 1740

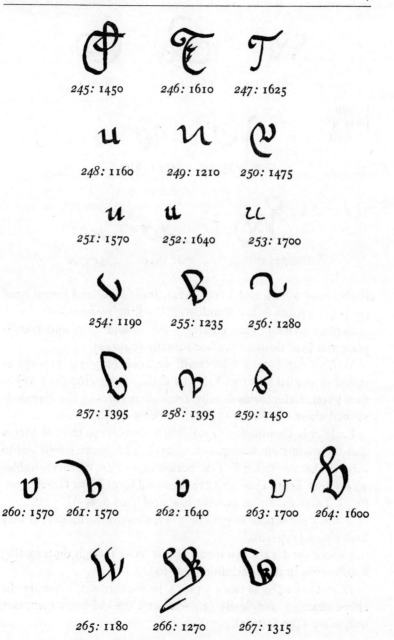

245: 1450   246: 1610   247: 1625

248: 1160   249: 1210   250: 1475

251: 1570   252: 1640   253: 1700

254: 1190   255: 1235   256: 1280

257: 1395   258: 1395   259: 1450

260: 1570   261: 1570   262: 1640   263: 1700   264: 1600

265: 1180   266: 1270   267: 1315

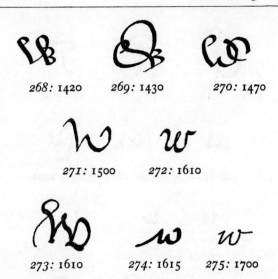

268: 1420   269: 1430   270: 1470

271: 1500   272: 1610

273: 1610   274: 1615   275: 1700

is also used after *o* and *a* (198, 202). Italic (200) and round hand (203–4) *r* return to the shouldered Carolingian form.

Scribes write *R* very currently till around 1600 and usually place the final downstroke horizontally (205–12).

Writers use long *s* with 'serif' or hook (213–14, 217–19) as initial or medial letter and short *s* dating from 1160 (215–16) as final letter. Later forms develop from these (220–9), the diamond-shaped short *s* of about 1440 (221) being distinctive.

Early *S* is Carolingian (230). Then about 1140 the tail curves and the main stem is duplicated (231). The centre swells out to form the beaver-tailed *S* of the period 1240–1320 which resembles an *m* (232). From 1300 till 1520 the usual form is like Greek *sigma* (233). Later examples present few problems (234–6).

T and *t* are simple to read (237–47) though the ligature *st* may look like *a* (237–40).

u and *v* (or *V*) are two forms of one letter though representing a difference in pronunciation (248–64).

W and *w* begins as two *v*'s (265). In the thirteenth century the shape changes completely (266–70) and the old form reappears only after 1490 (271–5).

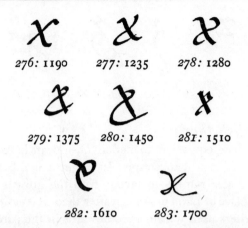

276: 1190   277: 1235   278: 1280

279: 1375   280: 1450   281: 1510

282: 1610   283: 1700

x is important because of its use in numerals (276–83) but is often so swiftly written that it is mixed up by unwary students with a *p* or *y*.

The tail of *y* curves to the right (284–8) prior to the adoption of italic styles around 1600 (289–90).

Scribes rarely need *z* (291–4). The letter may be confused with tailed round *r* (292).

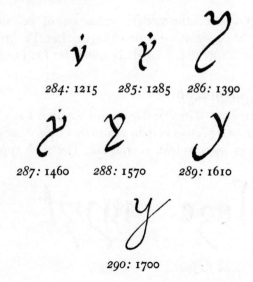

284: 1215   285: 1285   286: 1390

287: 1460   288: 1570   289: 1610

290: 1700

291: 1230   292: 1350   293: 1600   294: 1740

Old English thorn

The letter *thorn*, equivalent to modern *th*, appears in Anglo-Saxon and early medieval manuscripts. In origin it is a Scandinavian rune. The letter returns to favour with the growth of written English in place of Latin or French after 1420. It is easily confused with *y*. Writers used *y* from 1500 onwards in the particles 'the', 'they', 'this', 'that'. But people still pronounced the *y* as *th* and it is often better to transcribe it as such. *Ye Swanne Inne* is *The*

this 1320   *the 1451*

Swanne Inne. Of course the modern archaic use of 'ye', although still meaning 'the', should not be changed. Let *Ye Swan Inn* remain. Do not forget that *y* regularly stands for *i* as in *yt* (it).

Middle English yogh

Yogh is a descendant of insular flat-topped Saxon *g*. Early scribes employed *yogh* to represent certain values that now are shown by *g*, *gh*, *w* and *y* in again, kni*gh*t, *y*e and la*w*. The *yogh* appears in

lawe 1340   *myght 1380*

beyonde 1420

your 1451

English documents into the fifteenth century. But because *yogh* looks so much like *z* or sometimes *y* there is confusion when scribes abandon the *yogh* (which they do from 1250). Thus the *z* in Menzies is not really *z* but *g* (yogh).

Abbreviation

Abbreviation of words raises certain difficulties of reading. But we do not find such examples as £, &, or *recd* insuperable obstacles and can soon learn earlier practices too. As we have the apostrophe or full stop to indicate abbreviation, so earlier scribes employed signs. Their main mark, originally a straight line over or through an abbreviated word, indicates the deletion of some letters. It does not stand for specific letters though it often indicates the omission of *m* or *n*. The line through *li* (short for *libri*, 'pounds') has remained to this day in our £ sign. The mark curls up at the ends and by the fifteenth century is often like the modern apostrophe.

cum (with) 1263

So the universal mark of suspension can mean almost anything and sometimes means nothing when the writer uses it carelessly out

of habit. One of the commonest uses in Elizabethan times is to
mark the change from *-tion* to *-con* as in 'commendations'. But

commendations

writers just as regularly abbreviated without indication as in
'theyll' (they will) and 'thourt' (thou art).

There are various means of abbreviation. 'Suspension' means
that only a few letters of a word are written—perhaps just an
initial—before the word is suspended. We can show such a
shortening by ending with a full stop: B.B.C. stands for 'British
Broadcasting Corporation'. In old records you find *s, solidi*, 'shillings'; *d, denarii*, 'pence'; *li, libri*, 'pounds'; *T, testibus*, 'with
witnesses'; *m, manerium*, 'manor'; *anno r r, anno regni regis*, 'in the

solidi 1410   *manerium 1420*

year of the reign of king . . .' Examples of two or three letters
written before suspension are numerous especially in post-
medieval centuries. Thus *par.* stands for 'parish'; *pet.* for 'peti-
tioner' at quarter sessions; *bap.* for 'baptised'; *memo.* for *memoran-
dum*, 'it is to be remembered'. Suspension is, in medieval times
and later, indicated by a curved line over or through the last
letter, or by some appropriate flourish, or by a full stop. It is very
useful to scribes whose knowledge of spelling or Latin termina-
tions is faulty.

Perhaps as common is the 'contraction' of words often by
omitting vowels or the whole middle part of the word. Thus
Christus meaning 'Christ' appears in medieval deeds as (in Greek
letters) *Xps.* Very common are *do., ditto*, meaning 'the same'; *lb.,
libra*, 'pound weight'; *no., numero*, 'number'; *Mrs.* and *Mr.* for
'mistress' and 'master'.

Some scribes abbreviate with 'superscript' letters, small letters written above the line as in M^r meaning 'master'; w^t, 'with'; y^t, 'that', where y is really *thorn, th*; ye meaning 'the'; Matie 'Majestie'; y^{or} 'your'; M^{ris} 'mistris'.

Writers employ special signs to indicate abbreviations. These are not so much a shorthand as a general warning to expect an abbreviation. Thus the curved mark already mentioned does not always imply a missing *m* or *e* but its appearance clearly says: 'this word is abbreviated'. A flourish after the letter, turning down through the letter's last stroke, until 1650 stands for *es* or *is* especially in English plural nouns or words denoting possession, eg king's palace. But the mark also abbreviates words like *R, rex,* 'king'; *R, recipe,* 'doctor's prescription'; *d, denarius,* 'penny'.

kinges 1509   *recipe*   *penny 1460*

The sign for *er* is one of the commonest used in English as well as Latin until the seventeenth century. Notice the abbreviation of 'every' in the example. After *p* the mark always denotes *re*. Abbreviations following *p* are common and in such words as 'parish' or 'provided' appear into the eighteenth century. A line (possibly curved) through the tail of *p*—often merely a continuation of the tail curved backwards—abbreviates *per* and *par*. *Pro* is shortened by producing the bow of *p* round into a second bow.

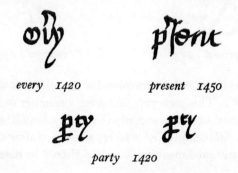

every 1420   *present 1450*

party 1420

provided

The sign for *rum* at the end of a Latin word occurs frequently. It is also used as a general abbreviation especially in place-names like Saresberia and Blandford Forinseca which when incorrectly extended with only a *-rum* turn into Sarum and Blandford Forum.

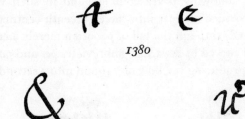

Sarum

Most medieval scribes write for *et* (meaning 'and') the sign devised by Tiro, freedman of Cicero, resembling a *z* or 7. 'Tironian notes' are a real shorthand but are seldom employed by medieval scribes. Later writers employ a ligature of *e* and *t* which is often regarded as a separate letter of the alphabet. *Etcetera* is written as *et* and *c*.

1380

ampersand 1130   *etcetera 1300*

Other signs include the semicolon for *us*, *ue*, and *et* which looks in time like a *z*. This sign may stand for a number of letters, for example, 'ounce' becomes *oz* and *videlicet* meaning 'that is to say' becomes *viz*. *Est* meaning 'is' is rarely shortened after 1250. Signs for *con.*, *ur.*, and *quod* meaning 'because' should be noted. The *ser* sign often stands for *sieur* and *seigneur* in French language manuscripts.

semicolon   viz   est

con   ur   quod   ser

Difficult letters

Certain letters should be treated as danger signals. For example the *s* and *f* are easily confused at certain periods when long *s* prevails. There is, however, a distinguishing mark.

                f has a line right through the stem
                s has a line only to the left

The double *f* is usually standing for capital *F*. Some people still preserve this usage in their surnames: ffoulkes. (See examples under *f* and *s*.)

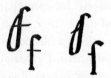

In medieval times *c* and *t* are almost indistinguishable, though the cross-stroke may yield a clue. The *t* grows higher than *c* in later hands and the cross-stroke stands out as in the modern letter. In secretary hands *c* is clearly accented. (See examples under *c*.)

Only in the eighteenth century were *i* and *u* finally adopted as vowels, *j* and *v* as consonants. Previously a scribe might write 'iunior' or 'neuer'. Sometimes *j* is used as a first and last letter, *i* as medial regardless of sound. In numerals the last minim is often made into a *j* as in 'iij'.

The reading of minims, the short perpendicular strokes of the letters *m, n, u, v, i*, is difficult when two or more come together in such words as *annum* meaning 'year'. Medieval scribes do not distinguish individual letters or dot the *i*. Thus 'June' and 'inne' may look identical. 'Minimum' is almost unrecognisable. There

minimum

are certain accepted renderings of words containing minims which must be learned: 'Fraunce' not 'Frannce'; 'graunt' not 'grannt', and so on. This is what the writer intended even if he could not at that time write *u* differently from *n*.

Numerals

Medieval scribes employed Roman characters as numbers in accounts, court rolls and most other documents. The form of the characters varies and the change can be followed under the letters *i, j, l, C, D* and *M*. Arithmetical calculations are difficult since there was no zero, and many mistakes occur in accounts. People used the abacus or the chequered cloth to aid their calculations. Even the king's treasury worked in this way, officials moving tokens from one square to another in the 'exchequer' department. The following are 1–6, 9–10 in Roman numbers. Letters indicating

1–6

9-10

scores (xx), hundreds (C) and thousands (M) are often written above the numerals.

Arabic numerals appear as early as the thirteenth century, mainly in informal documents, but are not at all common till Elizabethan times.

1-9, 0 c1380

Spelling

Spelling is of crucial importance when you are reading documents in English and a writer's choice of spelling must be observed. English was for long a spoken rather than written language, so spelling conventions have grown up haphazardly. Thus an Elizabethan scribe might use 'beleeve', 'beleive', and 'beleave' in one document without raising a contemporary eyebrow.

1. Scribes add the *e* at random to produce such spellings as 'kinge', 'newe', 'lesse', 'bargayne'. Plurals are formed similarly: 'frendes', 'girles'. Final *e* is often omitted: 'com', 'mak'.

2. One vowel sound is shown by several different letters: 'pleese', 'pleise', 'please' all appear. Very confusing is the interchange of *o* and *ou*. Thus 'cold' may mean 'cold' or 'could'. The *w* (double *u*) regularly replaces *u* as in 'yow', 'howse', 'abowt'. Nearly every scribe interchanges *i*, *y*, and *ie* as in 'verie', 'myle' and 'sive'.

3. Writers double single consonants and undouble double consonants at will producing 'loosse', 'shee', 'mannor', 'belleeve', 'runn'; 'lose', 'mil', 'unles', 'maner'. Vowels *e* and *o* are treated similarly: 'gode' for good, 'foteballe' for football. Notice that 'loosse' stands for the modern 'lose' whereas 'lose' is 'loss'. You can usually tell from the context what the writer intended.

4. As in medieval Latin *c* and *t* are interchanged. You come across 'gracious' and 'gratious', 'action' and 'accion' representing the changing pronunciation to a *ts* or *sh* sound.

5. One of the commonest interchanges is *c*, *k*, and *ck* as in 'publicke' and 'sik' (for 'sick').

Punctuation

Punctuation marks are employed from medieval times. Writers often make up their own rules. The virgule (/) serves many purposes (though mainly as a comma) till 1580. The semicolon is seldom seen until after 1700 but the colon is used from 1550 as a comma or full stop. Question marks from 1500 appear as in modern works and also to mark exclamations (the exclamation mark appearing after 1650). Quotation marks are rarely seen before 1630 and then to emphasise phrases rather than show speech. The full stop has many purposes at all dates apart from ending a sentence.

Proper names

Most proper names have Latin forms which are used in such documents as manorial court rolls until fairly recently. Thus John is Johannes. Even surnames can be Latinised: *filius Johannis* being Johnson; *Pistor* being Miller or Baker. Place-names like *Eboracum* for York and *Oxonia* for Oxford are common. Even today such forms survive. Oxford graduates are MA (Oxon). Bishops sign official missives with the Latin place-name. John Ebor is John, archbishop of York. Latin forms of proper names are in C. T. Martin, *The Record Interpreter*, second edition (1910).

Dating

During Saxon and Norman times the New Year began on 25 December. From about 1190 to 1751 Lady Day, 25 March, started the year. Only from 1752 did England revert to the Roman date, 1 January.

If your document is dated 1751 or earlier and relates to any day between 1 January and 24 March, take care. What we should call

29 January 1649 is by old style counting still 29 January 1648. People stayed in 1648 till 24 March. Modern historians often write this as '29 January 1648/9' to save confusion.

There is also the problem of eleven days by which in 1752 England had fallen behind the calendars of some European countries. James II left England before Christmas in 1688 to land in France and find Christmas already over. This difference may explain some puzzling dates especially in English-European correspondence. You should not be without C. R. Cheney, *Handbook of Dates for Students of English History* (1961).

When a document is undated estimate the approximate date by examining the handwriting. With a little practice you can see how secretary differs from thirteenth-century court hand. A manuscript with a reversed *e* dates from after 1330. The *r* without a shoulder is usually from the period 1260–1500. But remember that styles of writing do not change swiftly. A boy learning writing in 1320 from an old man may still be writing a Roman *e* in 1370. A scribe might also learn one script for Latin, another for English.

Transcripts

Study facsimiles of documents daily in order to become acquainted with scripts of every period. Any record office will photocopy manuscripts of your choice. Libraries stock published facsimiles such as those issued by the Essex County Record Office. Also recommended are F. M. Stenton, *Facsimiles of Early Charters from Northamptonshire Collections* (1930); C. B. Judge, *Specimens of Sixteenth Century English Handwriting* (1935); publications of the Palaeographical Society (1873–94) and New Palaeographical Society (1903–30); G. E. Dawson and L. Kennedy-Skipton, *Elizabethan Handwriting 1500–1650* (1968).

Reproductions of single manuscripts include *Domesday Book* (Ordnance Survey, 1861–4); *Gorleston Psalter*, edited by Sir Sydney Cockerell (1907); *Luttrell Psalter*, edited by E. G. Millar (1932); *Stowe Missal*, edited by Sir G. F. Warner (1906).

When transcribing a document, copy in the original language or dialect what lies before you. Never correct the scribe's supposed mistakes. Extend abbreviations which are correctly used and about which there is no doubt. Do not use brackets or italics to indicate the additional letters. Where there is doubt about the correct extension use a footnote to explain reasons for your final decision. There is, however, no need to alter common abbreviations like Mr or £sd. Never alter a writer's spelling in any language and certainly not in English documents after 1520. For manuscripts prior to 1520 it is allowable to modernise punctuation and capital letters, but after this leave capitals and punctuation exactly as they appear. Preserve Anglo-Saxon letters for as long as these are used, say to 1520. Then when writers use *y* for Saxon *thorn* you may write *y* or prefer *th*, though this latter is the only permissible change in modern transcription. When a scribe writes *ys* for 'is' or howse for 'house', you must use his spelling. Ignore marks of abbreviation that are used out of habit and not to show abbreviation. Thus Elizabethans often crossed their *l* as in 'parcel' meaninglessly. If you are certain there should be an expansion but are uncertain what the scribe intended use an apostrophe: scituat'.

Appendix I

SOME RECORD REPOSITORIES IN ENGLAND & WALES

THE following list is based on a handbook prepared by a joint committee of the Historical Manuscripts Commission and the British Records Association (fourth edition, HMSO 1971). By no means all local record offices are included below.

LONDON
There are at least one hundred repositories in London whose documents may be of interest. These include government, religious, banking, and borough archives, records of national institutions like the railways, of city Livery companies, of societies and colleges, and of religious foundations. Only a selection is listed here. Consult the Greater London Record Office for detailed help.

Public Record Office, Chancery Lane, WC2
Church Commissioners, 1 Millbank, SW1
Duchy of Cornwall Office, 10 Buckingham Gate, SW1
House of Lords Record Office, House of Lords, SW1
Principal Probate Registry, Somerset House, Strand, WC2
Department of Manuscripts, British Museum, WC1
Lambeth Palace Library, SE1 (Canterbury Archdiocese records)
Methodist Archives and Research Centre, Epworth House, 25–35 City Road, EC1
Society of Friends' Library, Friends' House, Euston Road, NW1
Westminster Abbey Muniment Room and Library, The Cloisters, Westminster Abbey, SW1

British Railways Board, Historical Records Office, 66 Porchester Road, W2
Corporation of London Records Office, Guildhall, EC2
Guildhall Library, Basinghall Street, EC2
Greater London Record Office (London Records), County Hall, SE1
Greater London Record Office (Middlesex Records), 1 Queen Anne's Gate Buildings, Dartmouth Street, SW1
Corporation Muniment Room, Guildhall, Kingston-upon-Thames
Southwark Diocesan Records and Lewisham Archives Department, The Manor House, Old Road, Lee, SE13
College of Arms, Queen Victoria Street, EC4
Society of Genealogists, 37 Harrington Gardens, SW7
Registrar General, General Register, Somerset House, WC2
Dr Williams's Library, 14 Gordon Sq, WC1
BEDFORDSHIRE County Record Office, Shire Hall, Bedford
BERKSHIRE County Record Office, Shire Hall, Reading
BUCKINGHAMSHIRE County Record Office, County Offices, Aylesbury
   Buckinghamshire Archaeological Society, County Museum, Aylesbury
CAMBRIDGESHIRE and ISLE OF ELY County Record Office, Shire Hall, Castle Hill, Cambridge
   University Library, Cambridge
   University Archives, Old Schools, Cambridge
CHESHIRE County Record Office, The Castle, Chester
   City Record Office, Town Hall, Chester
CORNWALL County Record Office, County Hall, Truro
   Royal Institution of Cornwall, River Street, Truro
CUMBERLAND Cumberland, Westmorland, and Carlisle Record Office, The Castle, Carlisle, and County Hall, Kendal
DERBYSHIRE County Record Office, County Offices, Matlock
DEVON County Record Office, County Hall, Exeter
   City Library, Castle Street, Exeter
   Cathedral Library, The Bishop's Palace, Exeter
DORSET County Record Office, County Hall, Dorchester
DURHAM County Record Office, County Hall, Durham
   Palatinate and Bishopric records, The Prior's Kitchen, The College, Durham
ESSEX County Record Office, County Hall, Chelmsford
GLOUCESTERSHIRE County Records Office, Shire Hall, Gloucester
   Bristol Archives Office, Council House, Bristol 1
HAMPSHIRE County Record Office, The Castle, Winchester
   City Record Office, Guildhall, Portsmouth
   Civic Record Office, Civic Centre, Southampton
   City Record Office, Guildhall, Winchester
   Cathedral Library, The Cathedral, Winchester

HEREFORDSHIRE County Record Office, The Old Barracks, Harold
    Street, Hereford
HERTFORDSHIRE County Record Office, County Hall, Hertford
HUNTINGDON with SOKE OF PETERBOROUGH County Record
    Office, County Offices, Huntingdon
ISLE OF WIGHT County Record Office, County Hall, Newport
KENT Archives Office, County Hall, Maidstone
    Cathedral Library and City Record Office, The Precincts, Canterbury
    Diocesan Registry and Cathedral Library, c/o Messrs Arnold, Tuff, and
      Grimwade, The Precincts, Rochester
LANCASHIRE County Record Office, Sessions House, Lancaster Road,
    Preston
    Public Library, Ramsden Square, Barrow-in-Furness
    City Record Office, Brown Library, Liverpool 3
    Central Library, St Peter's Square, Manchester 2
    Chetham's Library, Manchester 3
    John Rylands Library, Deansgate, Manchester 3
    Public Library, Museum Street, Warrington
    Local History and Archives Department, Central Library, Wigan
LEICESTERSHIRE County Record Office, 57 New Walk, Leicester
    City Record Office, Museum and Art Gallery, Leicester
LINCOLNSHIRE County Archives Office, The Castle, Lincoln
    Gentlemen's Society, Spalding
MIDDLESEX See under LONDON
NORFOLK Norfolk and Norwich Record Office, Central Library,
    Norwich
    Borough Record Office, Town Hall, Great Yarmouth
NORTHAMPTONSHIRE County Record Office, Delapré Abbey,
    Northampton
NORTHUMBERLAND County Record Office, Melton Park, North
    Gosforth, Newcastle upon Tyne 3
    City Archives Office, 7 Saville Place, Newcastle upon Tyne 1
NOTTINGHAMSHIRE County Records Office, County House, High
    Pavement, Nottingham
    Nottingham University Dept of Manuscripts
    Southwell Diocesan Registry, Church House, Park Row, Nottingham
OXFORDSHIRE County Record Office, County Hall, New Road,
    Oxford
    Archdeaconries of Oxford and Berkshire and Oxford Diocesan Registry,
      Bodleian Library, Oxford
    University Archives, Bodleian Library, Oxford
    Bodleian Western Manuscripts, Bodleian Library, Oxford
RUTLAND See LEICESTERSHIRE
SHROPSHIRE County Record Office, New Shirehall, Abbey Foregate,
    Shrewsbury
    Borough Archives, Guildhall, Shrewsbury

SOMERSET County Record Office, Obridge Road, Taunton
STAFFORDSHIRE County Record Office, County Buildings, Eastgate
Street, Stafford, in association with
Joint Record Office and Lichfield Diocesan Registry, Bird Street,
Lichfield, also in association with
William Salt Library, 19 Eastgate Street, Stafford
SUFFOLK Bury St Edmunds and West Suffolk Record Office, 8 Angel
Hill, Bury St Edmunds
Ipswich and East Suffolk Record Office, County Hall, Ipswich
SURREY County Record Office, County Hall, Kingston-upon-Thames
Museum and Muniment Room, Castle Arch, Guildford
SUSSEX West Sussex Record Office, County Hall, Chichester
East Sussex Record Office, Pelham House, Lewes
Sussex Archaeological Trust, Barbican House, Lewes
WARWICKSHIRE County Record Office, Shire Hall, Warwick
City Library, Ratcliff Place, Birmingham 1
City Record Office, 9 Hay Lane, Coventry
Borough Archives, Shakespeare's Birthplace Trust Library, Henley
Street, Stratford-on-Avon
WESTMORLAND See under CUMBERLAND
WILTSHIRE County Record Office, County Hall, Trowbridge
Diocesan Record Office, The Wren Hall, 56c The Close, Salisbury
WORCESTERSHIRE County Record Office, Shire Hall, Worcester
YORKSHIRE: EAST RIDING County Record Office, County Hall,
Beverley
Registry of Deeds, Beverley
YORKSHIRE: NORTH RIDING County Record Office, County Hall,
Northallerton
Registry of Deeds, Northallerton
YORKSHIRE: WEST RIDING West Riding archives and diocesan
records, Archives Department, Sheepscar Branch Library, Leeds 7
Brotherton Library, University of Leeds, Leeds 2
Yorkshire Archaeological Society, Claremont, Clarendon Road, Leeds 2
West Riding archives and diocesan records, Archives Department,
Central Library, Sheffield 1
Registry of Deeds, County Hall, Wakefield
Quarter Sessions Records, County Hall, Wakefield
YORK York Diocesan Records, Borthwick Institute of Historical Re-
search, St Anthony's Hall, York
British Railways Board Historical Records, British Rail Eastern Region
Headquarters, York
City Library, Museum Street, York
WALES National Library of Wales, Aberystwyth
ANGLESEY County Record Office, Shire Hall, Llangefni
CAERNARVON County Record Office, County Offices, Caernarvon
CARMARTHEN County Record Office, County Hall, Carmarthen

FLINTSHIRE County Record Office, The Old Rectory, Hawarden, Deeside

GLAMORGAN County Record Office, County Hall, Cathays Park, Cardiff

MERIONETH County Record Office, County Offices, Dolgellau

MONMOUTHSHIRE County Record Office, County Hall, Newport

PEMBROKE County Record Office, The Castle, Haverfordwest

Appendix II

SOME NATIONAL RECORD SOCIETIES

NAMES of some national societies that concern themselves with archives and history, publishing material from time to time. Addresses of these societies with details of their aims and policy may be obtained from the latest editions of *Whitaker's Almanack* and the British Council's *Scientific and Learned Societies of Great Britain*.

Local record societies represent regions of the country (the Surtees Society for the ancient kingdom of Northumbria); counties (Oxfordshire Record Society); towns (Greenwich and Lewisham Antiquarian Society); and dioceses (Lincoln Record Society). For addresses of some societies see the two reference books above. For examples of national and local society publications of documents and calendars see the volume-by-volume list in E. L. C. Mullins, *Texts and Calendars* (1958). Local societies are not listed below.

Alcuin Club (church records)
Anglo-Norman Text Society
Antiquaries of London, Society of
Antiquaries of Newcastle upon Tyne, Society of
Archivists, Society of
Army Historical Research, Society for
Baptist Historical Society
British Agricultural History Society
British Record Society (the society's *Index Library* lists wills and adminis-
    trations as well as other biographical and genealogical material)
British Records Association (to encourage the preservation and use of
    records and to give technical information and other advice about
    records)

British Society of Franciscan Studies
Business Archives Council
Camden Society. *See* Royal Historical Society
Canterbury and York Society (church records)
Catholic Record Society
Church Historical Society
Cymmrodorion, The Honourable Society of (arts, literature and science of Wales)
Early English Text Society
Ecclesiastical History Society
Economic History Society
English Church History Society
English Place-Name Society
Friends Historical Society
Genealogists, Society of
Harleian Society (genealogy, heraldry, parish registers and family history)
Henry Bradshaw Society (liturgical manuscripts and rare service books)
Heraldry Society
Historical Association
Historical Society of the Church in Wales
History of Science, British Society for the
Huguenot Society of London
Index Society merged with Index Library. *See* British Record Society
Inland Waterways Association Ltd
Institute of Heraldic and Genealogical Studies
Jewish Historical Society of England
List and Index Society (PRO lists and indexes)
Military Historical Society
Monumental Brass Society
Navy Records Society
Newcomen Society for the study of the history of engineering and technology
Parish Register Society
Pipe Roll Society (great rolls of the Exchequer)
Postal History Society
Presbyterian Historical Society of England
Railway and Canal Historical Society
Royal Historical Society, Camden Society (historical documents)
Selden Society (English law)
Unitarian Historical Society
Wesley Historical Society

BIBLIOGRAPHY

THE date which follows the title is generally that of the edition consulted by the author. Books are arranged under authors or editors.

ARCHIVE ADMINISTRATION
Fowler, G. H. *The Care of county muniments*, 1923
Jenkinson, C. Hilary. *A Manual of archive administration*, second revised ed with introduction and bibliography by R. H. Ellis, reissued 1965
Redstone, L. and Steer, F. W. *Local records: their nature and care*, 1953
Timings, E. K. 'The Archivist and the public', *Journal of the Society of Archivists*, April 1962

ATLASES
Gardner, D. E., Harland, D., Smith, Frank. *A Genealogical atlas of England & Wales* (1960), with gazetteer by Frank Smith (1968)
Speed, John. *Theatre of the empire of Great Britaine*, 1611 (facsimile ed relating to England 1953; facsimile ed of the 1676 ed relating to Wales 1970)

BIBLIOGRAPHY
The following reference works provide lists of books and periodicals that may prove of use in your researches.
Bestermann, Theodore. *World bibliography of bibliographies*
British union catalogue of periodicals
Davies, Godfrey. *Bibliography of British history, II: the Stuart period 1603–1714*, second ed 1970
Elton, G. R. *Modern historians on British history, 1485–1945*, 1970
Mullins, E. L. C. *Texts and calendars: an analytical guide to serial publications*, 1958

248

Read, Conyers. *Bibliography of British history, I: the Tudor period, 1485–1603*, second ed 1959

Somerville, Robert. *Handlist of record publications*, 1951

CHRONOLOGY

Cheney, C. R. *Handbook of dates for students of English history*, 1961

Poole, R. L. *Mediaeval reckonings of time*, 1918

Powicke, F. M. and Fryde, E. B. *Handbook of British chronology*, second ed 1961

DICTIONARIES

Dictionaries and related works that will be invaluable as you study documents. Languages, surnames, watermarks, seals and place-names are represented.

Bardsley, C. W. *Dictionary of English and Welsh surnames*, 1901, reprinted 1967

Briquet, C. M. *Les Filigranes: dictionnaire historique des marques du papier*, 1907, facsimile ed 1966

Cappelli, Adriano. *Dizionario di abbreviature latine ed italiane*, second revised ed Milan 1912

Committee of the International Council on Archives. *Elsevier's lexicon of archive terminology*, 1964

Ekwall, Eilert. *Concise Oxford dictionary of English place-names*, fourth ed 1960

Glover, R. F. and Harris, R. W. *Latin for historians*, third ed 1963

Gooder, E. A. *Latin for local history*, 1961 (with useful formulary of some common documents)

Kelham, R. *Anglo-Norman dictionary*, 1779

Latham, R. E. *Revised medieval Latin word-list*, 1965

Marshall, G. W. *The Genealogist's guide to printed pedigrees*, 1903

Martin, C. T. *The Record interpreter: a collection of abbreviations, Latin words, and names used in English historical manuscripts and records*, second ed 1910

Reaney, P. H. *Dictionary of British surnames*, 1958

Whitemore, J. B. *A Genealogical guide*, 1953

Wright, Joseph. *The English dialect dictionary; the English dialect grammar*, 1898–1905

Wyon, A. B. *The Great seals of England*, 1887

PALAEOGRAPHY

Your ability to read the handwriting of documents depends mainly on your own perseverance. Practise therefore on documents themselves or, of course, on clear photocopies. Study the following books which usually provide transcripts, translations and photocopies of original documents as well as descriptions of various types of hand.

R

Dawson, G. E. and Kennedy-Skipton, L. *Elizabethan handwriting 1500–1650*, 1968
Denholm-Young, N. *Handwriting in England & Wales*, 1954
Emmison, F. G. *How to read local archives 1550–1700*, 1967
Grieve, H. E. P. *Examples of English handwriting 1150–1750*, second ed 1959
Hector, L. C. *The Handwriting of English documents*, 1958
Jenkinson, C. Hilary. *The later court hands in England*, 1927
Jenkinson, C. Hilary and Johnson, C. *English court hand, A.D. 1066 to 1500*, 1915 (volume 1 is a treatise on the handwriting of medieval administrative documents and contains the text of documents reproduced in facsimile in volume 2)
Judge, C. B. *Specimens of sixteenth century English handwriting*, 1935
Wright, Andrew. *Court hand restored*, 1776
Wright, C. E. *English vernacular hands from the twelfth to the fifteenth centuries*, 1960

LISTS, GUIDES, CALENDARS, DIPLOMATIC

This section concentrates on documents themselves. A number of books deal with diplomatic, that is, the varying forms that documents take for different purposes century by century. Some documents or collections of manuscripts are published in full by photocopy, transcript or translation. Others are calendared, catalogued or merely listed. The literature in this section is extensive and the following books are listed merely as examples. Thus the chronicle of Richard of Devizes is not the only chronicle in print and not necessarily the most interesting.

Appleby, J. T. (ed). *Cronicon Richardi Devisensis de tempore regis Richardi Primi. The Chronicle of Richard of Devizes of the time of King Richard the First*, 1963
Bickley, F. B. and Ellis, H. J. (ed). *Index to the charters and rolls in the Department of Manuscripts*, 1900 (British Museum)
Birch, W. de G. (ed). *Cartularium Saxonicum*, 1885–99
Bond, M. F. *Guide to the records of Parliament*, 1971
Bond, M. F. *The Records of Parliament*, 1964 (pamphlet)
Born, L. K. (comp). *British manuscripts project: a check list of the microfilms prepared in England and Wales for the American Council of Learned Societies 1941–5*, 1955
British Museum, London. *A Guide to the British Museum*, 1968
British Museum, London. *Index to the charters and rolls in the Department of Manuscripts*, ed by F. B. Bickley and H. J. Ellis, 1900
Buckinghamshire County Council and Buckinghamshire Quarter Sessions Joint Committee. *Calendar of Quarter Sessions records*, ed by W. Le Hardy, in progress, 1933–
Burke, A. M. *Key to the ancient parish registers of England and Wales*, 1908
Camp, A. J. *Wills and their whereabouts*, 1963
Chaplais, Pierre. *English royal documents: King John–Henry VI, 1199–1461*, 1971

Cockerell, Sydney (ed). *The Gorleston psalter: a manuscript of the beginning of the fourteenth century in the library of C. W. D. Perrins, described in relation to other East Anglian books of the period*, 1907

Cornwall, Julian. 'An Elizabethan census' in *Records of Buckinghamshire*, volume XVI, part 4, 1959

Cranfield, G. A. *A Handlist of English provincial newspapers and periodicals 1700–1760*, 1961

Emmison, F. G. *Archives and local history*, 1966 (with photographs and transcripts of manuscripts)

Emmison, F. G. and Gray, Irvine. *County records*, third ed 1967

Emmison, F. G. *Guide to the Essex Record Office*, second ed revised to 1968, 1969

Finberg, H. P. R. *Early charters of Wessex*, 1964 (calendar and introduction)

Ford, P. G. *Select list of British Parliamentary papers 1833–99*, 1953

France, R. S. *Guide to the Lancashire Record Office*, second ed 1962

Galbraith, V. H. *An Introduction to the use of the public records*, 1934

Goss, C. W. F. *The London directories 1677–1855*, 1932

Guildhall Library. *London rate assessments and inhabitants lists in Guildhall Library and the Corporation of London Records Office*, second ed 1968

Hansard, T. C. *Hansard's catalogue and breviate of British Parliamentary papers 1696–1834*, 1953

Harley, J. B. and Phillips, C. W. *The Historian's guide to ordnance survey maps*, published for the Standing Conference for Local History by the National Council of Social Service, 1965

Hickes, George. *Linguarum veterum septentrionalium thesaurus grammatico-criticus et archaeologicus*, 1703–5

Historical Manuscripts Commission. *Calendar of the manuscripts of the Marquis of Bath, preserved at Longleat, Wiltshire*, 1904–8

Hoskins, W. G. (ed). *Exeter militia returns 1803*, 1969

House of Lords and Historical Manuscripts Commission. *Calendar of the manuscripts of the House of Lords*, 1870–94 (HMC); 1900 to date (HL)

Kemble, J. M. *Codex diplomaticus aevi Saxonici*, 1839–48

Leadam, I. S. (ed). *Domesday of inclosures 1517–18*, 1897

Leeson, F. A. *Guide to the records of the British state tontines and life annuities of the seventeenth and eighteenth centuries*, 1968

London Record Society. *London inhabitants within the walls 1695*, 1966 (an index prepared for use in the Corporation of London Records Office, with introduction by D. V. Glass)

Loyd, L. C. and Stenton, D. M. (eds). *Sir Christopher Hatton's book of seals*, 1950

Mabillon, Jean. *De re diplomatica*, 1681

Madox, Thomas. *Formulare Anglicanum*, 1702

Maitland, F. W. (ed). *Select pleas in manorial and other seignorial courts*, volume 1: reigns of Henry III and Edward I, 1889

Major, Kathleen. *A Handlist of the records of the bishop of Lincoln and of the archdeacons of Lincoln and Stow*, 1953

Miller, E. G. *The Luttrell psalter*, 1932

Munby, L. M. (ed). *Short guides to records*, series reprinted from the journal *History*

National Council of Social Service. *Historian's guide to ordnance survey maps*, 1965

National Library of Wales. *Handlist of manuscripts in the National Library of Wales*, in progress, 1940–

National Register of Archives. *List of accessions to repositories* (HMSO, annual)

Norton, J. E. *Guide to the national & provincial directories of England and Wales, excluding London, published before 1856*, 1950

Ordnance Survey. *Domesday Book* (facsimile), 1861–4

Owen, D. M. *The Records of the established church in England excluding parochial records*, 1970

Powell, W. R. *Local history from Blue Books: a select list of the sessional papers of the House of Commons*, 1962

Public Record Office. *A Guide to seals in the Public Record Office*, ed by Hilary Jenkinson, 1954

Public Record Office. *Guide to the contents of the Public Record Office*, 1963

Public Record Office. *Maps and plans in the Public Record Office relating to the British Isles c1410–1860*, 1967

Pugh, R. B. (ed). *Calendar of Antrobus deeds before 1625*, 1947

Purvis, J. S. *Introduction to ecclesiastical records*, 1953

Ranger, F. 'The National Register of Archives, 1945–1969' in *Journal of the Society of Archives*, volume III, pages 452–62

Record Commissioners. *Calendar of the proceedings in chancery in the reign of Queen Elizabeth*, 1827–32

Record Commissioners. *Rotuli hundredorum*, 1812–18

Record Commissioners. *The Statutes of the realm*, 1810–28

Record Commissioners. *Taxatio ecclesiastica Angliae et Walliae auctoritate P. Nicholai IV, circa A.D. 1291*, 1802

Record Commissioners. *Valor ecclesiasticus temp Henr VIII*, 1810–34

Royal Historical Society. *Anglo-Saxon charters: an annotated list and bibliography*, ed by P. H. Sawyer, 1968

Salter, H. E. (ed). *Facsimiles of early charters in Oxford muniment rooms*, 1929 (quoted sometimes as *Oxford charters*, contains charters prior to 1170)

Steel, D. J. and A. E. F. and others (comps). *National index of parish registers*, in progress, 1966– (published by Society of Genealogists; volumes 1–2 contain introductory matter)

Stenton, F. M. *Facsimiles of early charters from Northamptonshire collections*, 1930

Stephenson, Mill. *A List of monumental brasses in the British Isles*, 1926, reprinted 1964

The Times, London. *Handlist of English and Welsh newspapers 1620–1920*, 1920

Wanley, Humfrey and Hickes, George. *Linguarum veterum septentriona-
lium thesaurus grammatico-criticus et archaeologicus,* 1703–5
Warner, G. F. (ed). *The Stowe missal,* 1906
West, John. *Village records,* 1962
Wiltshire Archaeological and Natural History Society Records Branch.
Calendar of Antrobus deeds before 1625, ed by R. B. Pugh, 1947

DOCUMENTS AT WORK
The following books show how historians have used documents. Some of
the books are guides on the writing of histories.
Ashton, T. S. *An Eighteenth century industrialist, Peter Stubs of Warring-
ton, 1756–1806,* 1939
Baker, W. P. *Parish registers and illiteracy in East Yorkshire,* 1961
Barley, M. W. *The English farmhouse and cottage,* 1961
Beresford, M. W. *The Lost villages of England,* 1954
Beresford, M. W. *Lay subsidies (1290–1334; post 1334) and poll taxes
(1377, 1379 & 1381),* 1963
Beresford, M. W. *The Unprinted census returns of 1841, 1851, 1861 for
England & Wales,* 1966 (bound with R. L. Storey, *Wills*)
Beveridge, William (later Lord). *Prices and wages in England from the
twelfth to the nineteenth century,* 1939
Carr, E. H. *What is history?,* 1961
Celoria, F. *Teach yourself local history,* 1958
Chambers, J. D. *The Vale of Trent, 1670–1800,* supplement 3 to the
Economic History Review, 1957
Clark, G. Kitson. *Guide for research students working on historical subjects,*
1958
Coleman, D. C. *Courtaulds; an economic and social history,* 1969
Collingwood, R. G. *The Idea of history,* 1946
Cornwall, Julian. *How to read old title deeds XVI–XIX centuries,* Birming-
ham University Extra-Mural Studies Department, 1964
Court, W. H. B. *Rise of the Midland industries, 1600–1838,* 1938
Douch, R. *Local history and the teacher,* 1967
Emmison, F. G. and Humphreys, D. W. *Local history for students,* 1965
Emmison, F. G. 'The Relief of the poor at Eaton Socon, 1706–1834' in
Bedfordshire Historical Record Society, volume 15, 1933
Ernle, Rowland E. Prothero, 1st Baron. *English farming past and present,*
sixth ed with introduction by G. E. Fussell and O. R. McGregor, 1961
Eversley, D. E. C. and Glass, D. V. (eds). *Population in history,* 1965
Finberg, H. P. R. *The Local historian and his theme,* 1952 (printed also in
the author's *Local history*)
Finberg, H. P. R. and Skipp, V. H. T. *Local history: objective and pursuit,*
1967 (essential and exhilarating book for local historian)
Finberg, H. P. R. *West Country historical studies,* 1969
Fitton, R. S. and Wadsworth, A. P. *The Strutts and the Arkwrights,* 1958
Fleury, M. and Henry, L. *Nouveau manuel de dépouillement et d'exploita-
tion de l'état civil ancien,* 1965 (demography)

Galbraith, V. H. *The Historian at work*, 1962
Galbraith, V. H. *The Making of Domesday Book*, 1961
Galbraith, V. H. *Studies in the public records*, 1948
Gardner, D. E., Harland, D. and Smith, F. *Basic course in genealogy*, 1958
Gardner, D. E. and Smith, Frank. *Genealogical research in England and Wales*, 1956–64
Hatfield Workers' Educational Association. *Hatfield and its people*, twelve pamphlet volumes, 1961–4
Holdsworth, W. S. *A History of English law*, 1903–66 (volumes 13–16 ed by A. L. Goodhart and H. G. Hanbury)
Hollaender, A. E. J. (ed). *Essays in memory of Sir Hilary Jenkinson*, 1962 (seals, palaeography, archives, Public Record Office)
Hollingsworth, T. H. *Historical demography*, 1970
Hoskins, W. G. *Local history in England*, 1959
Institute of Heraldic and Genealogical Studies, Canterbury. *Parish register searching in England and Wales*, 1967
Iredale, D. A. *Your family tree*, 1970
Jackman, W. T. *The Development of transportation in modern England*, second ed revised with introduction by W. H. Chaloner, 1962
Jordan, W. K. *Charities of rural England 1480–1660*, 1961
Laslett, Peter. *The World we have lost*, 1965
Lawton, R. 'The Population of Liverpool' in *Transactions of the Historic Society of Lancashire and Cheshire*, volume 107, 1955
McKinley, R. A. *Norfolk surnames in the sixteenth century*, 1970
Maitland, F. W. *Domesday Book and beyond*, 1897
Prothero, R. E. *See* Ernle, 1st Baron
Pugh, R. B. *How to write a parish history*, 1954
Reade, A. L. *The Reades of Blackwood Hall*, 1906
Russell, J. C. *British medieval population*, 1948
Steer, F. W. (ed). *Farm and cottage inventories of mid-Essex 1635–1749*, 1950
Storey, R. L. *A Short introduction to wills*, 1966 (bound with M. W. Beresford, *Census returns*)
Tate, W. E. *The Parish chest*, third ed 1969
Vincent, J. R. *Pollbooks; how Victorians voted*, 1967
Walne, Peter. *English wills; probate records in England and Wales, with a brief note on Scottish and Irish wills*, 1964
Ward, W. R. *The Administration of the window and assessed taxes (1696–1798)*, 1963
Ward, W. R. *English land tax in the eighteenth century*, 1953
Webb, S. and B. *History of English local government*, 1903–29 (1. *The Parish and the county*; 2–3. *The Manor and the borough*; 4. *Statutory authorities for special purposes*; 5. *The Story of the king's highway*; 6. *English prisons under local government*; 7–9. *English poor law history*; 10. *English poor law policy*; 11. *The History of liquor licensing in England*)
Wrigley, E. A. (ed). *An Introduction to English historical demography*, 1966

PERIODICALS
American Archivist
Archives
Archivum
Economic History Review
The Genealogists' Magazine
History (especially the *Short guides to records*)
History Today
Journal of Economic History
Journal of the Society of Archivists
Local Historian
Population Studies

INDEX

257